On Society

On Society

ANTHONY ELLIOTT AND BRYAN S. TURNER

polity

First published in 2012 by Polity Press

Polity Press
65 Bridge Street
Cambridge CB2 1UR, UK

Polity Press
350 Main Street
Malden, MA 02148, USA

ISBN-13: 978-0-7456-4841-5 (hardback)
ISBN-13: 978-0-7456-4842-2 (paperback)

A catalogue record for this book is available from the British Library.

Typeset in 11 on 13 pt Bembo by
Servis Filmsetting Limited, Stockport, Cheshire.
Printed and bound in Great Britain by the MPG Books Group Limited

For further information on Polity, visit our website: www.politybooks.com

Contents

Acknowledgements   vi
Preface   viii

   Introduction   1
1 Society as Structure   29
2 Society as Solidarity   65
3 Society as Creation   100
   Conclusion   154

Notes   172
Index   184

Acknowledgements

The gestation of this book has been a long one. Some of the ideas contained here trace back to the late 1980s, when Anthony Elliott worked with the late Professor Alan Davies, the late Professor Graham Little and Dr John Cash at the University of Melbourne. The idea for an enquiry into society and the social initially arose when Bryan Turner and I first worked together in the UK during the early 2000s, at Cambridge and Bristol respectively. The actual development of a theory of society as a form of radical cultural enquiry commenced some years later, and our research has been sustained over recent years – mostly through virtual interaction, with occasional face-to-face meetings – between New York and Adelaide.

We are grateful to various friends and colleagues, some of whom read the book in part or whole and offered many valuable comments and suggestions. We must thank in particular Charles Lemert, Anthony Giddens, Robert Holton, Gerhard Boomgaarden, Nicola Geraghty, Jean and Keith Elliott, Atsushi Sawai, Masataka Katagiri, Daniel Chaffee, Eric Hsu, Anthony Moran, Kath Woodward, Sophie Watson, Peter Redman, Jack Barbalet, Fiore Inglese, Kriss McKie, Nick Stevenson, Carmel Meiklejohn, Paul Hoggett, Tom Inglis, Alison Assiter, Deborah

Maxwell, Conrad Meyer, Paul du Gay, Robert van Krieken, Bo-Magnus Salenius, Jennifer Rutherford, Jem Thomas, Riaz Hassan, Constance Lever-Tracy, Peter Baehr, Tom Cushman, Jonathan Imber, John O'Neill, Chris Rojek, Simon Susen, Stephen Turner, Gary Wickham and John Urry. Dan Mendelson provided terrific research support throughout much of the project, and David Radford assisted in the final stages with manuscript preparation and advice. An earlier version of these ideas was sketched out at a joint Flinders University and La Trobe Masterclass, and special thanks are due to John Carroll and Peter Beilharz. To underscore our major caveat in this work that the theories of structure, solidarity and creation cross and tangle in complex, contradictory ways, it was heartening to find colleagues locating social theorists in more than one (and sometimes all three) categories. We have, perhaps unsurprisingly, not been able to cover all the traditions of social thought, nor theorists, which many readers suggested. As such, there is no discussion of, say, William James, Charlotte Perkins Gilman, Anna Julia Cooper, Max Horkheimer, Antonio Gramsci, C. Wright Mills, Niklas Luhmann, Frantz Fanon, Immanuel Wallerstein, Judith Butler, Edward Saïd or Eve Kosovsky Sedgwick. Such a failing is, it might be argued, entirely in line with commercial requirements to write a book that isn't the size of a phone directory. Even so, perhaps we can address the work of such theorists – through the registers of structure, solidarity and creation – in some future study.

We would like to acknowledge the support of the Australian Research Council, a grant (DP0877817) from which assisted in undertaking aspects of this project. And finally thanks to staff at Polity, and also to Susan Beer for diligently undertaking copy-editing of the book.

Various aspects of the argument relating to the civil sphere in Chapter 2 appeared originally in Bryan S. Turner (2008) *Rights and Virtues*, Oxford: Bardwell, but these have been revised for this publication.

Anthony Elliott, Adelaide
Bryan S. Turner, New York and Sydney

Preface

The argument of this book is disarmingly straightforward, though hopefully at once intricately layered and sociologically provocative. Our central claim is that most discourses on society – emanating from the social sciences and humanities in particular, and public political debates more generally – can be located within one of the following categories or registers: (1) society as structure; (2) society as solidarity; and, (3) society as creation. Outlining these three registers, we seek to assess the strengths and defects of various versions of 'society' and the 'social' as expounded in the tradition of social and political theory. One core aim is to reflect on how these three interpretations of society, in broader socio-political and historical terms, intersect, interlock, conflict and displace each other. Another is to consider the sociological consequences of these visions of society for the major issues of our times – ranging across politics, culture, morality and religion.

The question of society – its explication, constitution, reproduction and transformation – lies at the core of sociology. The question – what is society? – is probably the first question students confront when commencing the study of sociology. In a curious paradox, however, the word 'society' denotes no specific identifiable or defining quality throughout the history of sociology; indeed, the concept has long posed (and continues to pose) a profound challenge to making the work of sociology intelligible. Historically speaking, the concept of society in sociology has been largely constructed as a separate, self-enclosed territorial container of social actions and social relations. This equation of society with territorial nation-states has functioned, as the German sociologist Ulrich Beck has argued, as a kind of 'methodological nationalism' – in which the discipline has been comfortable enough when examining national institutions and state borders, but embarrassed on the whole by the existence of, say, empire, colony or transnational corporations. This may well be one reason why the discipline of sociology has embraced a plurality of terms in conceptualizing 'society', ranging variously across 'social practices', 'social order', 'social system', 'social structure', 'social forces' and 'social worlds'. In assuming that society pre-exists the social practices and social relations it constitutes, however, these various frameworks have, in the most general terms, been unable to engage the possibility of a variety of differential forms of the social and of varied societies. That is to say, the theorization of society in sociology has, perhaps predictably, (re)produced the typical institutional patterns of Western modernity.

If it is true that 'society' emerges as one of the most opaque, baffling terms in classical sociological thought, it has arguably proved equally troubling to our own age of intensive globalization and multinational turbo-capitalism. For one thing, it is surely a paradox of our times that, while social relations increasingly no longer neatly fit (if indeed they ever did) within the territorial boundaries of nation-states, the discipline of sociology finds itself silent or evasive about a whole range of concrete social problems affecting contemporary societies because the notion of 'the social' has been recently subsumed within the interdisciplinary lexicon of globalism. Of course globalization has also been debated continuously – by neo-liberals who want to push it further, as well as anti-globalists who focus on the harm it does – particularly in the context of its consequences for national societies.[1] In this connection, the common perception is that globalization erodes vulnerable communities and corrodes national socialities. Negative public perceptions of the many problems relating to globalization have been intensified by the economic and social upheavals that have attended the global financial crisis of 2008 and subsequent worldwide credit crunch. Just as the emergence of industrialism in the nineteenth century was judged destructive of family and community, many critics today lament the erosion of a common culture and communal co-operation as a consequence of globalization. Communitarianism, as we show subsequently, has become influential precisely at the point at which community appears to be disappearing. However, the idea that we have moved from a generous world of the caring community or supportive society to a wholesale corrosion of social organization is equally a myth. Blinded by nostalgia for a bygone age, this viewpoint ignores the considerable evidence of flourishing global socialities and transnational communal loyalties. These include, to list just a few, socialities of global protest (such as Make Poverty History), worldwide socialities for the protection of human rights (such as Amnesty International) and socialities for the protection of the environment (such as Greenpeace). More recently, in early 2011, the waves of the Jasmine Revolution appeared to show the survival of social networks and communities despite years of state repression.

From one angle, it is hardly surprising that, as a consequence of globalization, multiple communal loyalties and diverse social interconnections are on the increase for contemporary women and men of the polished, expensive cities of the West. This matters because globalization brings lifestyle changes – new ways of engaging with others, relationships, work and politics – into the heart of what society actually means. Indeed, our day-to-day experience of 'society' seems now to have less to do with geographic location or place. In our third chapter, on creation, we explore a concept that we term Elastic Society, by which we seek to capture the many ways in which social relations are stretched over time and space. To continue with this metaphor, Elastic Society may be thin as social networks are extended through space, but it does not automatically follow that they are fragile. Elasticity can also imply resilience and versatility.

More and more, women and men are getting involved with communities – and developing new kinds of sociality (both face-to-face and online) – in non-traditional ways: participating in online voluntary networks, setting up community blogs or creating visions for sustainable futures, rather than just joining established political parties.[2] We have to recognize the paradox that anti-globalism is the basis of a worldwide community that is itself a product of the globalizing forces that it opposes. Such global changes, we argue in this book, present sociology with a fresh challenge. If it is to engage adequately with transformations in the scope and structure of society, it must develop an integrated and comprehensive theorization of the social at every level of social theory. It cannot simply recount nostalgic narratives of the corrosion of society, because the critics of these global developments have also to recognize the new forms of the social that are emerging from these crises around the environment, the climate, and the city. That said, nor can sociologists remain silent about a whole host of vital political issues which challenge contemporary societies – from migration to marginalization, and multicultural-ism to militarization. Here sociology needs to chance its arm. In the age of the Internet, for example, will off-line communities contract continuously as online social relations expand? With the world's population expected to reach around nine billion people by 2050, what kind of social relations are most likely in the major mega-cities? Against the backdrop of people living in sky-high, multiplex apartments and with work carried out online, will social-ity be eroded or renewed? This book seeks to open up such a line of sociological enquiry and to outline new theoretical perspectives for the critique of contemporary societies.

Our book is intended for students as an introduction to debates about society in the social sciences, but also for general readers who might find the topic interesting. This necessarily means we tread a precarious line between specialist debate and broad-brush presentation. We hope that some of the more demanding parts of the book do not come at the cost of lack of accessibility; if any such difficulties arise we would like to think this is partly a consequence of certain current trends in social theory which tend towards obscurantism or jargon, rather than to our presentation of the post-societal turn in social theory itself. In the end, our aim has been to engage sociological thinking about society with the most urgent global issues of our times.

Introduction

The golden age of 'society' is long dead. The foundational sociological perspectives on society developed by Ferdinand Tönnies,
Émile Durkheim, Max Weber, Karl Marx and Georg Simmel
– while still clearly of immense conceptual importance to the
discipline of sociology – have been seriously challenged by the
communications revolution and the world of intensive globalization. In our own time of corporate downsizings, out-sourcing,
leveraged buyouts, just-in-time deliveries and gated communities, can we still read classical sociology with some intellectual
benefit in order to understand the contours and consequences
of twenty-first-century society? The Internet world is perhaps
equally problematic for more recent social theorists, such as Talcott
Parsons, Erving Goffman, C. Wright Mills and Alvin Gouldner.
Their perspectives on industrial capitalism were of outstanding
value, but, we now face a deeply disturbing issue – is the very
foundation of society as such changing so rapidly and so deeply that
we can no longer draw fully and comfortably from the legacy of
sociology? Many of their ideas on 'society' remain of incomparable
significance, but our purpose in what follows is to acknowledge
the extent to which society has changed in the the late twentieth
and early twenty-first centuries. To be more precise have the social

changes of the last half century rendered the idea of society in American sociologist Talcott Parsons's *The Social System*[1] of 1951 wholly obsolete? Why, for example, has the notion of 'society' come in our own time to appear so problematic? Is it the case that society is no longer a vital preoccupation of the contemporary age? There is certainly no shortage of contemporary critics of 'society' – whether, say, theorists of globalization who see in the advent of the global electronic economy the dissolution of nation-state based societies, or postmodernists who promote a view of sociality that is progressively particularistic rather than 'society' writ large, which is viewed as repressively universalistic.

Consider the following critical voice on the concept of society, a critic chosen more or less randomly from the vast treasure trove of 'anti-society' literature. The 'category of society', so our critic reflects, 'is merely a term of convenience'. Whereas 'the term "society" was once supposed to fix bounds', designating an internally integrated unity, it in fact functions as 'merely an indefinite range of partially or wholly articulated associatings'. In the face of such sociological particularism, our critic goes one step further – in lifting sociological deconstruction to the second order. Society 'makes itself known to us in the form of incessant repersonalizations of persons'. We say 'society', but what we really mean to underscore are 'provisional co-operatings'. We say 'society', but what we mean to say are 'the rearrangings of arrangements'. 'Society' (read: a social situation or condition) is, in fact, the upshot of 'individualizings'. Who, exactly, is this critic? The voice sounds like an example of postmodern deconstructionism or a 'micro' theorist of everyday interaction? Hardly. In fact the author of these sentiments was American sociologist Albion W. Small, and his reflections on the imprecision of the concept of society date to 1912 – from an article published in *The American Journal of Sociology*.[2] While in our own time the discourses of postmodernism and globalization present themselves as troublesome for the concept of society, let us note from the outset then that 'society' – both as an analytical category in social science and as lived experience – has long caused conceptual strife.

This immediately raises a first-principle question: What, exactly, is society? Perhaps the one thing that can be said with some confidence is that there is remarkably little definitional consensus over the use of this word. We might note in passing that other social sciences have problems with fundamental concepts, such as 'scarcity' in economics or 'power' in political theory. However 'society' appears to suffer most from presuppositional chaos. Indeed, as we will shortly examine, leading social thinkers (both classical and contemporary) have used the term 'society' with abandon; we might almost say promiscuously. That said, Raymond Williams, a key figures in the founding of the discipline of cultural studies, in his authoritative *Keywords* reflects: 'Society is now clear in two main senses: as our most general term for the body of institutions and relationships within which a relatively large group of people live; and as our most abstract term for the condition in which such institutions and relationships are formed.'[3] Historically speaking, the relationship between the generalization and the abstraction has shifted dramatically, as there has been a rich diversity of social conditions in and through which societies are constituted, consolidated or closed. We can perhaps best grasp something of this diversity if we consider the following compilation of usages to which this most complex word has been applied:

Undoubtedly society is a being, a person.
Émile Durkheim

Society exists only as a mental concept; in the real world there are only individuals.
Oscar Wilde

Society exists where several individuals enter into interaction.
Georg Simmel

Society is a masked ball, where every one hides his real character, and reveals it by hiding.
Ralph Waldo Emerson

To regard society as one single subject (*Subjekt*) is to look at it wrongly, speculatively.
Karl Marx

A civilized society is one which tolerates eccentricity to the point of doubtful sanity.
Robert Frost

A society grows great when old men plant trees whose shade they know they shall never sit in.
Greek Proverb

Society is produced by our wants and government by our wickedness.
Thomas Paine

Man was formed for society.
Francis Bacon

A society is a type of social system, in any universe of social systems, which attains the highest level of self-sufficiency as a system in relation to its environment.
Talcott Parsons

Society is a continuous chain of role expectancies and behaviour resulting from role expectancies.
Joseph Bensman and *Bernard Rosenberg*

The social only exists in a perspective space, it dies in the space of simulation.
Jean Baudrillard

The modern political domain is massively, in totalitarian fashion, social, levelling, exhausting.
Julia Kristeva

A society is a cluster, or system, of institutionalized modes of conduct.
Lord Anthony Giddens

There is no such thing as society; only individual men and women and their families.
Baroness Thatcher

There are a number of points that might be noted about this list of definitions. For one thing, some of these definitions view society positively, others negatively, some are clearly ambivalent while others dismiss it entirely. The more positive of these definitions see society as an indispensable medium for the production of social relations, emphasizing the benefits of interpersonal relationships and the potential gains from intercultural communication. In this sense, society is viewed in a largely technical way, as a process that facilitates not only the constitution of identity and elaboration of forms of thought but also the reproduction across time and across space of social interactions (think, for example, of family life across generations) and of social institutions (think, for example, of schools, hospitals or churches). Some of these definitions, however, view society pejoratively – as the inculcation of false beliefs, mythologies or ideologies – and thus emphasize the role of economic and political forces in various forms of human exploitation. Others view the notion as just sheer escapism, a collectivist fantasy in the face of individualist realities. Tracing the semantic shifts at play in these academic and public-political definitions of society is one of the aims of this book.

Society: An Obsolete Term?

Society, certainly the notion of it and perhaps even the social reality to which it once referred, is now dead. Or so argue some of its more strident and prominent critics. Yet the notion of society, as sociologist Charles Lemert has brilliantly traced out, had long been in trouble.[4] This much is evident from the article mentioned earlier by Small, as detailed in his eloquent musings on the imprecision of the concept of society in 1912. In our own time, this strife of imprecision has been lifted up a gear, into a fully blown obsolescence. This we might date to French sociologist Jean Baudrillard's proclamation in the 1980s that society had dissolved into the hyperreality of simulacra. In more recent years, it is perhaps Ulrich Beck who best captures the alleged redundancy of the term: society today is just a 'zombie category', a ghostly word spoken from the mouths of individualized agents. An emerging consensus, at any rate, seems clear: 'Society' – just a fading memory.

The death of society; the end of the social; the fragmentation of the social system; the implosion of sociality – it is evident that society has become an unfashionable topic in contemporary debate. Or, more to the point, society is fashionable only if it appears with the coda of a farewell. One interesting sociological point here is that the unfashionable nature of all things societal appears to have gone global – an anti-society sentiment is now wall-to-wall, as it were. The current displacement of the concept of society in both academic and public discourse is equally evident from the political Left and Right. Conservatives lament that modern society is invariably coterminous with collective disorder, cultural discord and moral breakdown. One highly reactionary version of this conservatism extends the bleakness so far that the notion of society is emptied of all significance – rendered void, null. Perhaps the best known instance of this neoconservative lexicon which we have already quoted is former British Prime Minister Margaret Thatcher's 1987 assertion that 'there is no such thing as society. There are individual men and women, and there are families'.[5] Many liberals, to be sure, share this anxiety of any contamination of the individual by the (collective) social form. The American political scientist Robert Putnam seems to assume that every year brings with it increasing alienation, isolation and societal fatality as men 'bowl alone', while sociologist Richard Sennett speaks disapprovingly of societal 'corrosion' as a consequence of the impact on jobs and identities of the new economy. If modern society leads us to 'bowl along' this is because we hanker after a bygone societal era in which the interpersonal fabric of self and other was harmoniously sewn. At its starkest, there is, probably inevitably, a highly nostalgic imagination at work in many portrayals of our contemporary social decline. Political theorists like Hannah Arendt are fond of pointing out that in the classical world there really was no word for society as such and the *polis* was not dependent on a wider sphere of social connections. Society, on this view, has beat a steady, shamefaced retreat from its previous lofty, Olympian height in the face of various political forces – which run all the way from capitalism to globalization, from multiculturalism to post-feminism. In equal measure, the abandonment of the notion of society now looms large in various versions of social and political thought that assert radical credentials. For post-structuralists, the very idea of society smacks of closure, determination, and metaphysics. Indeed, the term is largely discarded altogether in postmodernist thought. French social theorists, notably Jean Baudrillard, have declared the implosion of society into 'hyperreality'. For various feminists and post-feminists, society as a concept is too masculinist, functioning as a kind of patriarchal signifier repressive of femininity and the Other. Meanwhile, for the political Left in general, it is a notion too closely linked to the dead-ends of liberalism, the complacency of the welfare state, and one certainly out of kilter with radical global assertions for political emancipation.

The wholesale rejection of the concept of society is, we believe, one very good reason for writing about it. Why have so many authors, on both the political Left and Right, along with cultural conservatives and progressives, declared the notion of society dead? Why are social theorists wary of using the term at all? And should society – as both theory and reality – now rest in peace? Can a robust defence of the concept of society be mounted, through a radical and controversial social theory? Or should society just be dissolved into the social/sociality couplet of contemporary critical discourse?

Images of Society

'Society' is widely regarded as one of the most fundamental words in public life and politics. In ordinary usage, the term 'society' is intricately bound up with images of a collective, common identity. 'Society' here implies value consensus, and as such serves as a kind of 'sorting device' for grasping connections and differentials of social norms between different societal types. When a person in ordinary conversation remarks, for example, that Japanese society is more formalistic and polite than American society, it is evident that the notion of society is imagined to distribute properties of a common identity to its inhabitants. Unsurprisingly sociology, as 'the science of society', has a particular and special interest in the concept and the reality. Sociologists have sought to grasp this internally integrated unity associated with the term 'society' through various terminological innovations: some speak of society as a 'bounded complex', some of 'societal totalities', while others refer to the fixed boundaries of 'social systems'. Yet if the term 'society' calls forth images of highly integrated unities or the 'systemness' of social integration – the idea that a society displays fixed boundaries which provide for a collective unity, one which separates that society off from other societies – it also is suggestive of disinterested interaction, rationalized relationships and some degree of alienation. If society means an integrated social system, it also signifies social association in the widest sense – and very often this latter sense of society is glaringly at odds with the former one. Émile Durkheim, in forging the central theoretical dimensions of French sociology, spoke of 'the division of labour' as the dominant pattern of social interconnectedness in modern societies – in a standpoint which remains suggestive of the ambiguous tension between social association on the one hand and societal unity on the other within the overarching concept of society.

When examining the idea of society in contexts of everyday life and ordinary usage, we find five broad standpoints (no doubt, more could be isolated), some of which reflect the imprint of more intellectual evaluations of the term in social, cultural, political and philosophical thought – of which more shortly. First, society can be equated with 'high society': to be part of society means having the 'right' social connections, or knowing the correct way to interact at a major public event. This is an understanding that symbolically equates society with status, style and the signifier of 'civilization'. A second understanding of society is one which underscores everyday living. Society just *is* that domain in which cultural issues of identity play out, where the search for self unfolds, and where ideologies of progressive self-development take hold. In this understanding, society is conceived as primarily a container for the self. Society is basically what goes on in everyday life. A third position on society is inspired by the spread of industrialization and modernization, in which society emerges as a thoroughly material process in which differentiation, division and domination come to the fore. Society thus is abstract, always with the upper hand over its varied human subjects. In this approach, the emphasis is on social determinism – society triumphs over individual agency. A fourth related understanding meshes society with the sacred. Against a backdrop of the aesthetic and ascetic twinned, society in this understanding can be religion, nationalism, the erotic, ethnicity, and the like. In this framework society is resolutely utopian, forging an imaginary reconciliation between the trials of social association on the one hand and the most fundamental questions of human existence on the other. Finally, a fifth understanding of society – in the sense of ordinary usage – has more recently emerged around globalization, new information technologies and the Internet, as well as postmodernism and 'Third-Way'-inspired politics, whereby society becomes cosmopolitan through and through. In this perspective, some affirmatively speak of a global democratization of society, while other sceptics lament the cultural spread of global capitalism.

If the term 'society' is fundamental to public political discourse, it is also foundational to the social sciences in general and the discipline of sociology in particular. Etymologically speaking, the very emergence of the term 'society' is bound up with the ambiguity or doubleness of collective unity on the one hand, and generalized social association on the other. 'Society' is commonly awarded its first socio-political usage in 1531, where according to the *Shorter Oxford English Dictionary* it designated 'association with one's fellow men'. Indeed one of its original meanings, which predates the origins of sociology and returns us to ancient Greece, is 'association', or the cultivation of community. Aristotle, in *The Nicomachean Ethics*, specifically contrasts human community or association (*koinonia*) – as foundational to the politics of a 'society of citizens' – with the private individual or household (*oikos*). This aspect of the associational nature of the social is very important. As we will see subsequently these references to the Greek meaning of 'society' and 'politics' becomes controversial at a later stage. We have already referred to the controversial political ideas of Hannah Arendt who argued that 'society' is in fact 'mass society' and alien to the Greek world which elevated the political over the social. At any rate, from the ancient Greeks onwards society was conceived as a kind of civic form or associational bond, referring interchangeably to economic relations, cultural relations or political relations. Prior to the Enlightenment, and specifically the formative years of sociology in France, there was still no conceptualization of society as a reality *sui generis*. It is perhaps ironic – given the idea that the word 'society' was alien to the classical way of understanding the relations between state and citizen – that 'sociology' is a combination of the Latin 'socius' (fellow or more expansively friendship) and the Greek 'ology' (or study of). Critics of the discipline often humorously claim that it is essentially confused in combining two separate worlds. More generously, we might say that sociology has a transcultural disposition to combine worlds.

If the word 'society' encodes momentous historical transformations – that is, a set of fundamental institutional changes that unfolded throughout Europe in the late Middle Ages and the early modern period – it also reflects a series of ideological tropes. These ideological tropes have been understood, received, reproduced and reconfigured in various versions of social thought, ranging from classical sociology to contemporary social theory, and extend to core conceptual distinctions between the meaning of societies, social systems, social relations and the social. Society in some versions of classical sociology, for example, functions as an encoding of the universal; the 'societal totality' is that which scoops up the individual within a large associational relationship in which social contract rather than blood relationship is central. In clearly demarcating territorial boundaries and forms of associational locale, society thus works to refine within each of us its cult of common identity, value consensus, and a progressive sense of historical development. In classical sociology, the word 'society' traces within its semantic contours a distinctive set of economic transformations from European feudalism to market capitalism, from traditional state sovereignty to a system of interlocking, demarcated nation-states. However, as the very word implies an ambiguity between societal unity and social association, society can distil the outlines of societal totality only at the gravest of costs to genuine cultural accord. A rift between society and community is thus opened, but also nostalgically encoded. As the German thinker Ferdinand Tönnies argued in his classic *Gemeinschaft und Gesellschaft*, '. . . society is only a transitional and superficial phenomenon'.[6] Society is realized through indifference, hostility and cool market relationships; its breeding of impersonal, instrumental relationships can thus be sharply contrasted with the more spontaneous, integrated forms of social association in small-scale communities.

Tönnies's contrast between *Gesellschaft* and *Gemeinschaft* is an ironic one, although this point has been often missed in the social sciences. For many standard sociological textbooks, Tönnies is invoked (if at all in the contemporary period) primarily to underscore that instrumental, impersonal relationships of large-scale modern societies have replaced traditional, hierarchal relationships of small-scale communities. Those that have drawn upon Tönnies's ideas to make this sharp sociological contrast are, it must be said, partly correct. In presenting a dichotomous conception of social change, Tönnies did emphasize that communities encompass tradition whereas societies constitute modernity. The battle between *Gesellschaft* and *Gemeinschaft*, he argued, represents a 'tragic conflict'.[7] However the emergence of society, and its recoding of community, is not for Tönnies a wholesale movement in which the latter is fully eclipsed by the former. Community is still with us; the development of modern, large-scale societies makes the search for community, in some ways, more pressing than ever. Clean divisions between society and community are but intellectual projections; the two, in fact, criss-cross, intersect and dislocate. We should also recognize the fact that Tönnies saw both of these as processes rather than static conditions. This is, perhaps, what Tönnies refers to when he writes 'the essence of both *Gemeinschaft* and *Gesellschaft* is found interwoven in all kinds of associations'. And yet – however interwoven – Tönnies does present community as spontaneous and society as mechanical. While we will be critical of Parsons at various points in our reflections that follow on the theory of society, we should note at this stage that in his final study of American society towards the end of his life, Parsons made exactly this point – combining both community and association in his *Societal Community*, in which he sought to capture the ways in which these two dimensions can be incorporated into a single social system.[8]

For Durkheim, by contrast, the problem is the reverse: society is not, in fact, impersonal and mechanical, but constitutive of moral individualism and integrative of social relations. Just as Tönnies believed that modern, large-scale societies are characterized by mechanical social relations and a kind of utilitarian individualism, so Durkheim held, inversely, that modern societies are generative of unifying forms of solidarity and advanced forms of moral individualism. Durkheim is thus, in effect, suspicious of Tönnies's conviction that only life in small societies can be morally sustaining. Durkheim opposes this melancholic nostalgia, which strips the present of its utopian vitality, noting that 'there is a collective activity in our contemporary societies which is just as natural as that of the smaller societies of previous ages'.[9] It is one of Durkheim's many original theoretical moves to question the notion that tradition and social forms of the past are necessarily to be celebrated. In a striking sociological interpretation, modernity for Durkheim turns the tables on mechanical social relations of the past, reconstituting a more expansive experience of community which is specific to large-scale, modern societies. In bridging the gap between society and community in this way, Durkheim is able to identify new forms of solidarity which are specific to modernity – that which he sees as the upshot of a socially developed division of labour and operationalized through what he termed the 'conscience collective', the collective conscience or consciousness. Of course, Durkheim's view of the possibility of recuperating the social was seriously damaged by the advent of the First World War, the rise of aggressive militarism and the slaughter of a whole generation of young French men, including his son Andre Durkheim. Modern mass warfare demonstrated only too well the destructive force of modern society.

The problem of defining 'society' has exercised many of the best minds in contemporary sociology. To take just one example, the American sociologist Robert Nisbet – who wrote so powerfully on the issues of community, conservatism and authority – offered an interesting reflection on the recent history of society.[10] Nisbet observed that, through much of the twentieth century, there had been both a negative and a positive definition of society. The negative perspective emerged in comparison to the idea of 'community'. Whereas society was loose, impersonal, mechanical and transitory, community was seen to be rooted in permanence, authority and intimacy. Nisbet acknowledged that this contrast had its intellectual origins in the work of Tönnies, namely the distinction between community and association. The second positive meaning, however, was situated in a contrast with the power of the sovereign nation-state. For many writers, society was the site of individual freedoms and liberties, but these were all too easily expunged by the intervention and growth of the modern bureaucratic state. One example was to be found in the work of the American philosopher and educationalist John Dewey who, in *The Public and its Problems,* had warned against the inroads of the state in the machine age on small communities.[11] Pluralists like the British political philosopher J. N. Figgis thought that freedom, depending heavily on the survival of voluntary associations, community and civil society was severely compromised by the growth of the state. In general Nisbet concluded that the majority of writers believed that modern society was in a state of crisis. The principal challenge to society was the development of the totalitarian state in both fascism and Communism. He concluded by claiming that the great question for his generation was whether the countries of the former Soviet Union could throw off the shackles of bureaucratic regulation and party domination to become free and vibrant sites for the renaissance of society.

Such dichotomous conceptions of social change – contrasting 'community' with 'association', 'community' with 'society' or 'tradition' with 'modernity' – served to drive the topic of society to the grandest of narratives in the social sciences during the twentieth century. The story of what this does to the social sciences themselves is one of our concerns in this book, a story we trace from Tönnies and Durkheim through Talcott Parsons and Erving Goffman to British sociologist Anthony Giddens and French-Bulgarian feminist sociologist and philosopher Julia Kristeva. In the current preoccupation with the 'death of the social', however, another (perhaps equally mystifying) conception of dichotomous social change is at work. This twenty-first-century conception of the obliteration of the social is, by turns, terrifyingly traumatic and euphorically utopian. In a world of do-it-yourself identities, online connections, gated communities, networked associations, widening inequalities, enforced migrations, the displacement of populations from war-torn regions, and government-outsourced private military contracts, it seems difficult enough to find a trace of the logic of 'society' at work anywhere. Society has become 'liquid' in the words of Polish sociologist Zygmunt Bauman, without shape or form. The social is now thought of as being elastic, when social connections are stretched through time and space by means of new technologies. 'Society', in the age of global capitalism, has been rendered (to re-invoke Beck's term) a 'zombie' category. And yet it is highly doubtful, we think, to believe that the social has simply been executed or liquidated. Rather, and perhaps akin to Durkheim's critique of Tönnies, it is our argument that – with the world now globally refashioned in the image of transnational corporations and agencies – new forms of society, sociality and the social are being constantly, if precariously, reconstituted. These new forms of the social can be discerned, we shall suggest, at varying institutional levels: locales, nations, regions and various forms of globalism.

The Critique and Reconstruction of Society: Arguments of this Book

Let us offer here a short summary of the organization and arguments of this book. The approach adopted is textual, hermeneutic and critical. Our aim is to review, interpret and critique the various schools of social thought which have elaborated ideas of enduring importance to the theory and reality of society. A particular feature of the book is the outline of a broad, interdisciplinary examination of the idea of society – ranging across perspectives in sociology, anthropology, politics, philosophy, psychoanalytical, and cultural studies. Having given in this Introduction an outline of the core concepts involved in debates over society – from 'the social system' to 'the social' – the remainder of the book will discriminate between the different meanings of society in an unorthodox fashion. That is to say, the discussion of society in the social sciences and humanities which follows is not organized in a chronological fashion, or in historical sequence. Our book is *not* a history of ideas and even less a history of social theorists. By contrast, the critique of society developed herein shifts back and forth between classical conceptions and contemporary approaches to society. Our approach is formulated partly to better capture the complexity of social-science narratives of the rise and decline of society. However, this approach is also the upshot of our sustained critique of 'the death of society', or the thesis of the age of the post-societal. This now brings us to the core of our argument and, specifically, the presentation of our own ideas concerning the reconstruction, re-evaluation and rebirth of society.

As a foretaste to the central argument developed in this book, we begin by suggesting that society – as both theoretical construct and lived reality – faces in three directions. These three conceptualizations – operating as both discursive constructions and pre-theoretic understandings – unfold around the turn of the nineteenth century and undergo various complex transformations through to the twenty-first century. These three distinct senses of society can be summarized as follows:

1. Society as structure, or upper-case Society.
2. Society as solidarity, or communities of concern, care and consensus.
3. Society as creative process, or the imaginary dimensions of communication and sociality.

These three versions of society will be examined at length throughout this book. In doing so, we will discuss the complex, contradictory ways in which these three senses of society intersect, interlock, conflict and occasionally displace each other. But for the remainder of this Introduction, we wish to provide a brief, skeletal outline of our approach to the critique of society through the conceptual prisms of structure, solidarity and creation.

First, there is society as structure – a conceptualization that designates the descriptive aspects of structured competition, conflict and rivalry and the normative aspects of refinement, morals and manners. What is typically emphasized in this context is the antagonism between society as commerce and cool market relations on the one hand, and the inculcation of a high-minded moralism in the framework of upper-case Society on the other. Society is meant to cultivate enterprise, facilitate the egoistic self-realization of individuals and channel human impulses within the context of industrial-capitalism's own this-worldly activities. From this angle, society as structure is abstract, alienated, deterministic and mechanistic. At the same time, however, it is vital that society becomes not too morally indifferent. There is a thin line, as it were, between initiative and isolation, activity and anxiety. Thus, society in this sense must also offer an antidote to unfettered competition and markets, tempering the ethos of individual contest and social control with a reminder of the civilizing influence of tradition as well as the political significance of rules, regulations and procedural law. If society on this view then means the market, commerce, exchange-value and the will to dominate, it also means moral refinement, social manners and self-control in order to ensure that the base or foundation of civilization is adequately protected. Action, power and social control are critical, but it is dangerous to assume that they are sufficient for the smooth running of society. Structured forms of social life can be produced only to the degree to which conflict and competition are kept in check through an integration of tradition, morals, manners and ethics in the name of the social whole. And it is this antagonism between the descriptive and the normative which we trace in various versions of society as structure – which run in a venerable tradition from Durkheim onwards – throughout Chapter 1.

Second, there is society as solidarity. In this interpretation of society, solidarity and societal unity are seen as in constant tension with the ruthless individualism of capitalism rather than as subservient to, or integrated with, it. If the societal community is understood to be at one with the logics of commerce in theories of society as structure, there is by contrast a considerable gulf between the economy and equality in theories of society as solidarity. In this view, society is an upshot of affect, sentiment and passion; society promotes concern for others, care of the self, civic bonding and communal integration. The constitution and reproduction of the societal community is a matter of engagement, dialogue, consultation and consensus; and since these all require a certain degree of cognitive open-mindedness and emotional reflexivity, it is perhaps easy enough to see why the ruthless individualism and emotional insensitivity bred by cool market relations is portrayed in this viewpoint as destructive in impact. This moral view of society as solidarity is the antidote to the problem raised so forcefully by the German philosopher Friedrich Nietzsche and partly adopted by Max Weber – namely, the problem of human resentment. One of the powerful sentiments identified by classical political economy before Nietzsche was the issue of individual sentiments. Resentment is as old as greed, but it appears to flourish in societies based on competition over status, where prestige and rewards are scarce for individuals. Social bonding may offer the panacea for competition around the scarcity of status where individual resentment is a corrosive force.

There are, to be sure, many different versions of society as solidarity in the literature of social theory – some of which we examine in detail in Chapter 2. One view of society in this idiom stresses the organic and the holistic. The opposite of inhuman and individualistic capitalist society, for Tönnies and his followers, was a solidarity, or social cohesion, which arises from a natural tendency towards communal unity itself. The societal community is, in the broadest sense, organic because mutual understanding is engendered, according to Tönnies, through the small child's earliest experiences of maternal care. Matrimonial relations, brotherhood, kinship, tradition: these are key terms for describing the organic, naturalistic life-forms of societal communities. In a gesture curiously pre-figurative of contemporary debates concerning the 'death of the social', it was just such a dissolution of the societal community in this viewpoint which was understood to go hand-in-hand with the growth of society as structure. Alienated and disenchanted, modern society opts for structure rather than the societal community – the values of social stability and integration in *Gemeinschaft*, or Tönnies's 'Community'. This inflation of the solidaristic dimensions of society also appears in more recent versions of social theory, but with the 'organic' traded for 'language' and the 'holistic' traded for 'universalism'. What matters most here in *not* the societal community, but the *society of communities*. Solidarity is the condition and outcome of which society is the product. Rather than producing societal harmony or value consensus, solidarity multiplies discourse, communication and symbolic interaction.

We introduce a further distinction in our discussion of solidarity, namely the idea of social solidarity that springs up, perhaps spontaneously and constantly like an underground spring. Everyday sociality is thought be nourishing and productive. There is indeed plenty of social research that suggests that the friendships and intimacies of everyday life offer us some protection from sickness and disease; isolated old men in inner-urban areas who have no social supports are prone to depression, self-harm and sickness.[12] This is the solidarity that emerges with the endless flow of the exchange of goods, but more importantly a consequence of the endless round of conversations that make life meaningful through both conflict and co-operation. This we term 'lower-case solidarity' to distinguish clearly from the top-down solidarity or upper-case Solidarity that is associated with nationalism – especially violent or reactionary nationalism. In modern times, we might also add to the list of upper-case Solidarity the spread of fundamentalist movements in many major religions. Hitler's Brown Shirts shared a common nationalist solidarity; the Moral Majority in the United States also have solidarity. But these forms of solidarity, which are often highly politic and repressive, are not spontaneous outbursts of intimacy and friendship that are shared by two lovers. These forms of solidarity are monitored by rules relating to membership that strictly control entry and exit. Indeed in many religious solidarities the exit of individuals is heavily regulated by notions of apostasy and punishment.

Finally, there is society as creation. Society in this sense arises when the social is constituted with explicit reference to its own self-implementation, design, construction or creation. This is, as it were, about as far removed as imaginable from upper-case Society's obsession with a God-given structure or politically necessary social order, and yet it is equally wary of the naturalizing of sentiment, the affections and communality in society as solidarity. This is not to say, absurdly, that society can go without structure, and nor is it a matter of dismissing solidaristic demands for societal unity as mere utopian fantasy. The term 'society as creation' designates that the self-institution of social relations, along with self-reflection on social life, is paramount. This can be a way of recognizing the constitutive role of imagination in one's own social world, or the constitutive role of imagination in other people's social world, or indeed the essential wellsprings of the imaginary in society more generally. In this tradition of thought, society – always under interrogation, both analytically and as lived reality – is all about invention, ingenuity, innovation and imagination. At its best, this recasting of the social in full-blooded aesthetic terms underscores the centrality of autonomy, singularity, sociality, the unconscious and the new to creative living. At its worst, this version of society becomes complicit with a postmodern corporate culture which automatically celebrates (and indeed markets) all things new throughout shopping malls and cyberspace – which is to say, both locally and globally.

The three distinct senses of society outlined in this book do not easily separate out. That is to say, these versions of society – structure, solidarity and creation – cross and tangle in complex, and often contradictory ways. This is certainly true of how society has been signified as an analytical feature of social science, at least with reference to the three major forms of the concept throughout human history – namely, tribal societies, class-divided societies and modern nation-state societies. Especially important among intellectual evaluations of 'society' – and this is arguably so whether the societies in question were simple or primitive on the one hand, or complex and developed on the other – is the degree of 'systemness', or integral wholeness, attributed to external forces in meeting the satisfaction of people's material needs and wants. This is certainly true of society-focused social theories, from Durkheim's heavy emphasis on society as a whole to more recent versions of structural sociology and systems theory. No matter the degree of 'systemicity' attributed to society as a substantive entity (conceived usually as closely allied with either biological processes or informational metaphors), however, all structured conceptions of society make some reference – however minimal – to the beliefs, values, feelings and dispositions of the members of any

Table I.1 Domains of the Social

Types of Social Relations	Ideological Registers	Modes of Interaction	Identity and Difference Vested in Forms of Personal and Social Life	General Orientation of Social Conduct
Structure	Enclavement	Hierarchical Societies	Self Against Other	Understands society principally in terms of rules, regulations and legal processes
Solidarity	Stickiness	Interactive Societies	Self-Other Continuum	Focuses upon the importance of community, consensus and cooperation
Creation	Elasticity	Innovative Societies	Self and Other	Seeks communication and dialogue, and regards curiousity, stimulation and play as fundamental

given society. This is to say, if societies are to function with an adequate degree of systemicity there must be some basic sense of 'common identity' (which is not necessarily a value consensus) or 'sense of belonging' to a wider collectivity. It is important here to re-emphasize that, in conceptualizing social association, social scientists theorize the orderly roles of structure, the 'natural' sentiments of solidarity, and the inventiveness of creation differently. This issue comes out clearly in post-Parsonian attempts to rethink the classical ideas of status and role in which symbolic interactionism argued that 'role' is always a process in which actors endlessly struggle to make sense of the norms that allegedly define role performance. But the critical point is that these different versions of society appear as contradictory, strained, sometimes overlapping and, usually, unstable. When it comes to sociological thinking about society, for whatever analytical purposes, social scientists can be 'half-in, half-out' of the versions of society we are sketching.

In our scheme – structure, solidarity, creation – we avoid the trap of thinking that a particular theory or theorist can *only* fit into one of our categories. Obviously theories can in actual practice draw on any combination of them. As a result, we do not want to follow the old binary divisions in which, for example, Durkheim allegedly believed in consensus and Marx emphasized conflict. We avoid any simple opposition between structure and creation. In this respect, we are sympathetically following the British sociologist David Lockwood's strictures in *Solidarity and Schism* when he comments, in a discussion of institutions, that it would be wrong to conclude 'that the only alternative to the normative functionalist explanation of order is to revert to equally over-simplified solutions in terms of coercion and advantage, of fear and cupidity'.[13] He went on to observe that we should avoid the 'no less onerous assumption, apparently favoured by "conflict" theorists, that the structure of values and norms is of negligible importance in accounting for social disorder'.

If this is the case for theorizing 'society' as an analytical feature of social science, it is equally true of 'society' in the more ordinary sense of the word – as a feature of practical social life. Society in this sense arises whenever these three pre-theoretic stocks of knowledge – that is, structure, solidarity and creation – open up possibilities of action within social life at the same time as they limit or constrain other ways of acting in the world. Hence, 'society' is not just some academic set of theoretical pronouncements issued by social theorists, but a set of possibilities and constraints on human action used in the reproduction and transformation of social relations. We have now entered, as it were, society at street level. Understanding that the three distinct senses of society which we elaborate are deeply embedded in the production of everyday social life is one of the main contentions of this book, and it is worth developing the point a little further here.

Notwithstanding fashionable pronouncements about the death of society, there are many, varied ways in which these three senses of society play out – interlacing and dislocating – in contemporary times. While contemporary societies of the West are remarkably different in contour and consequence from industrial society as conceived by Durkheim, Weber and other founders of sociology, there are still various orderly roles and legal duties which exist and may usefully be termed 'structured society'. Whenever a person completes their tax return, lodges an application for a passport, pays a fine on a parking ticket or makes a (regular) payment on their mortgage to a bank, it is arguably the case that structure arises as a normative means of imagining that society. It is equally easy to invoke social practices that bring societies of solidarity or creation to mind. Solidarity is a set of social relations encompassing trust, tact, tragedy and tradition. Expressing sympathy for a grieving friend, joining in the self-effacing work of charity fund-raising, or consulting with colleagues to ensure a fair work outcome for all: these are instances of the experience of the comfortable and comforting unity of solidaristic societies. In the everyday world these practices – signing cheques, going to a party or supporting a fan club – are ways in which society is constantly re-produced.

In *The Future of Society*, the British sociologist William Outhwaite argues that the notion of society that became important for the early stages of the development of sociology already had certain problematic qualities.[14] Society was typically associated with socialism, especially in the case of Auguste Comte – one of the founders of the discipline of sociology – and Henri de Saint Simon, whose early writings were to be influential to many nineteenth-century sociologists. This association between a political agenda and a science continued in the work of Émile Durkheim, especially in his reflections on the role of the state. Whereas Durkheim, again in a French tradition, associated society with social solidarity, the German wing of early sociology took a very different direction. Outhwaite notes correctly that Weber, for example, rarely used the word society and was more interested in community. Both Weber and the German sociologist and philosopher Georg Simmel rejected the idea of society as an objective structure, preferring to think of society, in Weber's case, as 'sociation' or *Vergesellschaftung,* or 'community-formation' (*Vergemeinschaftung).*

Possibly as a result of American confidence after the Second World War, functionalism treated society as a well organized system, and formation of interconnected parts that moved, after disturbance, towards an equilibrium. In the more unstable 1960s and 1970s, these notions of society came under critical scrutiny from conflict sociology, interactionism, and ethnomethodology. 'Society' came to be seen as something that was fleeting, constructed and unstable.

'Society' had been associated pre-eminently with 'modernity', and as uncertainty about the consequences of modernization increased in the late twentieth century, so too questions were asked about 'society'. With increasing migration, the fabric of society became more complex and questions about society increased in intensity. The work of the French sociologist Alain Touraine can be taken as a good example of uncertainty about social life, specifically his reflections in *Can We Live Together? Equality and Difference*.[15] We can argue that attitudes towards social differences divide into two opposed camps. Social and political theory has been divided between a politics of difference that encourages us to recognize the cultural hybridity brought about by globalization and a theory of global citizenship that attempts to discover new patterns of social solidarity. The emphasis on difference celebrates the diversity of identities in a fragmented world by abandoning a strong theory of equality. The emphasis on social equality attempts to preserve some element of Enlightenment universalism in order to take up a defence of justice, but has difficulty in formulating a comprehensive view of tolerance. More specifically, the politics of identity is accused of abandoning any commitment to justice and equality, while the notion of universal rights is often perceived as inexorably Western and blind to local demands for recognition and respect. In some respects, this tension between individual differences and social equality reflects a tension between liberalism and socialism in the context of the development of sociology. Touraine's comprehensive inquiry into equality and difference, published in France in 1997, was a bold attempt to find solutions to these real polarities.

With globalization, culture can no longer control social organization, and social organization can no longer regulate technological and economic production. As a result, culture and economy, and the symbolic world and the instrumental world, have drifted apart. Out of the ruins of the institutions of modernity a new social world is emerging in which there is a global system of communication and at the social level a retreat to identity-based groups – communities, sects, cults and national associations. Outhwaite treats globalization as the social process that has done much to undermine the notion of society as a viable concept for sociology. The paradox of globalization is that local identities are intensified in a context of expanding global networks. The new communalism does not, however, derive its legitimacy from the sovereignty of the people, but from charismatic sources (gods, myths and traditions). The idea of global citizenship has little sociological purchase in a world of fragmented but intense communities. The erosion of national sovereignty and the growth of charismatic communities make living together increasingly tenuous. This view of the divisive force of identity, especially religious identity, was eventually the basis of a theory that shaped academic notions of foreign affairs, namely the thesis of 'the clash of civilizations' by the American political scientist Samuel Huntington, which we will discuss in Chapter 1.

Touraine remains suitably sceptical about existing solutions with respect to the growing cultural complexity of modernity. The attempt to revive some version of secular republicanism to address diversity results in social exclusion. The problems of French republicanism with respect to the Islamic tradition of veiling for women only became apparent in the next century. By contrast, the postmodern recognition of difference adequately confronts the collapse of nation or class as agents of progress, but the postmodern solution is only valid as a response to cultural diversity. For critics, postmodernism was notoriously apolitical; its creed ruled out any systematic policy options by a unified state. It was in short silent about the question of equality. In any case, without political solutions, the market will effectively regulate collective life.

Another response is to rely on procedural democracy to establish codes of public conduct that will contain cultural and ethnic conflicts. This solution is minimalist, because it safeguards public order, but it fails to ensure effective and meaningful communication. In short, those modern institutions and cultures that maintained modern society as a consequence of the French and American Revolutions are no longer relevant to a global context in which the corporate economy dictates the conditions of politics and communication. We have seen this problem acutely in the media crisis that has surrounded News Corporation and the unravelling of the Murdoch Empire in 2011. Sociologists who argue that the basis of democratic participation rests on communication channels in civil society must provide some effective legal defence against media monopolies. The benevolent political leader of the Enlightenment is dead, and his role in politics has been replaced by global financiers, bankers, innovators and public relations analysts. If the new Hobbesian war is between global corporate strategists and the charismatic leaders of ethnic communities, then the solution must be to reintegrate culture and economy in order to resist the agencies of global capitalism.

Touraine's response to 'demodernization' (namely the separation of culture and economy) is guided by two principles. The first is the importance of protecting personal life from fragmentation by preserving the possibility that the narrative of one's life-story is not simply an incoherent and contingent series of events – a coherent biographical narrative helps the individual to become an actor. The basis for a new politics is thus the project of the Subject, who resists both the globalized world of media technologies and narrow confines of communal membership. Touraine provides a study of the sociological conditions by which Others are recognized as Subjects and the institutional safeguards that are necessary to protect the freedom of the Subject and foster communication between them.

His approach to the problem of society is divided into the production of the self and living together. Tourraine draws on the sociology of social movements to study the transformation of the modern self and the production of the Subject. In hypermodernity, the Subject is torn apart by the contradictory forces of the market and the community. Because the traditional democratic notion of the individual and the general will is no longer adequate, new social and cultural movements provide contexts within which the individual can become an effective agent. Touraine's quest (which implicitly follows the political theory of Jean-Jacques Rousseau) for alternatives points ultimately towards educational means to protect the Subject from the social disintegration of late modernity. The school for the Subject requires an education that will enhance the freedom of the individual to become a Subject, but education must also recognize heterogeneity and promote the dialogical dimensions of communication. Education must remove the concrete obstacles to equality that would prevent the Subject achieving personal coherence. This recognition, often referred to in the philosophical literature as 'recognition ethics', will require effective policies of multiculturalism and regulatory mechanisms that prevent or contain communal conflict flowing from cultural particularism. Unfortunately for Touraine's solution, commitment to multiculturalism as a social policy had in the first decade of the twenty-first century been abandoned by the major European societies (France, Germany and Britain) and in many small European societies (Denmark, Norway and Finland) as right-wing nationalist parties have become increasingly important in political life. The problem behind these political developments has been migration and the growth of the Muslim diaspora. Interestingly he condemned Islamic fundamentalism as the principal illustration of archaic communalism without any sensitivity to the social complexity of fundamentalism as a protest against the consumerist face of modernity. Touraine of course emphasized the importance of cultural understanding, because 'a multi-cultural society can exist only if no majority ascribes a universal value to its own way of life'.[16]

For Outhwaite the problems of multiculturalism are the product of globalization. The sociology of globalization was more prominent in British than in American sociology. He comments on the main theorists of globalization: John Urry, Martin Albrow, Anthony Giddens and Roland Robertson. Perhaps the key figure in the critique of 'society' was Urry. His position was summarized as 'globalization involves replacing the metaphor of society as *region* with the metaphor of the global conceived of as *network* and as *fluid*'. This theme was also an aspect of the work of German social theorist Niklas Luhmann, who developed his own approach to the idea of a global system of societies.[17] Outhwaite eventually seeks a solution that (1) does not deny the reality of the nation-state; (2) does not embrace an out-of-date notion of society within a specific territory; and (3) does not assume that society will have much solidarity. From the standpoint of our scheme, it might be said he recognizes that both structure and solidarity are now problematic.

Outhwaite sees the modern problem of sociology in terms of a question posed by the British sociologist Nicholas Gane:

> Could it be that 'society' (which tended to be theorized as being contained within the territorial limits of the nation-state) is all but dead, or is it possible that (capitalist) society is recasting itself in new global, post-national directions? Or might it be that the social itself is no longer confined (if it ever was) within the limits of society or the nation-state, and is increasingly fluid and diverse in form?[18]

We have tried to answer this question in this book by suggesting that new forms of sociation (the principle of creation) constantly emerge with new means of communication. We argue that these new forms of sociation can have dramatic political consequences and hence they are not necessarily trivial forms of the social (for example, WikiLeaks and the Arab Spring). We suggest however that these types of sociation will have minimal solidarity – they will not be, in our terminology, 'sticky'.

Finally, our discussion of the three faces of society involves a philosophical (and possibly existential) concern to debate the implications of nostalgia. It is all too easy to assume the role of intellectuals as the carriers of a dismal science, but such an attitude is ultimately unhelpful and defeatist. Our purpose is to seek out those instances in the modern world where the social, conceptualized as creative everyday processes of sociality, is constantly being rebuilt and re-assembled in the face of formidable odds – the decline of neighbourhood, the erosion of active citizenship, the decline of public institutions, the commodification of the everyday world, the commercialization of religion, the loss of innocence. The list of 'bad news' is more or less endless, but a pessimistic or nostalgic surrender to fate is not a laudable position. In our view it is not a defensible or coherent position. Why would we write this book to underline pessimism? Surely it would be more consistent not to write at all. We attempt to explore at least one aspect of such sociable repair through an examination of the networks and connections made possible by the Internet. What type of sociality might arise out of the globalization of communication; is a new cosmopolitan virtue possible? At the point of writing this book, democratic alongside potentially destructive social forces are reshaping modern Tunisia, Jordan and Egypt after decades of one-man or one-party rule, in large part through the networks and social movements made possible by Facebook and Twitter. While academics may rightly lament the decline of a book culture and civilized standards of literacy, we cannot ignore the progressive potential of the Internet for the regeneration of democracy, not to mention society.

1

Society as Structure

Sociology is born as a discourse of social order, norms and structure. Anyone who considers the history of European social theory must be struck by the intriguingly high priority assigned by it to issues concerning the primacy of society over the individual. In its most influential formulation in French social thought by Émile Durkheim, the reciprocity intrinsic to modern social solidarity produces a basis of social order. For Karl Marx, the increasing instrumentalization of both nature and humanity under capitalism is the upshot of an imposed universal, abstract law – compressing all social relations to the dictates of the capitalist division of labour. German sociologist Max Weber downgraded the question of social order in favour of individual action and meaning, but nevertheless spent a lifetime pondering how the two spheres intersect. Weber, while promising to rid sociology of collective concepts, constantly analysed structures of power, authority and exchange. For Ferdinand Tönnies, in a contrasting fashion, modern society is portrayed as superficial and fragile – because it is not grounded in lasting values and durable structures. In modern social theory, from the German philosopher and sociologist Theodor Adorno's formulation of the 'totally administered society' to Talcott Parsons's emphasis on the social cohesion of modern societies, the terms structure, order and norms are granted theoretical privilege. In the current debates on globalization, cosmopolitanism and culture, structure would also appear to remain an important category for the analysis and critique of transnational spaces.

To assert the centrality of structure to the general theory of society in sociology might seem, at first glance, too unqualified a gesture. We do not suggest, however, that classical social theory was fully held in thrall to the concept of structure to the exclusion of other ways of conceiving of the social. The truth is that various other theoretical concepts and political doctrines were mobilized throughout the history of sociology to capture the complexities of societies in quite specific ways. In the course of this book, we chart the adventures not only of *structure*, but also *solidarity* and *creation,* in the discourse of the social. It would also be foolish to suppose, even where the language of structure has reigned supreme in social theory, that an emphasis on social order and moral norms fits neatly into a conservative political tradition. For again the truth is more complex. Certainly in what follows we seek to map a combination of social and historical factors to develop the argument that the discourse of society as structure has been informed by many political traditions – especially the doctrines of liberalism, conservatism and socialism.

Notwithstanding these qualifications, however, sociological conceptions of society as structure arose – generally speaking – against a background of disorderly behaviour and disruptive events in European cities and urban spaces. From the French Revolution of 1789 to the outbreak of the First World War in 1914, Europe had been subject to profound revolutionary changes in the transition from the *ancien regime* to the emergence of modern industrialism, and as such social theory became primarily concerned to understand social order and the social conditions that produced normative order. We shall see a little later, especially in the work of Durkheim, how such a detour through problems associated with the disruption of social norms brought about by urbanization and rapid social change was politically necessary in the intellectual context of French society during the late nineteenth and early twentieth centuries. Yet this intellectual response to the disorientation of values and beliefs in modern society was not the only distinguishing trope of classical sociology. For in a striking theoretical move, classical sociology was also founded upon the quest to define and differentiate 'the social' from 'the natural'. Critical of attempts to understand social phenomena in terms of the natural endowments of human beings, sociology substituted 'institutions' for 'instincts'. Sociology came to insist on the reality of the social world, but it also sought to distinguish itself from economic, political, and even cultural perspectives.

This centrality of the social, as opposed to some raw explanations in terms of nature, lies at the root of the critique of culture launched by classical sociology. However classical sociology involved not only the quest to define the social as a field of distinct intellectual endeavour, but also to grasp the social as a moral phenomenon distinct from individualism – especially the form of individualism that emerged primarily in British social theory. In fact we can read much of (continental) social theory in the late nineteenth century as a critique of British liberalism in politics and utilitarianism in economic thought. The key figure here was the English philosopher and sociologist Herbert Spencer whose doctrine of state and individual was the object of much of Durkheim's critical attack through the notion of solidarity. British political economy from the Scottish social philosopher Adam Smith onwards had argued that the market, the division of labour and competition through international trade would result in the benefit of all. Spencer and the utilitarians of the nineteenth century inherited from the English jurist and philosopher Jeremy Bentham the idea that progress could be measured in simple quantitative terms as the happiness of the individual. The role of government was to remove the hurdles to general happiness. European sociology had a much darker vision of society and history with Weber famously predicting a night of icy darkness rather than utilitarian felicity. Continental social theory has been throughout critical of the 'Manchester School' as both naive and utopian. For Durkheim at least, a set of countervailing forces was necessary to offset the destructive force of economic individualism.

If the character of sovereignty defines the political, the social is defined by trust. Trust is the social dimension that underpins social relations, especially contractual relations in the social sphere.

Just as money is the medium of exchange in the economy, trust is the medium of reciprocity in the social field. Classical sociology, or at least those versions that render society as structure, was the study of the institutionalization of relations of trust, respect and hierarchy – in the family, religion, the law, customs and so forth. This emphasis on the orderliness of society has often led to the view that writers like Durkheim were inevitably conservative but such is not the case. Durkheim argued for example that the state had a moral function to play in steering society out of the crisis of anomic values. As a result his emphasis on the state over the individual was socialist not conservative.

It is important to note in this context that there were various levels of analysis in the classical tradition. Because the debate with economics as a science was central to much of nineteenth-century social thought, it is hardly surprising that Marx and Weber approached their task of analysing capitalist society in terms of a model of economic action. The economic model involved the idea of rational actors satisfying their wants in a competitive market. Social action was modelled on a similar set of notions, but sociologists sought to study social collectivities (such as social classes), questioned the rationality of economic behaviour (by including notions such as ideology and the non-rational), and questioned the idea of needs and wants (by demonstrating their cultural relativity). Whereas economics involved the study of the rational selection of means and ends in conditions of scarcity, sociology emerged as the study of the conditions of trust that underpinned social institutions, and they saw these social bonds as underpinning economic contracts. In economics, money provides a measure of the distribution of rational choices, whereas trust is only an indirect or proximate measure of social solidarity. In short, sociology – in contrast to classical economics – developed much richer or thicker notions of behaviour and action, but at the cost of precision, measurement and predictability. And yet it is precision and predictability that sociologies of structured society most prize. As we will shortly see, the emergence of anxieties about an increase in the disorientation of values and beliefs are consequences of a decline in trust in modern societies. Low trust is viewed as signalling the erosion of social order in various sociologies of society as structure. The general response to such developments across the expensive, polished cities of the West from this sociological orientation has been one of alarm.

The dynamic, exhilarating project of society as structure represents, from one angle, a long political tragedy – one marked by the unspeakable sufferings of women and men subjected to various 'civilizing forces', from capitalism to colonialism. Indeed, modernity's drive for order, control and predictability represents at once a very particular kind of global history – roughly speaking, the West – and its absolute negation. Such a paradoxical conception of society rests on a radical split between descriptive and normative senses of the social. Society as structure has nourished and destroyed simultaneously. The development of bureaucracy in modern societies was for both sociologists and philosophers of the nineteenth century the process par excellence that defined order and predictability. Weber thought it was inevitable and associated its growth with the triumph through Germany and then Europe of Prussian values and institutions. Military discipline and military bureaucracy became the basis of military success as warfare became industrialized. Japan, in its rush to modernize, absorbed German military organization and technology with devastating success, as the Japanese demonstrated in the war with Russia in 1905.

On the one hand, the modernist dream for certitude, nowhere fully realized but long sought after, would seem a key source of social, cultural and political inspiration from industrialization to imperialism. On the other hand, modernist transformations of ideology have functioned to generate a sense of society that is itself lacking any particularity or specificity. The scientific revolution of the early modern period decentred the social in a dramatic fashion, producing a set of values or criteria universalistic in scope and thus which served to inform ways of knowing any authentic way of social life whatsoever. In the realm of social theory, such a connection between the concrete and universal is part and parcel of what we term the discourse of society as structure. Structured society is the worldview of organized social relations, involving cultural codes and social scripts objectifying prescriptions, prohibitions and performativities. In this vision of the social as organized and organizing, society is at one with universal rights and responsibilities, and

more often than not social imperatives are conceived in terms of
law and order.

Society, or the political state, or community, is viewed in
this frame of reference as a supra-collective foundation, exercising legislative authority and making juridical pronouncements in
the name of universal humanity. At its best, society as structure
expresses a realist bent, anchored as it is in social context and security, and concerned above all with economic prosperity or social
order. At its worst, society as structure is conformist, utilitarian,
shallow and passionless. Weber's notion of society as an iron cage
captures this sense of standardization and rationalization at its most
bleak and pessimistic moment. Capitalism expanded the market
but at a substantial cost to human happiness. In fact from Weber's
perspective, happiness could not be of any concern to sociologists
but only to utopian reformers of industrial society. Weber was
particularly critical of romanticism and of those utopian thinkers
who felt they could oppose the march of modernization, com-
plaining in particular about the young disciples around the German
poet Stefan George who imagined they could defy the progress of
rationalization. Their poetic protests were merely ineffectual waves
smashing on the stubborn resistance of rocks.

If society originally means organized social relations, it suggests
both regulation and continuity. The social is what encourages
choice, change and the construction of personal identity, but the
ground from which it does so needs to be consistent, structured
and sanctioned, which in turn leads to an ongoing preoccupation
with obedience, control and the collective. 'Society' here can be
traced to a certain type of discourse which belonged to the general
spirit of Enlightenment, with its vision of linear, progressive self-
development 'without history', an ideology that from the German
philosopher Immanuel Kant onwards was dubiously established at
the very heart of historical society itself. Society as structure, in its
grand narrative of universal humanity, is written in capital letters:
Progress, Property, Science, Freedom and the Family. These ideals
governing the discourse of society appear neither removed nor
wholly at one with the actual texture of daily social life. Rather,
like the Freudian superego inflicting harsh rebukes upon the conscious self, the cultural ideals of society as structure imply a radical

split between the subject who speaks and lays claim to the organized and organizing rules of social order, and the Other denied access to instituting rules and thus deprived of the status of subject. This is, in short, the core of the Ethnocentrism of society, which is given its political axes and force through a series of dichotomies: civilized/savage, self/other, normal/mad, man/woman, adult/ child. From this angle alone, society as structure represents an adventure story that continues fully into the present day, profoundly shaping some of the key global political conflicts of our age. Indeed, society as structure is a worldview arguably pivotal to those forms of politics conceived in the mould of the West versus the rest.

Of course, generalizations are always dangerous, especially when dealing with the Enlightenment. One of its leading figures was the Swiss philosopher Jean-Jacques Rousseau, who endlessly complained about the destructive impact of society – by which he meant the rapidly urbanizing and commercial world of Paris – on the innocence of the child and, in *Émile*, created many of our contemporary ideas about protecting the emotional world of the sensitive child from the adult world of competition around status and wealth. Rousseau was especially critical of the rise of the modern theatre which was a site for competitive displays of wealth. Rousseau thought that the good citizens of Geneva would be corrupted by the world of Parisian capitalism. But there is no simple way to interpret Rousseau, who also defended the idea that we can find freedom in the general will. Liberals such as the British social and political thinker Isaiah Berlin have condemned Rousseau as an enemy of freedom. However, Rousseau's argument was to reject the notion that the selfish actions of individuals can produce a common good and proposed that the general will can never be a simple aggregate of individual selfish desires. One further point about Rousseau is that he believed that freedom and virtue of the individual were much more difficult to secure in large than in small societies. In short, the emerging idea of society as structure had a good deal to do with the growth of population and the rise of large cities like Paris, London and Berlin.

Self-constitution and concentration of activities within the *milieux* of society may certainly emanate from the stylization of the individual subject. But this interplay between self and society may also be experienced as a force exerted upon the day-to-day lives of citizens by the political centre. In social theory, all modern forms of society have consisted of a plurality of organizations; in particular, the concept of the 'state' – as an apparatus of government or power – has special resonance in those versions of social theory that have sought to comprehend society as structure in its origin and nature. For the state to effectively subordinate social systems to their rule, it must socialize its citizens in the proper cultural attributes of a national community and instill particular sorts of expression of cultural identity; and it is this which the state/civil society relation designates in a celebrated tradition from German philosopher Georg Hegel to Marx. In civil society and specifically the bourgeois version of the civil sphere, individuals are viewed as primarily self-seeking and atomistic, driven by their own particular interests; but the state is that political field which facilitates the emergence of a series of defined communities or ethical clusters in which egoistic conflicts and social divisions can be overcome; in short, upper-case Society suppresses diversity (whether gender, race or class) in order to create an imagined community of sameness. Hegel's dialectic of the universal and particular in *Phenomenology* – the state is 'the Universal that has expressed its actual rationality', representing 'the identity of the general and particular will' – anticipated much of the direction that the state/civil society debate was to assume in social thought.[1] For Hegel, the connection between the impersonal power of the political and the civil spheres of society is easy to see: the state actualizes and deepens forms of 'the universal' which are lacking in civil society. The state, writes Hegel, is 'the embodiment of concrete freedom, in which the individual's particular interests have their complete development, and receive adequate recognition of their rights'. In this tradition of thought, the individual subject adopts a state sanctioned identity by rising above prosaic particularity, through elevating culture over politics, to realize a kind of 'universal freedom'. The state incarnates reason, not by scooping up civil society but by embodying certain of the universal qualities upon which it is predicated.

In turning Hegel on his head, Karl Marx's sociological thought involved a sustained reflection of the relation between universal

and particular, and in his political writings at least the problem of
the social is dramatized in terms which emphasize that the state
rests upon civil society. In his 'Critique of Hegel's Doctrine of
the State', Marx levels the charge of 'political formalism' against
Hegel.[2] Hegel's political thought, says Marx, conceptualizes how
the state is a kind of universal instructor in civility, instilling
within the individual self a supreme sense of the abstract equality of individuals. The formalism of this position for Marx is that
such a politically harmonious account of the state/society relation can be purchased only at the cost of denying the concrete
particularities of, and differences between, individuals. For Marx,
Hegel's doctrine of the state is, in fact, a portrait of bourgeois
society, in which a lethal cleavage appears between the subject
of civil society in his or her immediate material specificity and
the abstract, rights-bearing person of public political life. Marx,
in his reflections on the emancipation of the Jews, was critical
of the abstract notion of the 'rights of man' arguing that without
economic emancipation these rights were merely empty promises.
By contrast, Marx posits that the state/society relation moves
at the uneasy conjuncture of class and culture, society and the
symbolic. For Marx the state is linked, not only to class (whose
dominant composition it reflects), but to the fundamental structures of 'social division'. Marx saw that at the root of society lies
a certain divisive force between the dominant and the dominated,
of which class relations or the relation between state and civil
society were symptomatic. Society for Marx is generally ignorant
of the fundamental feature of social division, and this he traced
to the intoxicating hold of ideology. According to Marx, there is
always within society an imperative need to forge representations
of unity, to project a kind of 'imagined community' by which the
historical is portrayed as natural, the particular is disguised in the
universal, the contingent is effaced in necessity. As one of Marx's
key innovators contends:

> Ideology maintains the illusion of an essence of society, staves off the
> double threat which weighs upon the established order by virtue of
> the fact that it is divided and the fact that it is historical; it imposes
> itself as a discourse rational in itself, a closed discourse which, masking

the conditions of its own engendering, claims to reveal that of the empirical social reality.[3]

The mechanisms by which the state regulates and stabilizes society – repression, sublimation, disavowal – have been traced in considerable detail in various Marxist and neoMarxist formulations. The whole Marxist problematic of a dynamic social field regulated and repressed by state institutions remains wedded, however, to the wider modernist dislocation between the universal and concrete, form and content.

The ideas of individual and society are pivotal to the tradition of social theory, so much so that they may seem definitive of the discourse of sociology itself. Yet with consideration of the state/civil society relation in Western philosophy during the eighteenth and nineteenth centuries, the key to the autonomous realization of human powers thenceforth centred upon a fine balancing of the universal and concrete. In the case of sociology, given its preoccupation with explaining the rise of both industrial capitalism and the modern state from the traditional texture of old European societies, the domain of the social as a totalistic entity was to be contrasted not with particularity but with the individual. The emancipated society, wrote Marx, will be possible only when 'real, individual man resumes the abstract citizen into himself and as an individual man has become a *species-being* in his empirical life, his individual work and his individual relationships'.[4] Society for Marx, but also as we will see in a moment for Émile Durkheim, consists in an immediate relation between the uniquely, specific individual and the universal. However as British literary theorist Terry Eagleton has rightly argued, such an interfusion of universal and individual has absolutely nothing beyond itself: there is not anything beyond the universal, and the individual is likewise a kind of microcosm of such universalism. As Eagleton writes, 'nothing could more closely resemble the universe than that which is purely itself, with no external relations. The universal is not just the opposite of the individual, but the very paradigm of it.'[5] What the social does then, in universalizing the individual, is realize the spirit of specific human powers from within, or at least this is so according to the discourse of society as structure.

In this sense, the more actual social relations appear constitutive and organizing of human experience, the more the idea of society becomes a form of universal identity at work within each of us as human subjects. As Durkheim puts it in his *Division of Labor*:

> Social life comes from a double source, the likeness of consciences and the division of social labor. The individual is socialized in the first case, because, not having any real individuality, he becomes, with those whom he resembles, part of the same collective type; in the second case, because, while having a physiognomy and a personal activity which distinguishes him from others, he depends upon them in the same measure that he is distinguished from them, and consequently upon the society which results from the union.[6]

In the shift from mechanical, pre-modern societies to organic, modern societies, individuals find themselves functionally separated members of the whole; however the expansion of the division of labour stimulated by the progress of industrial life also renders individuals, paradoxically, increasingly interdependent. If the industrial world divides people from each other and promotes social differences, it also oversees the regulation of a new morally cohesive code and its further development. Moral regulation and refinement may be an ongoing exercise in adjustment to the independent power of social facts, but this need not imply a denial of agency and will in social action. If we are independent beings, free to develop individual sources of action, we are also part of a complex *conscience* on which our sense of morality and ethics go to work. If, morally, modern individuals increasingly act as self-cultivators – as free and rational subjects – then a loss of social cohesion perpetually looms – and society hovers on the brink of an anomic condition. But freedom is not necessarily an obstacle to the realization of collective values and hopes, since organic solidarity in Durkheim's view promotes interpersonal dependence connected to external events. And it is precisely this ambiguous or doubled dimension of modern society that critics of Durkheim overlook in making the charge that his theory of the social denies the individual subject and can accommodate no conception of agency. Agency and individualism are in fact for Durkheim involved at the deepest level of structure, with complex interaction between objective and subjective worlds.

Durkheim is a major figure in the discourse of society as structure – though his work and legacy is not without various theoretical contradictions and tensions, which in turn have generated some massive misunderstandings from a range of critics. His sociological vision continues to play a profound role in shaping contemporary thought about the nature of modern life, and anybody who wants to understand the concept of society must take Durkheim seriously.[7] Durkheim's search for a rational and positivistic theory of morals was a legacy not only of the Enlightenment project, but a variety of streams of European thought. He was for example deeply influenced by Rousseau who had developed the idea of 'civil religion' as an essential ingredient of a society that was becoming increasingly diverse and complex. Against the enduring conflicts between Protestants and Catholics, Rousseau developed his own version of Deism in which he claimed that religion can be useful (or in sociological language functional) in providing an integrative framework for citizens – and in his case the citizens of Geneva. The stability of society as much as the happiness of the individual would require detailed training and observation of the child who must be protected from the evils of society. As we have seen, it was on these grounds that liberals like Isaiah Berlin complained that Rousseau, through the idea of the general will, came to the conclusion that where necessary the individual should be forced to be free. As a result Rousseau was one of the 'most formidable enemies of liberty in the whole history of modern thought'.[8] To our knowledge, Berlin did not subject Durkheim to the same withering criticism, but Berlin was ultimately hostile to the French philosopher and social thinker Henri de Saint-Simon for similar reasons: the triumph of structure over individual liberty. Durkhiem's focus on education, civil religion, the importance of shared values is all part of this intellectual dependence on Rousseau.

These sociological orientations were famously identified by Robert Nisbet, who uncovered at work a deeper conservative political tradition.[9] These conservative themes included the primacy of the social over the individual; the necessity for moral restraint over human passions; the importance of authority in the organization of communities; the dependence of society on religious values; and the organic character of social relations. What Nisbet calls 'conservative' can in fact be treated quite simply as 'Rousseau's social and political theory'. In what follows, we are going to concentrate on the theme of the primacy of society over the individual – a core dimension in the broader sociological worldview of society as structure. Although we will suggest that there is much to commend in this interpretation of Durkheim, we shall ultimately depart from this standard account of Durkheimian sociology in order to offer an alternative standpoint.

In conceiving of society as an organic whole and not as an aggregate of individuals, or the general will and the individual will, Durkheim has often been identified as a founder of 'structural-functionalism' as a distinctive school of sociology. Certainly Durkheim's view of historical change was primarily in terms of the dichotomy between mechanical and organic solidarity which he explored fully in *The Division of Labor in Society*. The interpretation of Durkheim as a social theorist who laid the foundations for the analysis of social integration in social systems was promoted most forcefully by Parsons in a number of major publications, such as *The Social System*.[10] In so doing, Parsons promoted the idea – in a fashion similar though somewhat less directly than critics like Nisbet – that Durkheim has to be seen as a theorist of social stability and social integration. For example, Parsons argued that Durkheim's account of solidarity in *The Division of Labor in Society* in terms of the conscience collective in mechanical solidarity throughout primitive societies, and of social reciprocity in organic solidarity throughout advanced societies, was a major solution to the Hobbesian problem of social order in the utilitarian tradition. Durkheim's analysis of the integrative functions of religious practice in both making and sustaining social communities provided Parsons with a theoretical source in classical sociology for his own emphasis on the importance of common values in the social cohesion of modern societies. In Parsons's early academic career, Weber's analysis of capitalism had been the primary intellectual stimulus for Parsonian sociology, but as Parsons moved more towards an analysis of the allocative and integrative requirements of a social system Durkheimian issues appear to have become increasingly important.[11] Thus, Parsons's appreciation of the significance of the psychological internalization of values, which he took from fellow American sociologist Charles Cooley, was now supplemented by Durkheim's analysis of the integrative function of common beliefs to produce the cornerstone of Parsons's 'middle period', namely the internalization and socialization of values in social integration.

It may also be, however, that this stress on social order and cultural cohesion does more than reflect the orthodox realms of Durkheimian sociology. For it also gives shape to the construction of classical sociology as a canon in itself. In the conventional paradigm of introductory textbooks for undergraduate sociology courses, there developed a tripartite version of classical sociology: Marx was a theorist of conflict and social change; Weber was a social philosopher of action and meaning; and Durkheim was a sociologist of social order, moral systems and political stability. Consequently, it took the academy many years to arrive at a more complete and mature interpretation of Durkheim's sociology. This shift in understanding arose partly as a result of a renewed emphasis on Durkheim's political sociology and his awareness of the political contradictions of the state in modern society.[12] The Durkheim revival has also been connected with the recognition of the centrality of religion to modern societies and the criticisms of the secularization thesis that was dominant in sociology through much of the second half of the twentieth century. However, this revival of interest in Durkheim has been shaped not by religion as social glue but in terms of the 'clash of civilizations' in which religion is seen to be pivotal in the conflicts within civil society.

The core of such a re-reading of Durkheim's sociology, broadly speaking, runs as follows. If society is to be an effective moral force, it must implant itself in subjectivity itself, if cultural order is to be secured. Thus for Durkheim's sociology to be both descriptive and normative, part of Enlightenment's very dynamic of social progress rather than only a sociological account of its historical unfolding, then the fashioning of society as a transformative political force appropriate for moral development and ethical judgement arises as key to the theory of social evolution. The answer for Durkheim is the state, which he theorizes in relation to political authority and social values. For Durkheim, the modern state is of particular value as a moral organization: the sociological issue is whether the state can be regulative and transformative of the moral individualism which has developed in modern society. Unlike Max Weber who conceived of the state in terms of the monopoly of power within a specific territoriality, Durkheim sees the state as the spontaneous embodiment of the complex social whole, functioning to provide us with norms relevant to personal and ethical behaviour. The state thus offers the overall guidance of society. Durkheim does not believe in the possibility of a state in which citizens somehow automatically identify with the principle of common social life. The degree of complexity in social organization that modernity ushers into existence makes any such link between the level of values and of institutions untenable, and in any event the 'cult of individualism' means that different individuals, groups and classes will experience their relations to the social whole differently. Notwithstanding this, however, the state embodies, through the organ of government, the enshrinement of individual rights and freedoms, making possible the flourishing of the individual.

'The state', writes Durkheim, 'is the very organ of social thought.'[13] We can only understand this argument by realizing that here, as elsewhere in Durkheim's sociology, he is attempting to counteract the arguments of Herbert Spencer. For Durkheim, the contemporary development of the state is not incompatible with the growing importance of the individual and individualism. But for Durkheim this has to be the regulated, morally organized and controlled individual and not the individual of either romanticism or calculating Manchester economics. The state is an essential feature of the evolution of individual rights, because it is only the state which has sufficient authority and collective power to create and protect individual rights. There is nothing about the state which must produce a political tyranny, and indeed it is the modern state which has liberated the individual from particularistic forms of domination, which were typical of feudalism.

What is projected by Durkheim as a universally valid relation between state and society in modern times is, however, a very specific reckoning of the contours of the social as theorized in the

discourse of society as structure. Durkheim renders the state as a
kind of Supreme Being, relentlessly shaping the day-to-day lives
of those individuals who are its citizens. Apart from the question
of the dubious nature of this conception of the political reach of
the state and, putting to one side the very forceful criticisms that
have been made of Durkheim's assumption that the state intrinsically represents the interests of those it rules, note that society on
this view is itself universal and thereby denied any specificity. The
state/society relation here is rather the set of values or criteria
which ought to inform any aspect or process of social and collective life. 'Durkheim', writes W. Watts Miller, 'goes beyond the
distinct, empirical (even if socially developed) individual to invoke
the person. One reason is that regard for each of us as different
individuals requires regard for everyone as a person, with the same
status and dignity. But it is also to look, in modern individualism,
for something that transcends us as individuals – a force that can
command respect but also inspire us and mobilize faith, and that is
a common faith.'[14]

Society is thus called structure in this frame of reference
because the social is primarily conceived of as organized with
social systems stabilized, partly by institutional shaping and partly
by self-regulation. 'Stabilized social relations' refers to a society of
discipline, of rule-following, of knowing not only the right thing
to do, but when and how to do it. Society here is, by and large,
conceived as a structure of rules, regulations and repetitions; such
rules provide a means of escape from our capabilities for self-
interrogation and critical reflection, and to that degree displace the
particular critical and reflective capabilities from which we might
explore our own subjectivities and our relation to others and the
wider world. Yet subjective distance from human creation would
appear an inevitable consequence for those theorists of structured
society who posit the social as outside of themselves, and indeed in
some versions of society as structure the creativity of common life
is displaced altogether. This, to repeat, is not simply a conceptual
dilemma, but presses in on individuals in their day-to-day social
lives. 'Actors', writes the American sociologist Jeffrey Alexander,
'experience the fear of obliteration from the forces they have
themselves created, from the isolated and demanding self, from the

impersonally organized society, from an omnipotent God, from the rationally re-organized forces of nature.'[15] One powerfully disabling consequence of certain versions of society as structure, therefore, is to cast the social in anti-subjectivist terms and in particular, to render human subjects as mere ciphers of culture and social practice.

In this commentary on Durkheim, we have noted that he adopted a positivist epistemology in which social facts are things, that is phenomena existing outside of the individual and exercising a regulatory force over the individual. Secondly, we have argued that Durkheim, especially in his early lectures on the sociology of education, adopted much of Rousseau's social theory about protecting the child from the corruption of modern society and Rousseau's political theory of civil religion, citizenship and the state. We might conclude thirdly with the observation that, while Durkheim was critical of Kant's theory of knowledge, he followed Kant to some degree in his ethical theory. Within the autonomous individual, there is always a capacity for self-regulation and moral reflection and therefore the moral individual is not somebody who is wilfully self-indulgent and egotistical, but an agent who in following an internal moral impulse can live in harmony with his/ her fellow beings. There is no space here for a Robinson Crusoe figure or the claim that man is an island unto himself. Thus in Kant, Rousseau and Durkheim there is the paradox that people are most free when they are at their most social. It was this idea that Berlin – the great exponent of modern liberalism – found to be 'sinister'.

The Ruins of Structure: On the Politics of Nostalgia

In *The Sociological Tradition*, Nisbet argues that sociology was an aspect of diverse intellectual movements which were responses to the industrial and the French Revolutions.[16] While liberalism and socialism were influential, the most significant force shaping early sociology was in fact conservatism. The key 'unit ideas' of sociology, such as the problem of authority, the sacred, community and organic wholeness are primarily aspects of this conservative legacy. Thus, sociology was an intellectual response to the sense of a lost community, the disappearance of the sacred as a source of values, the isolation of the individual in the city, and the resulting crisis of meaning. In this sense, sociology was a nostalgic reflection on the loss of authenticity, personal spontaneity, social wholeness and community.[17] We must be careful here in our use of terminology, because in the modern world 'conservatism' might be easily identified with reactive, backward-looking thought. The idea has also become associated in Britain with former Prime Minister Thatcher's hostility to trade unions and in the American context 'conservative' is largely identified with neoconservatism, from the legacy of former President Ronald Reagan. But as we have noted, Durkheim favoured state regulation and supported economic guilds and professional bodies to regulate trade and industry. Durkheim is, to use Frank Pearce's terminology, a 'radical conservative' who was distrusted by, for example, the Catholic Church. Durkheim's family background lay in rabbinical Judaism and in France this heritage automatically identified with cosmopolitanism, Paris intellectuals and the political Left. Durkheim was thus a radical conservative in his (socialist) critique of rampant individualism and the disruptive force of industrial capitalism.

In broad terms, four major dimensions can be identified as regards the analysis of society as structure as a nostalgic reflection on the loss of community and integrative culture. Firstly, there is the sense of historical decline and loss, involving a departure from some golden age of 'homefulness'. The messianic message of Old Testament Judaism and New Testament Christianity typically involved some sense of a lost space and lost time from which contemporary social systems can be measured and found wanting; in this sense, the Abrahamic religions are fundamentally nostalgic in their theology of grace, as a description of the Fall of humanity from a perfect union with God. This Judaeo-Christian background has had a profound impact on Marxist sociology and critical theory, which promoted a cataclysmic vision of history as a violent progression of revolutionary events into an unknown future from a garden of perfect harmony. This was radical conservatism writ large and found tragic expression, for example, in the work of critical theorists such as Walter Benjamin, who in the face of rising European fascism combined a mystical Jewish tradition with secular Marxist theory. The result was an eschatology or theory of the ends of history that saw the present in terms of a wind of total destruction.

The second component of the nostalgic reflection on society is a sense of the absence or loss of personal wholeness and moral certainty. In this dimension, human history is perceived in terms of a collapse of values which once provided the unity of human relations, knowledge and personal experience. This nostalgic theme contains a theory of secularization in which the sacred canopy of religious certainty is fractured by catastrophic social processes, typically the emergence of markets, capitalist relations and urban cultures as the negation of rural naivety. We can find this theme prominent in the philosophy of Rousseau in his nostalgic version of the social contract as the loss of genuine experience and the rise of an artificial world of spectacle and theatre. The modern period as the loss of God was announced by Nietzsche in the discourse of Zarathustra on the death of God. In historical analysis, the nostalgic theme pervaded the work of the Hungarian economist Karl Polanyi whose concept of 'the great transformation' involved a melancholic vision of economic change.

The third aspect of nostalgia as concerns society as structure is the sense of loss of individual freedom and autonomy with the disappearance of genuine social relationships. With the death of God and the loss of moral coherence, the isolated individual is increasingly exposed to the constraining social processes of modern institutionalized regulation, which gradually undermines the individual, who is strangled within the world of state bureaucracies. This theme was the classic basis for Weber's metaphor of the iron cage in which individuals were merely cogs of modern social processes. For Weber, the modern world meant the loss of both charisma and tradition, and the overwhelming spread of rational bureaucracies. This sociological tradition was inherited by the Frankfurt critical theorists, who described modern society as an administered world where the isolated individual is wholly subordinated to the rationality of instrumental reason and capitalist relations of production. This theme of administration was also to surface in the late French historian Michel Foucault's notion of the carceral.

The final aspect of nostalgia in versions of society as structure is the idea of a loss of simplicity, personal authenticity and emotional spontaneity. The primitive emotions which were once celebrated in peasant festivals have been subdued first by the culture of the court and finally by the restraint of bourgeois society. The festivals and ceremonials of peasant culture were once a collective celebration of primitive pleasures and, in this sense, the work of the French Renaissance writer François Rabelais can be seen as the final tribute to peasant culture in the face of market relations and the restraints of the emerging system of courtly manners. The primitive gluttony, spontaneity and orgiastic abandonment of the premodern table have collapsed with the spread of refined manners and personal restraint through the new gastronomy of taste.[18] From Freudian psychoanalysis, critical theorists such as Herbert Marcuse claimed that civilization was also bought at the cost of personal freedom and sexual spontaneity; contemporary civilization was a political system of surplus repression.[19]

The British philosopher Alasdair MacIntyre's historical sketches of philosophical and social changes in the development of modernity raise the suspicion that there has never been a society in the past that was blessed by coherent values and authoritative moral solutions to human dilemmas. MacIntyre only offers rather distant examples – ancient Greece and the warrior cultures of northern Europe and Iceland – of societies in which fact and value were not separate and in which personality and meaning were neatly combined in the social structure. The modern period of historical decline in MacIntyre's scheme of things hangs on the construction of the moral theory of Thomas Aquinas. One criticism of MacIntyre would be that these societies of warriors and the Thomist institutions and values of the Middle Ages were themselves hierarchical and sharply divided, for example between clergy and laity and between warriors and peasants. The historical evidence at least raises a question about the degree to which these societies were characterized by some coherent moral system or a dominant ideology.[20] MacIntyre's work is underpinned by a pessimistic criticism of the present and a nostalgic view of the past.

Nostalgia plays an important role in critical theories of modernity and is not in any simplistic sense a form of cultural conservatism. MacIntyre's type of nostalgia is neither passive nor inert.[21] He offers us a philosophy of resistance to the individualism and emotivism of modern societies. Furthermore he does not believe we can return to the distant past and his main solution is to turn to community as a shelter from the corrosive individualism and social instabilities of a market-driven social order. Is this plausible and convincing? One obvious counter-argument is that critics of modernity from Tönnies onwards have looked towards community (*Gemeinschaft*) as a more satisfying and authentic world in opposition to the associational structures of capitalism (*Gesellschaft*), but to employ this contrast between community and association, we need to have a more adequate understanding of Tönnies's account of social change. MacIntyre interprets Western culture as a decline from the communal life of the past to a society dominated by the market, but this tendency to divide the world into a communal pre-history and an associational present is to invent an exaggerated notion of social history as the Fall. Rather we should think, following Tönnies, of community as process. To understand the community–society distinction as a process may enable us to avoid a pessimistic nostalgia about the past that cripples political action in the present. If we see history as the Fall, then we rule out the possibility of the ongoing re-creation of community in advance. From this angle, MacIntyre's position in which moderen communities are fragile and limited seems valid. Whereas society in the past was 'sticky' – difficult to join and almost impossible to leave – modern societies are fluid and fragile, and as a result they offer little support for communal life.

The response to the loss of a coherent community of moral authority may be to look towards civil society, civility and citizenship as secular forms of belonging that might offer a more optimistic view of the present.[22] In historical terms, 'civil society' was specifically the product of bourgeois European society and etymologically connected to burger culture through the notion of *Bürgerliche Gesellschaft*, which for Hegel was distinct from *citoyen*. Whereas a citizen was regarded as simply a member of a state, the traditional view of civil society also included the ideas of civility and civic duty. *Gesellschaft* from *Geselle* indicates a shared space and is associated with the idea of companionship or friendship.[23] Society is that space within which the companions are sociable and for Aristotle these relationships are the true basis of the *polis*, since without trust and friendship the competition (*agon*) between rational actors in the public domain can destroy political life through ceaseless interpersonal contest. It is consistent with MacIntyre's argument that we have in fact lost this understanding of the political importance of friendship, but it was particularly significant in the rise of German sociology in works by Otto von Gierke on premodern fellowships (*Genossenschaft*) and pre-eminently in Tönnies's *Gemeinschaft und Gesellschaft*. This distinction between community and association reminds us that German sociology was concerned to understand the tensions between two different types of will-formation in the civil sphere or in Marxist terms between the destructive force of class interests and the need for reciprocity and trust, or between scarcity and solidarity. Weber's sociology of social relations in *Economy and Society* was heavily influenced by the work of Tönnies. The sub-title of *Gemeinschaft und Gesellschaft* was 'Basic Concepts of Pure Sociology'. His basic sociological principles contrasted the 'natural, warm-blooded primeval community with the cold, modern society governed by monetary relations',[24] but perhaps the main point about the theory was to examine a process namely *Vergemeinschaftung* (development of communal relations) and *Vergesellschaftung* (development of associative social relationships). This basic idea has in fact shaped much of the critical literature on modern society and the principal exponent of this tradition in modern sociology is the German sociologist and philosopher Jürgen Habermas in *The Structural Transformation of the Public Sphere* (1989) – an account of the growth of bourgeois society in terms of 'discursive will formation' and its decline under the influence of modern media, which is considered in more detail in the next chapter.[25]

What emerges from this discussion is that the contrast between the past and the present is sociologically problematic and in addition that the implicit theory of the Fall prematurely cuts off the idea that community may in fact be an endless process rather than a fixed historical point. While the roots of modern communal processes are fragile and the prospects of restoring communal life are dim, we must leave open the possibility of communal renewal. While recognizing that modern societies are indeed characterized by excessive individualism, low social capital and thin social relations, the social world, from the perspective of critical sociology, can always be open to renewal and reinvention.

While MacIntyre is overtly engaged with the legacy of Weber, his argument about community and resistance to individualism appears to draw more profoundly from the legacy of Durkheim – a figure who rarely or never makes an appearnce in MacIntyre's oeuvre. Certainly MacIntyre's emphasis on the importance of community has a distinctively Durkheimian flavour. In *The Elementary Forms* Durkheim argued that the roots of the social are ultimately in the sacred.[26] If we accept the direction of Durkheim's sociology, the ultimate roots of community are sacred and therefore the forms that bind people together into communal bonds are indeed religious forces. Critical theorists recognize that the sacred roots of collective culture are being eroded by globalization in the form of commercialization and commodification; we are faced with the prospect of the unending McDonaldization of society. In a modern commercial society, the citizen becomes merely a passive consumer of goods and services. There is in short an elective affinity between the passive citizen, modern spirituality and individualism. The 'chain of memory' that is constitutive of communal relationships has been broken by the evolution of possessive individualism in capitalist societies.[27] This interpretation of our modern dilemmas – relativism, moral incoherence, the destruction of the environment, the celebration of greed – does indeed involve a metaphysics of nostalgia, but the nostalgic imagination is defensible and at least intelligible, when it can also become a creative response to the end of the communal.[28]

Enclavement, Sequestration and New Structures of Winners and Losers

We suggested earlier that any attempt to define society *in toto* from an extrapolation of certain imaginative features specific to the discourse of society as structure is bound to fail. For the social and our current practices of sociality, we contend, are not merely a function of structure; they are also, as we will examine throughout this book, an upshot of theoretical and normative discourses also circling around solidarity and creation. Notwithstanding this more pluralistic way of conceiving of the social as well as the analysis of society, however, the question remains as to how we should distinguish one kind of discourse of society from another. In the remainder of this chapter we turn to consider certain institutional transformations recently occurring throughout contemporary societies of the West, and consider the trope of 'structure' once more in specific political terms. This means asking whether particular social practices, personal lifestyles, political struggles and cultural norms occurring in certain areas of the globe fit with the conceptions of society outlined in the notion of upper-case Society.

The call for structure in classical sociology, we have suggested, was among other things a response to the political problem of disorderly behaviour in European cities and urban spaces. The rise of the city – especially capital cities like Paris, London and Berlin – and the urbanization of the West obviously played a large part in the rise of European sociology. The notion of anonymous relations between strangers in cities was important for both Weber and Simmel, but it was also crucial in the so-called 'arcades project' of critical theorist Walter Benjamin. In the United States, while small towns remained important to the social fabric as we can see in the famous studies of the Lunds, sociologists became fascinated by the social problems of Chicago and New York, which were seen to be virtual experiments in migration, multiculturalism, zoning, policing and regulating. The so-called Chicago School consequently became a foundational group in the emergence of American sociology and in a much later period the New York intellectuals such as Irving Kristol and Daniel Bell were also a product of what we might call the 'city imaginary'.

Europe in the period of classical sociology was still a parcellized territory of competing principalities and warring states, of which the discourse of society as structure was designed to map how the bourgeois enlightenment could be politically developed to instill a proper and profound respect for civility, civilization and civil society within its re-socialized rule-following subjects. The answer was to come in the form of nation-state citizenship and nationalist ideology, as that most immaterial of political representations for the creation of individual identities appropriately drilled in the arts of structured social life. For in the traditional terminology of sociology, citizenship-building was also, and necessarily, nation-building. The creation of institutions of citizenship in legal, political and social terms was also the construction of a national framework of membership within the administrative structures of the state – a historical process that dominated domestic politics in Europe and North America through much of the late eighteenth and nineteenth centuries. The production of an institutional framework of national citizenship created new national identities and replaced regional and sub-national cultures. Citizenship identities during the rise of the European cities had been local and urban, but with the rise of nationalism they became increasingly connected with strong nationalistic cultures that demanded greater domestic coherence. Nationalism embraced negative images of outsiders and, as a result, modern politics became a politics of friend or foe, along the lines suggested in the political theology of German political theorist Carl Schmitt. National identities and social citizenship thrived in a period of international conflict and competition. The rise of the national state was signalled by bureaucratic mechanisms which increased the power of the state over the individual; we think here in particular of the growth of universal taxation, sovereign legal systems and the creation of the passport as a document that firmly marked the difference between citizens on the one hand and guests and aliens on the other. The rise of the fiscal state with its budgets and bureaux indicated the conversion of peasants into urban dwelling citizens; the state required a rational budgetary system if it was to police the streets and create hygienic policies to rid the city of disease and infection.

In our own time of advanced globalization, declining national-state regulatory power and turbo-capitalism, however, the discourse of society as structure has undergone dramatic change. Today the question of the continued relevance of society as structure centres on two, interrelated forces: globalization, which is not (as yet) a definite or specific political society to which the ideals of structured and organized Society could be attached; and the development of political forms of neoliberalism, privatization and deregulation, which on the one hand fits hand-in-glove with the ethos of society as structure, while on the other eats away at some of its most cherished values. Certainly as this new century unfolds and against the political backdrop of 9/11 and the war on terror (to which we shall turn shortly), the failure of political elites recently converted to neoliberalism to ameliorate the economic burdens, social contradictions and emotional damage done to and suffered by the various outcasted enclaves of the polished, expensive cities of the West has served to engender astonishingly high levels of social unrest and civic alienation. From this angle, the discourse of society as structure appears as both condition and remedy; indeed, contemporary politics and social policy is full of reckonings designed to combat these social disorders which, in fact, spring directly from an altogether idealized version of upper-case Society – as structured, ordered and rule-following.

If the discourse of society as structure laid a foundational basis for the territorial boundaries and secure social spaces of national cultures and nation-states, this same discourse now threatens to scupper world order (or, at least, a certain set of values by which economics, politics and law have been set out and understood). For the national circuits by which cultures have been intermeshed with a rule-based and order orientated institutional political mechanism under the rule of upper-case Society became fundamentally shattered during the course of the late twentieth century – due in large part to the conditions and consequences of advanced globalization. Transnational capitalism erodes national societies, in a manner similar to how it weakens national economies, as a result of the institutionalization of diverse forms of cultural globalization, cultural interaction and transnational infrastructural flows.[29] In order to grasp what this means for the whole discourse of society as structure, we need to see that globalization involves much more than merely a wave of new technological innovations, information revolutions and the intensification of the mobility flows of people, goods, finance and patterns of investment. It is rather that the global opening up of communicational circuits that cross national borders with ease (read: at the click of a mouse) map directly onto

urgent political issues of human security, social well-being and
societal order, including those issues of securitization which arise
most obviously as a result of new terrorist networks and rogue
states. From the viewpoint of upper-case Society, the terror attacks
on the World Trade Center and the Pentagon of 9/11 represent
not only political violence of epic proportions and thus a crime
against humanity; it represents also, and above all, an attack on
Western society as such. After 9/11, the 'war on terror' thus became
a kind of shorthand for the defence of Western society – or, better,
of Western civilization.

What has happened in our time, however, is not just that the
West has become locked into a political battle with societies which
appear uncivilized in the eyes of those conservative and neoliberal guardians of the American security doctrine of unilateral and
pre-emptive war. There has always been a fundamental cleavage
between those that see themselves as the custodians of society as
structure (or, Western civilization) on the one hand, and those
excluded from the terrain of upper-case Society. It is rather that
9/11, and recent wars in Afghanistan and Iraq, as well as the wider
war on terror which has now spread to political hotspots across the
globe, have served to compound anxieties that upper-case Society
no longer has a monopoly on the economic, political and cultural
contexts of institutionalized affairs. From the vantage point of the
discourse of society as structure, today's so-called world order now
hovers on the brink of coming completely apart. From the breakdown of law and order to the rise of extrajudicial outlaw killings
sanctioned by rogue states, the distinctive way of life associated
with society as structure is threatened to its core – which is one
key reason why the defining political axis of our age has become
that of distinguishing the West and its Others. Nothing, after all,
could be more elementary than the project of re-establishing the
difference between Western civilization or society on the one
hand, and other forms of social life (inferior, degraded, distaste-
ful) on the other hand. Accordingly, and through a powerful
resurgence of the discourse of society under the unilateral control
of the United States, we have witnessed in our own time some
powerful national regulations of global flows – or, at least, *attempts
to regulate global flows*. Just as the economy becomes increasingly

global (especially in terms of the flows of finance, investment and commodities), so nation-states and their bureaucracies have in many respects become more rigid in defending the principle of sovereignty. There has been, as a result, a profound contradiction between the economic requirements of flexibility and fluidity and the state's objective of defending its territorial sovereignty. In particular with the growth of a global war on terror after 9/11, states, rather than becoming more porous, have defended their borders with increasing determination. From a historical perspective, it is useful to remind ourselves that the flow of people has become more rather than less restrictive. The American sociologist John Torpey, for example, has argued that 'the invention of the passport' as a method of surveillance and regulation was a product of twentieth-century statehood.[30] In a similar fashion the sociologist Saskia Sassen, in *Guests and Aliens*, demonstrates how the free flow of workers in Europe, that had been traditional during harvest time, was changed by the transformation of such guests into political aliens.[31]

It is not difficult to see in the American security doctrine of unilateral and pre-emptive war, initiated under the leadership of former President George Bush, the discourse of society as structure. The norm of structure, *pace* that of solidarity and creation, does not consist in permitting material and economic progress to go hand in hand with contemporary patterns of cultural exchange as well as the flow of people, objects, information and opinion within and across national borders. It consists rather in re-asserting the need for capital market liberalization to be maintained and structured through the ordering, monitoring, and regulated patrolling of national borders to ensure that residential populations are 'protected' against the perceived risk of mobile populations. This, in short, is the re-assertion of upper-case Society against societies. This promotion of economic globalization through the institutional exclusion and negation of 'voices' (other peoples, races, nations) is what one of us elsewhere has termed the emergence of 'the enclave society'.[32] The creation of an enclave society involves a framework of political power in which governments and other agencies seek to regulate spaces and, where necessary, immobilize flows of people, goods and services. The hubristic doctrine that

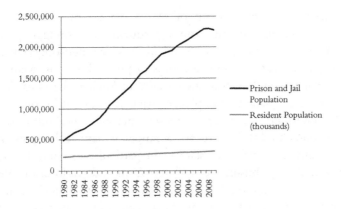

Sources: US Census Bureau, Population Division; US Bureau of Justice Statistics

Figure 1.1 Incarcerated Population vs. Resident Population, USA.

'threatening' others need to be sequestrated, excluded and closed off from the core rights, entitlements and business of society has been pursued in recent years through three interrelated processes: (1) the military–political; (2) the social and cultural; and (3) the biological. Seeking to exercise governmentality, often in extreme form, over populations by enclosure, bureaucratic barriers, legal exclusions and registrations, contemporary processes of 'enclavement' function then, as a set of strategies and tactics for both domestic and international regulation. Thus alongside the growing mobility of persons and rising competitiveness of the market in the era of advanced globalization, we also witness the emergence of an immobility regime of gated communities (for the elderly), ghettoes (for migrants, legal and illegal), imprisonment and a range of related practices (tagging) for criminals and deviants. Indeed, there has been a dramatic rise in the number of incarcerated people residing in the United States over the last thirty years especially – see Figure 1.1.

The sharp increase in numbers of incarcerated in the USA is suggestive of the broader contours of enclavement processes – as an operational mode of the discourse of society as structure. In this sense, the politics of society as structure makes a fetish out of spatial closure. Nowhere is this more obvious than in the regular, routine

and relatively benign forms of spatial closure that characterize
modern societies: security zones, frequent-flyer lounges, prayer
rooms and no-smoking areas in airports, women-only railway
carriages in Japan, or private rooms in public hospitals. Many of
these practices and institutions are ancient (such as the Great Wall
of China and quarantine in plague-stricken medieval Europe), but
with modern information technology, microbiological innovations
and nanotechnology, there are a range of new techniques that
are becoming available to states – in particular to control global
flows of slavery, business crime, terrorism and warlordism. New
information technologies are thus at the very core of enclavement,
allowing the guardians of society as structure to penetrate ever
further into the fabric of daily life for the purposes of attempting to
control, order and regulate it. And yet the complaint, sometimes
heard from fringes of the traditional political left, that we now
live in a world of total surveillance seems as misplaced as ignor-
ing the detailed policies that promote processes of enclavement
throughout the world today. The present age combines both the
desire for security through enclavement and the frustration arising
from every attempt to better insulate upper-case Society against its
multivarious Others. The more Western society closes in on itself,
through bio-technological and communicational mechanisms of
enclavement, the more a climate of fear takes hold. It is contemporary enclavement strategies which chop the world into tightly
regulated segments, sequestrating off from structured society the
dangers presented by those suffering from homelessness, unemployment, disease and infection. But in a tragic irony, every
attempt to assign these sequestrated Others determinate meanings
fall short of desired levels of security. The ego-ideals permeating
upper-case Society, it would seem, know no limit.

It is not difficult to trace the causes of the rise of the enclave
society. These would surely include the globalization of crime
and disease, 'the return of the state', securitization, measures
against illegal migration, political paranoia, technical innovations, and so forth. At the level of the global order, however,
the umbrella notion that explains these developments is 'the war
on terror'. Culturally speaking, the more 'the war on terror' has
been exported by the US to the rest of the world, the more it has

fanned a new xenophobia that shape, societies of fear. While the creation of physical and bureaucratic fences to control migrants has been much discussed, the biological dimensions of enclavement are perhaps the most interesting. Following the reflections of Italian social theorist Giorgio Agamben on 'bare life', we can foresee a new apparatus of bio-sequestration, exclusion and regulation.[33] Guantanamo Bay is probably the ultimate conversion of city life into the camp. These developments constitute a global process of enclavement resulting in an immobility (not a 'mobility') regime.

This re-assertion of 'society as structure' as a dominant ideology and master strategy has been an effective way for the West to deflate its own anxieties concerning the strength and durability of its belief-systems and core values. Much the same insecurity and anxiety happens in the organization of political enclaves within the West itself. Contemporary enclavement comprises three principal forms: (1) sequestration; (2) storage; and (3) seclusion. The isolation or sequestration of populations could be regarded as the most basic form of social regulation with the aim of protecting host populations from infectious disease or from dangerous persons who are regarded as morally or biologically undesirable. In the 1930s, European campaigns to achieve 'racial hygiene' promoted the idea of national fitness and eugenics strategies included negative measures such as sterilization to biologically sequester the unfit. Negative eugenics, being obessesed by the notion of human degeneration, became preoccupied with the problem of the mentally ill and the disabled. These measures were not only part of a fascist ideology but were also embraced by social democracies as aspects of public health policies.[34] For eugenics, before Hitler's Germany, the management of human propulations was no more sinister than breeding animals to improve productivity. Such practices that sequester special sections of the population may be regarded as essentially illustrations of what Max Weber understood as rationalization. By contrast, the creation of gated communities to protect the elderly or the vulnerable is designed, not to keep out threats from the outside, but to protect local communities, especially the elderly, from internal dangers (possibly from self-harm). With the rapid ageing of the populations of the developed world and increasing life expectancy, a range of strategies has also emerged for the management of the elderly, increasingly seen as a surplus and burdensome segment of modern society; these include the growth of overseas retirement villages, homes for the elderly and increasingly luxury cruise ships. Whereas Foucault in *Madness and Civilization* was struck by the Ship of Fools which transported the insane from port to port in the hope that the motion of waves would calm their troubled minds, geriatric luxury cruises now transport the rich but elderly in search of cosmetic cures for their failing bodies.[35] Because it is unlikely that the deeply aged will ever return to the labour force, these strategies are best conceptualized as forms of 'social storage'. Finally, there is a range of new laws and technologies that allows states to categorize and track individuals who are deemed to be dangerous to the rest of society, in order to bring about their bureaucratic control through spatial seclusion. The unemployed, the unemployable, the undesirable and the unwanted typically fall into the category of persons whose actions can come to be regarded as examples of 'offensive behaviour'.[36] In the United Kingdom, the Anti-Social Behaviour Act of 2003 gave extra-ordinary powers to various local authorities to create zones from which persons deemed to be likely to cause an offence can be excluded. These zones were also designed to prevent youths from simply 'hanging about'. The Act also introduced penalties for beggars by making begging a modifiable offence. The Act creates provisions, not to solve or remove crimes, but to put them outside the social world of virtuous citizens, thereby achieving an emotional seclusion.

Agamben has argued that the state of emergency historically was best illustrated by the concentration camp, starting with the use of such camps by the British authorities in the war against the Boers and then by the Nazi concentration camp. This site of detention is one in which law is suspended and the inmates exist without the conventional protection of rights. For Agamben, the state of emergency has become a normal method of the exercise of sovereignty, even by liberal democracies. His arguments have been highly controversial, because he claims that the Patriot Act recognized a state of emergency and that Guantanamo Bay has the same legal and political status as the Nazi concentration camps. When the state of emergency becomes permanent in an unending war against terrorism, then the city becomes merely a camp, and the inmates of these extra-judicial zones are fully exposed to 'bare life' – that is, they are expelled from *bios* to *zoë*. These camps offer the state the opportunity of indefinite containment for anybody who is deemed to be a potential threat.[37] The principle of indefinite detention which Guantanamo expresses means that the camp offers the state a strategy of indefinite political storage whereby, even were the inmates to be tried and found not guilty, they could still be detained. The inmates are not covered by the Geneva Convention according to White House lawyers since they did not belong to 'regular armies'. When questioned about the legal status of the 'detainees', Donald Rumsfeld said that his aim was to keep these people off the streets rather than answer abstract points of law. In this sense, the inmates are in 'permanent storage'.

Even so, the political tension between Society and societies is one that no amount of sequestration and storage can adequately contain, let alone repress; and it is for this reason that the contemporary custodians of society as structure remain on full alert for *potential enemies* near to the gates of Western civilization. With the global development of diasporic communities, the stranger is now both proximate and distant, because he or she is involved in a global network of communities extending around the world. Migrant labour is typically connected to economically marginal societies or communities, and their remittances are often necessary to support such distant communities. Where migrant labour does not become integrated into the host community through marriage, work or citizenship, they can remain isolated from the mainstream. Indeed, with some forms of multiculturalism, cultural differences become institutionalized and produce fragmented, isolated and underprivileged social groups. Their children become part of a diversified, marginalized, urban underclass. These migrant communities have been increasingly augmented by a flow of stateless people, refugees, asylum seekers, boat people and the victims of failed states and civil wars. These marginal communities of the diaspora are also known as parallel communities because they exist alongside, but without connection to, the mainstream host society. The growth of global cities has been accompanied by an underclass of illegal or semi-legal migrants and refugees who work primarily in the informal economy, and come to constitute a disprivileged 'weight of the world'.[38] The stranger is now an anonymous, displaced person without citizenship rights, and a member of an underclass that is seen by the state as simply a recruiting ground for criminals and terrorists. The stranger in the global economy is somebody who is recruited not to service in the formal economy of society, but to a life in prisons, detention camps, inter-state zones, departure lounges and a variety of other intermediate, quasi-legal arenas. Terrorism has obviously contributed significantly to this fear of the stranger in our midst who is not connected to us and whose face may be obscured by the hijab, the burqa, or chador. Because the bombings in London were performed not by outsiders, but by citizens, the aftermath of 7/7 may be, at least for Europeans, more significant than 9/11. The bombings and attempted bombings in London were undertaken by the children of migrants and asylum seekers, who were, at least formally, British citizens. In the new xenophobia, as the 'friendly stranger' has become 'the hostile stranger', every citizen has become a potential enemy within. The essential political condition for the rise of the new xenophobia is a situation in which the majority feels that it is under attack and that its culture and way of life are threatened by social groups whom it does not understand, with whom it cannot identify and consequently does not recognize. The threatened majority harbours the suspicion that its own state protects strangers through liberal laws that allow criminal activities to flourish.

Dominant ideologies in our own time – from the twenty-first-century American security doctrine of unilateral and pre-emptive war to the globalized 'war on terror' – attempt to provide some legitimacy for such devices as sequestration, storage and seclusion to re-assert the imagined unity of upper-case Society. Yet there are other ways, too, in which the discourse of society as structure has unfolded on a global level. A good deal of fundamentalism, for example, can be cast in just this light. A major feature of many fundamentalist movements is the desire to restore family values, improve Christian education and protect children from lifestyles that are simultaneously anti-American and anti-Christian. We can see the development of the Christian Right as a delayed response to the failure of the Vietnam War and a critique of the values of the radical student movements of the 1960s. This perception of the erosion of American values was at the heart of the Moral Majority that was formed in the 1970s under the leadership of evangelicals such as Jerry Falwell. The original inspiration for this movement came from political groups that were frustrated with the Republican Party, and it included Protestants, but also Roman Catholics, Mormons and Pentecostalists. American domestic and foreign policy had to be based on the Bible and, in order to restore America to its true mission, it was necessary to struggle against the 'moral minority' that exercised power over the government. The New Christian Right, as they came to be known, were against abortion, against gay rights, and against drug liberalization. In fact, there was a significant emphasis on problems relating to sexuality. More recently they have led campaigns against gay marriage and the ordination of gay clergy. Fundamentalists regarded feminism as a 'disease' and equated homosexuality with pederasty. It was 'secular humanism', a catch-all phrase that included feminism and liberalism, that had emasculated American men. In this respect, fundamentalism was able to address a range of popular anxieties about male impotence, high divorce rates, female self-assertion and low birth rates.

American fundamentalism responded to this cultural and political crisis in a number of ways. From the late 1980s, there were aggressive, and occasionally violent, campaigns against abortion clinics by so-called moral 'rescuers'. On the educational system, Christian creationists led an attack on evolutionary science and Darwinism in an effort to assert the literal truth of Genesis. In terms of family life, fundamentalists re-asserted what they thought to be the biblical view of marriage, namely the importance of male headship. For example, the Southern Baptist Convention meeting in 1988 amended its Baptist Faith and Message Statement to declare that a woman should 'submit herself graciously' to the leadership of her husband. The result of the amendment by the largest American Protestant denomination was to jettison the principle of an egalitarian family. This assertion of male leadership was seen to be a necessary step in restoring the family, which is seen to be fundamental to the continuity of Christianity and to the health of the nation. In practice, Christian interpretations of what leadership actually means in day-to-day terms are variable and pragmatic, but the influence of these fundamentalist ideas has been significant, as illustrated by President Clinton's eventual confession of sinfulness to a breakfast meeting of Christian leaders following the Monica Lewinsky affair.

While American fundamentalism has been predominantly a Protestant religious movement of the southern states, there has also been a remarkable convergence of opinion between fundamentalism, the political right, Catholic conservatives and, ironically, some sections of the women's movement around pro-natalism. These diverse movements have in various ways rejected liberal America in favour of the regulation of pornography, anti-abortion legislation, the criminalization of homosexuality and the virtues of faithfulness and loyalty in permanent sexual partnerships. In short, these values confirmed a religious view of sexual and marital relationships that transcended denominational affiliation. Fundamentalism can be interpreted in this respect as a sustained struggle between a conception of society as structured, disciplined and organized and other, more fluid conceptions of society. More recently still, the rise of the Tea Party has rejected the social policies of the Obama administration on such matters as health reform and opposed much of his foreign policy with respect to treaties with Russia. This conservative movement has in many ways repeated much of the political populism of the past and at the same time thrown up new figures such as Sarah Palin. Are these movements critical of society as structure? On the one hand they wish to 'take back our liberty' by reducing the size of the state but on the other hand they wish to exert more control over illegal immigrants.

2

Society as Solidarity

From Ferdinand Tönnies to E. P. Thompson, and from Georg Hegel to Jürgen Habermas, the humanities and social sciences have been preoccupied with ideas about community, social solidarity, fairness and social justice as good in themselves. Social-science discourse has especially concentrated on solidarity, its constitution, its nurturing, and the realization of these solidaristic processes into a single social whole or community of sentiment. Solidarity, a key term in the development of theories of society, represents a social discourse which turns on care, concern, sentiment, affection, tenderness, sympathy and love. In an increasingly secular age, where social relations are all too often reduced to the purely instrumental and contractual, it is human fellowship, lived experience and the natural affections that become valued and in need of protection. During the course of the twentieth century, following after the carnage and destruction of two world wars, the movement towards collective solidarity became entrenched in many European societies and other countries as a result of the legacy of Keynesian social welfare models. During this time, there was a general consensus that social citizenship should be supported through the state provision of public utilities and pensions – which, in turn, would provide normative kinds of support towards nation-state solidarity. These developments gave rise within the register of solidarity to the emergence of what we call 'sticky societies' – that is, societies in which there was sufficient 'glue' to override conflicting interests around economic or political power. Such societies are difficult to join (other than through the primary ties of family and locality) and difficult to leave. Any departure from such societies is widely interpreted to be apostasy, disloyalty or treachery. Sticky societies of the twentieth century were forms of solidarity held together by the thick ties of locality, language, religion and culture. During the course of the late twentieth century, many of these thick ties came under mounting pressure – from multinational corporations, from the neoliberal economic reforms of the 1970s initiated by the governments of Ronald Reagan and Margaret Thatcher, and from globalization. And while the register of solidarity remains a fertile breeding ground for contemporary explorations of the social, it is arguably the case that sticky societies have suffered all kinds of despair and defeat in the early years of the twenty-first century.

Like societies of structure, the cultural climates of solidarity are politically loaded. In a class-divided social order, for example, ideologies of civic-mindedness and communal virtue are most likely to appeal to the economically well-off and culturally well-heeled – a point not lost on various radical thinkers who have warned that a 'communal' view of the social can easily collapse into bourgeois idealism. On the theme of embourgeoisement, the Scottish philosopher Francis Hutcheson offers a catalogue of such communally minded social types: 'an honest trader, the kind friend, the faithful prudent advisor, the charitable and hospitable neighbour, the tender husband and affectionate parent, the sedate yet cheerful companion'.[1] There is then, as we explore in this chapter, a specific performative style or distinct sensibility which underpins the rise of solidaristic societies – one which represents a new form of cultural politics in which differences between self and others can ideally be minimized, or at least substantially mitigated. The performativities constituted in conditions of society as solidarity are less a matter of rules and regulations, than an intensity of interpersonal and communal relationships. What matters from this standpoint is not winning and losing but belonging and sharing.

Before we delve more deeply into social theories of solidarity and community sentiment, however, we need to outline some of the core attributes permeating visions of society as solidarity a little further. At the outset we should also note that the notion of 'solidarity' has a certain historical specificity, namely that it was a prominent feature of much French social theory from the late eighteenth century onwards. It was specifically deployed in critical debates with English utilitarianism, individualism and Manchester economics. Roughly speaking, the solidarity and sentiment vision of society concentrates on transposing aggression into its opposite, namely sympathy or love. It is now communal sensitivity, rather than ruthless individualism, which mediates the relation between self and society. In the ideal society of solidarity, practices of kindness, care, mutuality, supportiveness, discretion, and self-effacement are paramount. The mode of conduct appropriate to those practised in the arts of solidaristic social life is one geared to the Other: listening carefully to others, caring for others, acting in the interests of other persons. Such altruistic social practices range all the way from befriending the needy to championing the poor. The cult of solidaristic society, however, constructs such practices with reference to a variety of justifications, or assumed foundations, in the ordering of social life. Solidaristic cultures, and the social theories produced by such societies, tend to be enamoured by the naturalistic or organic. Thus, talk of human nature and natural sentiments loom large in discourses of society as solidarity. So too, perhaps somewhat ironically, does talk about democracy, dialogue and discursiveness. This anchoring of solidarity in both the natural affections and dialogic communities produces some interesting political tensions or conundrums, which will be analysed in some detail throughout this chapter.

In the society of solidarity, moral codes are thought to be communally embedded and spontaneously synchronized across diverse groups of individuals. In the domain of lived experience, such a conception of society requires a style of subjectivity in which nature and cultural naturalness, spontaneity and social convention, seamlessly interconnect. The conduct of life in conditions of society as solidarity, in other words, is lived out as concern, longing, devotion, a love of others, compassion and charity. Such cultivation of concern for others is the very essence of solidaristic societies, and this ethos is enshrined in a range of social and ethical theories. The Scottish philosopher, Adam Ferguson, in his *Essay on the History of Civil Society*, wrote that 'love and compassion are the most powerful principles in the human breast'.[2] Weber, in his writings on the sociology of religion, postulated *Liebesakosmismus*, translated as 'the acosmism of love' or 'world-denying love' – a love, without distinction, for all: friends, strangers and enemies.[3] In seeking to shift the language of social solidarity up a gear to the realm of globalization, Jürgen Habermas reconfigures political community in terms of a 'postnational constellation' – one in which a universal democratic community, operating against the backdrop of multicultural societies, can achieve 'solidarity among strangers'.[4] In our own time of multinational capitalism and global governance, Jeffrey Alexander also sees democratic solidarity as intricately interwoven with a universal moral community, although one focused principally of effecting 'civil repair of intimate injustice'.[5]

The question of how the world of social relations is conceptualized within the viewpoint of society as solidarity is a question that pertains not only to social theories, ethical categories and politics, however. Like all imaginings of society, the register of solidarity is one that is in constant engagement, dialogue and tension with other versions of the social. In order to contextualize frameworks of solidarity in sociology and social theory, we must thus also reckon into account the social conditions that have spawned this turn to both 'naturalistic' and 'refined' communal sensibilities. In a world of intensive industrialization, widening inequality, untamed capitalism, techno-industrial warfare, deepening poverty and thorough-going ecological risks, it is sometimes immensely difficult to see the liberating consequences of communal solidarity as having impacted upon societies in any lasting sense. Against this backcloth, social and political frameworks geared to the realization of solidarity have arguably emerged precisely in order to contain the anarchic and destructive forces of industrial capitalism. It is perhaps not surprising that the struggle against bureaucratic

Communism and the Party machine in Poland was undertaken by shipyard workers under the umbrella of the Catholic Church and in the name of Solidarity. The call to solidarity then, in a nutshell, has arisen as a response to society as structure. A framework of solidarity, built on either the natural affections or dialogic communal sensitivities, explicitly contrasts with the ruthless, egoistic individualism of society as structure, or upper-case Society. (There are also interesting ways in which society as solidarity intersects with societies of creation, but aside from some passing comments this is a matter that shall be deferred until the next chapter.)

In this chapter we examine some of the conceptual experiments undertaken and the sociological conclusions drawn by a range of social theorists reflecting on the topic of solidarity. In the first section of the chapter, we start with classical sociology, focusing in particular upon Ferdinand Tönnies's foundational reflections on *Gemeinschaft*, or community. Tönnies's thought on the topic of communal solidarity is resolutely organicist, averse as it is to social modifications of, or refinements to, social cohesion and cultural unity. In Tönnies's view, the origins of solidarity are obdurately organic and particular, located in the earliest family experiences of a child with its mother, types of patriarchalism and also other experiences of natural devotion such as religion. This ardent naturalism – Tönnies's underscoring of the organic and emotional elements of community solidarity – has important consequences for an understanding of the social. However, it would be misleading to focus our discussion of communal solidarity exclusively in terms of organic relations and naturalism. In the discourse of society as solidarity, there are various shifts of register, especially towards notions of love, care, intersubjectivity, communication, language and culture throughout the twentieth century and into the twenty-first century. In the second section of the chapter, the focus ranges from early Christian theology – where we consider community in the light of Saint Paul's universalistic cosmopolitan vision of society – to Nietzsche and beyond. In the third section of the chapter, there is a dramatic shift from the theological to the dialogical. The shift is made through a consideration of Jürgen Habermas's compelling account of political solidarity, specifically in terms of his theorization of global transformations or postnational constellations promoting 'solidarity among strangers'.[6] In a similar idiom, we also turn briefly to critically examine Jeffrey Alexander's insistence on the intricate links between civil society, solidarity and civic repair. The final part of the chapter turns from social theory to politics more explicitly, with a consideration of communitarianism and its impact upon public and social policy. Throughout the focus is on conceptualizations of society as solidarity, the narrative of which we trace from Tönnies's portrayal of organic communities to the optimism of Alexander's model of social repair. This is a narrative, we suggest, which becomes progressively more complex in scope, which in turn suggests major transformations in the dynamics of contemporary societies. As society grows more complex and fragmented, sociological representations of it become richer but equally more problematic.

Classical Sociology and the Value of Solidarity

The classical distinction in German sociology between 'community' (*Gemeinschaft*) and 'association' (*Gesellschaft*) – or between the thick communalism of pre-modern societies versus the thin solidarity of modern industrial society – was contextualized in our Introduction. It is in the work of Ferdinand Tönnies that the contrast between 'community' and 'society' arose as the early analytical cornerstone for conceptualizing society and its paths of development. In fact, it is Tönnies who, in many ways, defined what the modern sociologist understands by 'community' – a closely knit social group, based on a local neighbourhood, with strong emotions of membership and the absence of individualism. The dominance of society over community expresses the decline of communities based on social solidarity and binding emotions of belonging.

Solidarity for Tönnies does not so much spring up in communal relations rather it is just *there* from the outset. It is what comes naturally, located as it is in nature. According to Tönnies, a sense of solidarity with others, with the community, is organic. It is not surprising, then, that Tönnies's rendering of *Gemeinschaft* emphasizes commonality: caring for others, sharing with friends, the valuing of reciprocal relationships. Solidarity is thus deeply rooted in the connections between self and community; it is the baseline that guides our actions and our interactions with others. Indeed, for Tönnies the solidarity of *Gemeinschaft* is what allows collective, communal processes to come about at all.

If the foundation of solidarity is resolutely organic, the communal location in which solidaristic sentiments are harmoniously realized is the family. Tönnies focuses on familial relations – husband and wife, and especially parent and child – in conceptualizing the constitution of reciprocal relationships. In examining the small child's early interactions with its mother, Tönnies underscores the deep and lasting emotional bonds fostered – which he views as essential to more mature forms of communal concord or consensus. 'Children', writes one of Tönnies's acolytes, 'are naive and harmless; they live in the present and need to be protected.'[7] Notwithstanding the clearly contentious aspects of Tönnies's views on the relationship between women and children, what must be underscored here is the organic and natural in the framing and maintaining of care, concern and community writ large. The intense emotional bond between mother and child is vitally significant because it is the bedrock of deeper ethical concern for others in the community.

It is important always to consider the fine grain of an argument or classification, especially a classification as distinctive and influential as Tönnies's community and association distinction. At first glance one might easily miss the point that Tönnies was deeply influenced by Karl Marx and through most of his life regarded himself as a Marxist. Tönnies published his *Gemeinschaft und Gesellschaft* in 1887 and he brought out a biography of Marx (*Marx Leben und Lehre*) in 1920.[8] Tönnies visited the German socialist philosopher Friedrich Engels in London in June 1894, exchanging correspondence with him about Spinoza's philosophical materialism. Tönnies departed from Marx in arguing, with the German historian Otto von Gierke, that medieval society was a commune devoid of social class conflicts. But he did regard capitalist society as competitive, individualistic and divisive. In breaking the relationship between man, community and land, capitalism exposed the worker to economic exploitation, disease and poor health. The dominance of the arbitrary will (*Gesellschaft*) over the essential will (*Gemeinschaft*) was irreversible. His famous distinction can therefore be interpreted as the contrast between a capitalist *Gesellschaft* and a communist *Gemeinschaft*.

The City of God: From St Paul to Nietzsche and Beyond

There is another sense in which the term 'solidarity' has functioned as a critique of theories of society. This can be distilled by a consideration of early Christian theology and especially the Christian doctrine of brotherly love. The idea of an ideal society based on love is clearly an important legacy of Christianity. The primitive church projected a vision of society not based on revenge or violence, but grounded in mutual respect and love – a reflection on earth of Christ's unworldly message of loving our neighbour and turning the other cheek. The Christian Church has struggled throughout its history to celebrate the idea of *agape* or disinterested, charitable and asexual love from *eros* or destructive, selfish and aggressive sexual excitement. It has tried, perhaps unsuccessfully, to institutionalize *agape* in celibacy and especially in a celibate priesthood.

When the small and insecure early Church began to grow in the context of the declining Roman Empire, Christians were faced by not only the power of the Empire, but by its claim to be the vehicle of a superior civilization. St Augustine's notion of the celestial City was one solution to this conundrum since Augustine argued that there are in fact two societies – the secular society in which power is necessary to control the evil passions of men, and a sacred city of the future in which Christian citizens will live in harmony and peace. Augustinian theology recognized a sharp distinction between the secular *polis* and the *ecclesia* thereby recognizing two forms of citizenship or loyalty between *civitas Dei* and *civitas terrena*. The solidarity of brotherly love was confirmed and demonstrated in the common meal or Eucharist of the believers.

The early Christian community was therefore caught between the philosophical traditions of Greek society, the classical world of the Roman Empire and the prophetic and scholarly legacy of Judaism. Recent philosophical research about early Christian theology has been stimulated by the Jewish intellectual Jacob Taubes and French socialist philosopher Alain Badiou, who have both treated St Paul not so much as a major theological thinker, but as a political theorist and statesman. Paul is in particular treated as 'our contemporary' because of his universalistic cosmopolitan vision of society in which there is neither Jew nor Gentile, male nor female, slave nor freeman. In other words, the solidarity of the Church was not based on the old law but on a new dispensation that would overcome human divisions. Paul stripped the Christian message down to its basic premise – Christ is risen! – and argued therefore that the new Christian society of love would transform and transcend the Jewish notion of the Law, just as it would overcome Jewish ritual. Whereas the old law was the product of a vengeful divinity, the new bond between humans was transformative and empowering. The new society was held together not by a narrow observance of the Law but by a communal meal at which Christ was present. The solidarity of the Church and the relationship between the believer and Jesus was founded on a simple meal of bread and wine that could transcend the everyday jealousies and rivalries that beset all social groups. This conception of the social was thereby developed to overcome the narrowness of the quarrels and feuds between the Jewish and the Gentile Christians, between those who had been present to witness Jesus in the flesh and those like Paul who came afterwards. In the process of this healing ministry, Paul also elaborated the idea of selfless, caring and sustaining love (*agape*) and selfish, careless and often destructive love (*eros*).

This Christian doctrine of brotherly love and community has down the centuries provided a vocabulary for criticizing earthly society – St Augustine's secular city – for its selfish individualism and inhumanity. It provided, for example, much of the motivation that drove the Quakers and the Clapham Sect to oppose slavery, and it has generally provided a model for communal life and communitarian values. But it has equally been attacked by critics who emphasize the judgemental and self-righteous possibilities within

Christian moral teaching. In modern times, Nietzsche has provided an influential critique of the Christian notions of morality
and society that are especially relevant to our account of society
as solidarity. If Christians see the perfect society as one driven
by *agape*, Nietzsche treats these moral notions as merely a smoke
screen for resentment. Here then is an interesting opposition that
should be considered in this chapter – solidarity as the outcome of
charity and society as a power structure brought about by resentful
sentiments of the poor against the rich and the powerful.

Nietzsche's opposition to 'Socratism' (abstract rational thought)
was energetic, but his critical impetus was reserved overwhelm-
ingly for an attack on St Paul, because Paul, not Jesus of Nazareth,
is credited with the invention of Christianity, and it is the latter
which has primarily been responsible for the metaphysical creation of a spiritual world that is fundamentally antagonistic to
'the little things' of the everyday sensual world. Paul is accused
by Nietzsche in *Daybreak* of an 'intractable lust for power (that)
reveals itself as an anticipatory revelling in *divine* glories. This is
the *first Christian*, the inventor of Christianness!'[9] It is through this
invention of Christianity that Paul is also blamed for inventing
consciousness, guilt, self-hatred and remorse as the most destructive forms of resentment. Paul is the arch Priest in this respect as
the supreme despiser of the body. There is an irony here however,
as Jacob Taubes points out, because Paul was in fact also bringing
about a revaluation of values.[10] Paul was responsible for creating a
new world of values that would transcend the constrained world
of Jewish legalism and launch Christianity as a force that shaped
the Western world. Nietzsche, according to Taubes's interpretation, has to attack Pauline Christianity as a doctrine of weakness
borne out of the social situation of a pariah group overwhelmed
by feelings of resentment. Against this legacy of Socratic rational-
ism on the one hand and a Pauline theology of resentment on the
other, Nietzsche offers his counter position in the *Twilight of the
Idols* of 'the innocence of Becoming'[11] against resentment against
time.

In modern philosophy, the British sociologist Gillian Rose
provided an insightful understanding of Nietzsche in *Judaism and
Modernity*.[12] She was intent on rescuing Nietzsche from simplis-

tic accusations that he was an anti-Semite. Her argument had a number of components. First, Nietzsche invariably distinguished between priests and prophets, regarding the former as the principal carriers of resentment. Talmudic Judaism survived as a consequence of the political struggle of the rabbis against the priestly stratum. Nietzsche's criticisms were not directed against rabbinic Judaism but against the religion that had been created by priests. She argued that these distinctions are important in understanding Nietzsche's stance as a psychologist who was concerned to understand in the idea of the slave revolt the relationships between power and impotence. Here again it is Paul who is signalled out as the Priest of priests and who in the doctrine of the justification by faith alone prepared the way for Luther to revive Christianity on the foundation of the priesthood of all believers. This treatment of Judaism and Christianity points to the dynamic dimension of Nietzsche's philosophy in the opposition between the man of resentment (the underman) and the man of heroic self-creation (the overman). Through this dynamic analysis of asceticism, 'Nietzsche could understand morality both as the "slavish" invention of the Jews *and* as the source of their tremendous capacity to create good out of suffering.'[13] Judaism lays the foundations for Christianity but only through Paul's struggle to transform the old Law of Judaism. In *Daybreak*, Paul is referred to as the 'first Christian' and 'without the storms and confusions of such a mind, of such a soul, there would be no Christianity; we would hardly have heard of a little Jewish sect whose master had died on the cross'.[14]

These very contradictory assessments of religion and specifically the role of Paul underline the fact that the human response to adversity can be either deeply creative (the revaluation of values), or massively negative and destructive (the role of the underman of resentment). Suffering can lead to nobility of response; as Nietzsche said, whatever does not kill me makes me strong – helps me to grow. Alternatively suffering can produce resentment when the victim imagines the oppressor as pure evil and when the self is credited with all goodness. The result is a culture of reaction in which the 'man of *ressentiment* is clever, scheming and secretive, he cherishes his memory of offence, and fixes and idealizes his evil enemy as his own deed'.[15] Society as solidarity, with its cult of care and concern for others, might seem just the opposite of this. Yet the call for community is largely a way of attempting to give the slip to the superego's ferocious destructive powers, with the suffering of *ressentiment* thought to be buried through the condition of solidarity (whether the call is peace, love, togetherness or community).

This intellectual goal of understanding the changing nature of the individual in modern society was also overtly the aim of Nietzsche's philosophical investigations – which we will consider in more detail in the next chapter. The target of his critical thought was the disappearance of the heroic individual who had achieved self-mastery through struggle against conventional morality and modern society. The *Ubermensch* was precisely somebody who had achieved self-mastery through discipline in a confrontation with hypocrisy and convention. At times Nietzsche argued in a manner wholly parallel to Weber that the heroic individual was cultivated in the ancient world, in warrior societies and in the military, but had become unmanly in the standardized and rationalized world of modern capitalism. The *Ubermensch* was the charismatic figure capable of breaking through the dead weight of tradition to challenge society with the vision of new values. In terms of Weber's theory of charisma, Paul's conversion was the charismatic event that turned the course of history.[16] The further irony is that it is Paul whom Nietzsche most resents.[17]

Nietzsche and Weber also shared in common a view of the world as characterized by endless struggle. Against the view that the ancient world was one of tranquillity, Nietzsche showed that Greek society was characterized by an endless struggle between eroticism and passion (Dionysus), and rationality and formalism (Apollo); a healthy life for the individual would require some reconciliation of these two dimensions of human nature. The problem with modern society was that an industrial civilization and a mass society had eclipsed the opportunities for heroic individualism. Nevertheless, against modern nihilism, Nietzsche preached a 'revaluation of values', a critique of culture that would open up the possibility of recreating heroic men.

Nietzsche's social philosophy, rather like Weber's, emphasized the idea of endless struggle, both individual and social, as necessary for growth and renewal. His criticism of Christianity was based on the notion that Christian asceticism was destructive of the heroic life of masculinity and warrior societies; it was a religion of the dispossessed and the weak, and hence it could not contribute to the health of the individual. The healthy individual had to overcome and reject the illusions and the sickly life of the world-denying monks and priests. Nietzsche's ethic was to reject all manifestations of nihilism and no-saying philosophies embracing a manly ethic and a yes-saying philosophy. At the root of Nietzsche's ethic of action and personal renewal was a stinging criticism of the destructive resentment because resentment, unlike rage, turns inwards and corrodes the life of those who resent, rather than those who are resented.

Christian theology was held to be responsible for the whole mythology of personal freedom that attempts to glorify the meek and humble against the powerful and strong. It interprets meekness as merit. The characteristic slave type of morality is therefore one of resentment, but it is only when it assumes a Christian – that is priestly – direction that it becomes parasitic and negative. The slave morality of Pauline Christianity has to posit an external world that is evil against which it is reactive, not active. Insofar as Christian asceticism shaped the modern world in terms of Max Weber's theory of inner-worldly asceticism, it is a modernity that breeds resentment in which the individual comes to resent any deviation from piety and to resent others who deviate from social conventions. The ascetic is somebody whose swollen will-to-power is directed inwards at self-mastery and against this ethic of personal and inward domination and mastery Nietzsche offers an ethic of 'letting be'.[18]

Not all those who have reflected on community and solidarity have been so resolutely negative. As we saw in the earlier discussion of nostalgia, Alasdair MacIntyre contends that we live in a world in which the only philosophical justification for any action is based on emotivism: it is good if it feels right. Like Weber and Nietzsche, MacIntyre thinks that we have arrived at this impasse because of the death of God that signifies the erosion of a community in which moral principles could exercise any collective force with some degree of authority. This argument runs throughout MacIntyre's philosophy but it found its most obviously sociological expression in *Secularization and Moral Change*.[19] Looking at British society in particular, he argues that during the industrial revolution, social classes had some degree of internal communal integration and each social class had its own religion and morals. Class solidarity was the basis of a degree of shared values. With urbanization and the gradual fragmentation of communal life, the virtues associated with class position finally evaporated. We might add to MacIntyre the observation that in Britain at least, the communal solidarities that underpinned social class have further evaporated with the social changes brought about during the Thatcher years when union membership declined rapidly, the working-class communities of old industries such as mining and ship-building collapsed and a new individualism flourished on the basis of individual consumerism. Mrs Thatcher's famous claim there is no such thing as 'society' – there are only individuals and families – became the justification for treating money as the only sure guide of what people really wanted in life. Comic actors during the Thatcher years celebrated 'luvely money' as the justification for everything. These social changes that accompanied the marketization of social relations have resulted in greater income inequality and lesser social trust.

These authors – Nietzsche, Weber and MacIntyre – are all deeply influenced by Christianity and by Pauline theology in particular, even when they seek overtly to reject that influence. Their picture of the good society – as beyond nihilism, before the iron cage, or before fragmentation – is deeply Christian and at the same time deeply nostalgic. In the case of MacIntyre his view of society and his philosophical framework were increasingly derived from Aquinas. His understanding of solidarity was taken from a Catholic tradition that condemned individualism, usury and selfishness. These critics of modernity yearn for social solidarity or community based on collective co-operation, but they argue that a society of love is no longer available to us. The modern world is fragmented, divided by social class and corrupted by selfish motives. Their criticisms present a sharp opposition (in Augustinian terms) between a city based on secular and selfish values, and the city of God, a community with institutionalized *agape*.

Communicative Solidarity: Habermas

Perhaps the most renowned contemporary advocate of solidarity is Habermas. One can trace the mesmerizing power of the notion of solidarity in Habermas back to his earliest work, *The Structural Transformation of the Public Sphere*. The public sphere, argued Habermas, emerges in the life of the *polis* in ancient Greece – constituted as an energetic, dialogical arena in which discourse and reason are fundamental elements. The development of mercantile capitalism in the sixteenth century, according to Habermas, transformed the meaning of 'public opinion' away from the domain of courtly life as embedded in the traditional texture of old European societies and toward the expansion of market economies and newly defined spheres of division between the state and civil society. In the societies of early or market capitalism, a mediation between differentiated spheres of the state and civil society unfolded as individuals went about the daily business of interpersonal interaction, business dealings and civic association.

The emergence of a full-blown bourgeois public sphere, contends Habermas, occurred only in the wider social context of salons, clubs and coffee houses which were then spreading throughout the cities of early modern Europe. In particular, newspapers and journals were used by various educated elites when interacting to debate and questioning political authority and the conduct of the state. 'Newspapers', writes Habermas, 'changed from mere institutions for the publication of news into bearers and leaders of public opinion – weapons of party politics.'[20] Under these social conditions, critical debate flourished. The heyday of such collective forms of solidaristic discourse or rational comprehension was, however, shortlived. For the rise of an electronic, mass media – with its array of seductive advertising, spin doctors and trivialization of politics – signalled a major impediment to processes of democratic communication as well as to rational forms of ongoing political dialogue and solidarity.

It is perhaps not difficult to see in the early Habermas the influence of Tönnies's lament for the disappearance of community, or the solidarity of social life, under the modernizing pressures of society, or *Gesellschaft*. Etymologically, *Gesellschaft* comes from *Geselle*, indicating a shared space and subsequently associated with the idea of companionship or friendship.[21] Here again the connection with sociology is straightforward since, at root, sociology is the study of companionship (from *socius*). Society is that space within which the companions are sociable and, for Aristotle at least, these relationships are the true basis of the *polis*, since without trust and friendship the competition between rational actors in the state may well destroy political life through endless interpersonal conflicts. In this connection, Tönnies's distinction between community and society reminds us that German sociology was concerned to study the tensions between cooperation and competition (in fact between two different types of will formation) in the civil sphere, or in Marxist terms between the destructive force of class interests and the need for reciprocity and trust, or between scarcity and solidarity.[22] From this angle, Habermas's *The Structural Transformation of the Public Sphere* – as an account of the growth of bourgeois society in terms of 'discursive will formation' and its decline under the influence of modern media – clearly takes its cue from this classic dichotomy which has dominated sociological thought.

In his more recent writings, Habermas has continued to defend the centrality of solidarity and in particular processes of what he terms 'collective will formation', but this time on a global level. His suggestion is that, today, social solidarity – which social science has theorized primarily at the level of the nation-state – must be shifted up a gear in order to comprehend the emergence of cosmopolitan values entrenched in important sectors of international and transnational processes. Such a radicalization of democracy, comments Habermas, is not necessarily abstract; the flowering of culturally cosmopolitan sentiments of belonging, inclusion and shared interests is already emerging from the weakening of the nation-state under the pressures of advanced globalization. In terms of the debate specifically over Europe, Habermas argues in favour of a pan-European public sphere that presupposes a European civil society, complete with interest groups, non-governmental organizations and transnational social movements. Transnational mass media can only construct this multi-vocal communicative context if, as is already the case in smaller countries, national education systems provide the basis of a common language – even if in most cases it is a foreign language. The normative impulses that first set these different processes in motion from their scattered national sites will themselves only come about through overlapping projects or a common political culture.

Just as Habermas in his early writings argued that the salons and coffee-houses of eighteenth-century Europe provided the social ground for the development of political forms of solidarity, so in his more recent writings he underscores the ultimate political value of public participation and the widest reaching democratization of transnational decision-making processes. Only popular processes of communication and practical discourse, reflecting the impress of collective will formation, will adequately generate forms of cosmopolitan solidarity geared to the pluralization of democracy emerging at the level of transnational or global social policies. For Habermas, such democratization is socially desirable, especially in terms of the development of post-conventional learning patterns in the realms of society, personality and culture. As he writes:

> The artificial conditions in which national consciousness arose argue against the defeatist assumption that a form of civic solidarity among strangers can only be generated within the confines of the nation. If this form of collective identity was due to a highly abstractive leap from the local and dynastic to national and then to democratic consciousness, why shouldn't this learning process be able to continue?[23]

While there are various points that might be made at this juncture, note Habermas's emphasis on the political possibilities of a 'form of civic solidarity among strangers' that might arise as a consequence of patterns of multilayered governance and overlapping communities of political fate associated with the forces of globalization. Is this wishful thinking? Possibly, some might say; perhaps even utopian, as others have argued. Putting aside these considerations here, we instead wish to concentrate on Habermas's emphasis concerning the institutional requirements of cosmopolitan solidarity and focus in particular on how this conception of an open global society exemplifies the doctrine of society as solidarity.

'Habermas's social theory', comments the American philosopher Max Pensky, 'is largely silent concerning the culturally specific forms of reaction, aversion, legitimation and accommodation that arise as strategies to compensate for the loss of traditional meaning in modern societies.'[24] But what, exactly, fuels the emotional undercurrent, at once individual and collective, of post-traditional forms of solidarity? In an age of intensive globalization, transnational mobilities and multinational capitalism, how exactly does a passion for solidarity manifest itself in concrete social relations and civic society? And does the notion of 'solidarity among strangers' – in the sociological context of the global electronic economy – adequately capture the complex, contradictory ways in which individuals navigate and narrate their increasingly mediated, virtualized experiences of the social today? Habermas's views about a European project based on justice and communication have become increasingly distanced from the views of European leaders. The idea of European cosmopolitanism – recognition and celebration of differences within a shared value system – is now open to serious questioning and debate.

Violence and Solidarity: The Idea of Civic Repair

Solidarity is not just about 'talking things over'. Whatever the sociological merits of Habermas's vision of communicative ethics, solidarity can also mean that people need to 'come together' strategically, undertaking new forms of social action if ethical wrongs have any chance of being put right. An interesting formulation of the link between communal forms of social action and civic repair has been recently advanced by Jeffrey Alexander. In *The Civil Sphere* (2006), he argues that we need a new concept of civil society as the 'civil sphere' – a field of values and institutions – to create a space for social criticism and democratic integration.[25] He further argues that such a sphere depends for its survival on social solidarity, including such emotions as sympathy for others and that solidarity is *par excellence* the subject matter of the discipline of sociology. Therefore, the importance and the social function of sociology as a critical discipline is hitched to the survival of the civil sphere, and not just sociology but *cultural* sociology in particular.

What is Alexander's account of this tradition? For Alexander the civil sphere is bounded by the 'non-civil' institutions of state, religion, family and community, which are seen to be particularistic and sectoral, rather than universalistic and societal. Because the solidarities of the civil sphere constantly fail, there is an important role for civil repair – social and political acts that are designed to rebuild confidence, solidarity and trust. The demand for justice, especially in modern social movements from the black civil rights campaigns onwards, is an important component of this civil repair. Alexander rightly takes the American political philosopher John Rawls's (1921–2002) *Theory of Justice* to be the turning point of modern political philosophy but complains justifiably that Rawlsian theories of justice have little underpinning from empirical sociological research. Rawls does not show, for example, in *The Law of Peoples* how an 'overlapping consensus' might actually come into existence through social processes.[26] His central theme is that we should conceive civil society as 'a solidary sphere, in which a certain kind of universalizing community comes to be culturally defined and to some degree institutionally enforced'.[27] Against earlier versions of the theory of civil society in classical political economy, he wants to distinguish clearly between capitalist markets and civil society. Capitalist forces are not the only or most damaging threat to the civil sphere which is all too frequently overwhelmed by racial hatred, misogyny, patriarchy, or the monopolistic power of political elites, experts and bureaucrats. In these situations, social movements demanding a restoration of justice or a defence of civility and solidarity against efficiency and hierarchy can lead to civil repair. The civil sphere is then characterized by a series of sentiments or civil motives (reasonableness, calmness and self-control), by civil relations (open, trustworthy and deliberative) and by civil institutions (rule regulated, lawful and inclusive). The civil sphere is also illustrated by the idea of 'the public' and above all by civil associations such as AARP (the American Association of Retired Persons) or by NAACP (the National Association for the Advancement of Colored People) and other organizations that articulate and defend minority interests.

This view of America's civil sphere clearly echoes the classical work of French political thinker Alexis de Tocqueville, but Alexander tries to distinguish between the public-minded, more universalistic associations of the modern period and the voluntary associations that were central to Tocqueville's analysis of American democracy. He associates a neo-Tocquevillian position with the work of Robert Putnam and the idea of social capital or social investments in society. Putnam's work, especially in *Bowling Alone*, offered a powerful criticism of the disturbing social consequences of modern individualism – epitomized in isolated teenagers just watching the TV.[28] Alexander offers an effective criticism of this Putnam legacy by noting that not all voluntary associations contribute to trust, democratic sentiments or generalized solidarity. There is nothing especially liberal and democratic about the Boy Scouts. How does the National Rifle Association or the National Federation of Independent Businesses contribute to civil repair? Do societies such as the Masonic League promote the interests of the people as a whole?

The problem – which Alexander recognizes only too well – is that associations can only contribute to democracy and inter-personal trust if they are 'intertwined with the full range of communicative and regulative institutions'.[29] One criticism of Alexander might be that he fails ultimately to provide a solution to this issue and in particular neglects how the institutions of secular citizenship as public institutions connecting the private citizen to the state through such mechanisms as taxation and public service are a necessary brake upon the exclusionary solidaristic forces of the family, the tribe, the sect and the secret society.

Alexander notes the fact that one can easily identify societies that have strong civil society components but weak or compromised democratic structures. Italy provides one illustration where, through much of the twentieth century, local, familial and religious connections and organizations counteracted the possibilities of more democratic institutions at the national level; or modern Thailand where the strength of Buddhist associations such as the *sangha* and the monarchy stand in the way of any reasonable political settlement with its Muslim minority. Another illustration might be offered by Israel, where it appears that the very strength of associations outside the state – primarily the associations that are connected with the ultra-Orthodox community – makes the conduct of effective democratic government deeply problematic. But these illustrations may begin to create analytical problems for which the theory of 'civil sphere' may not produce ready-made solutions.

Alexander's analytical attempt to resolve the legacies of different versions of civil society theory over a vast period of time is impressive, but we might take a more pragmatic view of his text – the proof of the pudding is in the eating. In this perspective we can read *The Civil Sphere* as a series of case studies showing the importance and vitality of the liberal, democratic sphere for the proper functioning of politics. These case studies are a model of sociological observation, and they are designed to study the contradictory forces unleashed by any human society between inclusive forces and exclusionary pressures around the 'We' and 'Them' divide. To illustrate these elementary forms of social life, Alexander turns to social movements as movements of civil repair. Once more, he is not content merely to appropriate existing social movements theory but rather wants to recast it better to serve his normative and analytical purposes, claiming that the classical model of social movements needs to be given a deeper cultural and historical foundation. He notes that in modern societies, where notions of justice are often embedded in local and particular contexts, successful morally powerful social movements must present an idealized picture of the community as a whole if they are to command any generalized attention. In short, the particular interests of localized movements must be translated into society-wide interests and values if they are to mobilize society for civil repair. In the space of this chapter, it is not possible to provide an account in detail of the examples Alexander presents, but they illustrate how through the evolution of the women's movements into feminism, with its notions of gender universalism, the issues of gender found a wide and powerful public. Furthermore, the movement for racial equality for black Americans 'played an enormous role in the civil repair of racism that crystallized in the Civil Rights movement of the 1950s and 1960s. It supplied economic and organizational power and an ideology of solidarity in the struggle against white oppression.'[30] This transformation of black opposition was eventually translated into a legal apparatus such as the Civil Rights Act of 1964 which began the process of making segregation and discrimination on the basis of race a crime.

The great social and political problem of our times is the problem of securing public security and cultural cohesion in societies that, primarily as a result of global migration and transnational movements, have become deeply differentiated and divided by ethnicity, language and religion. Many conservatives and liberals, even in a society such as the United States which is constituted by migration, believe that multicultural policies have destroyed national identity and moral coherence. It is argued by critics of cultural liberalism that enthusiastic support for cultural difference has resulted in the erosion of national identity, thereby increasing social and political tensions over social membership. These criticisms were associated with the work of the American sociologist Nathan Glazer on American multiculturalism.[31] Although Glazer rejects the label of 'neoconservative', his complaint that America has been 'balkanized' has become associated with what is seen as the national retreat[32] from racial justice. These arguments amount to noticing that recognition (of the validity and worth of cultural differences) may lead to neither justice nor solidarity. While this debate has been important in American politics, in Europe in 2011 David Cameron in Britain, Angela Merkel in Germany and Nicolas Sarkozy in France all declared that multiculturalism had failed because European migrants had formed parallel communities that were not well integrated and these separate communities had become a significant security threat.

Alexander agrees that empirically speaking modern civil spheres are deeply fragmented and that ethnic particularism in non-civil spheres does contribute to this fragmentation, but he holds to the utopian vision of a genuine public sphere in which multiculturalism can in fact enhance universalism, rather than destroy it. For example the eventual inclusion of Jews in American society provides some confidence that the public sphere can operate in an ethnically differentiated society. For example, he takes the current increase in Christian and Jewish marriages as being an indicator of progressive change.

Alexander's principal defence of multiculturalism is normative in the sense that he claims that it is a moral preference, but he also aims to show empirically that it can also be a celebration of diversity and hybridity, rather than merely a process of containment and assimilation. There is evidence, he claims, for the view that public recognition of various 'primordial qualities' – repressed sexualities, minority religious identities, subordinated genders, and minority languages – can enhance, rather than undermine civility. Increasing marriage rates between phenotypically distinctive racial groups, a decline in the public acceptance of racial stereotypes, and cultural indications of the erasure of a white hegemony (at least in popular culture) are examples of public recognition These cultural signs of a wider sentiment of inter-ethnic solidarity are reinforced by regulatory measures, primarily in terms of legal enforcement. In sum, Alexander celebrates the idea of social solidarity as the positive dream of all social reform and recognizes that ultimately the civil sphere is a project – 'a restless aspiration that lies deep in the soul of democratic life'.[33]

From a sociological point of view, there are at least three ways of formulating democratic theory as a perspective on participatory politics: social capital, citizenship and civil society. Alexander's theory of the civil sphere pays a lot of attention to the first two, but says relatively little about modern citizenship. As we have seen, he gives one of the most telling criticisms we have of social capital theory and develops a morally and sociologically powerful defence of the idea of the civil sphere theory. However, while citizenship is frequently implied in his argument, he does not provide either a critique or a defence of the idea of citizenship as necessary to building and defending solidarity. There is consequently little emphasis on rights and duties as foundations of the public sphere. He clearly recognizes the importance of a regulatory regime in defending universalism against prejudice and parochialism. Can social solidarity be defended however without a well grounded set of citizenship institutions? How will public institutions be funded without the universal obligations of taxation? In Britain, the public as a discursive democratic space depends heavily on the BBC, public libraries, museums and the universities, but these institutions are under constant threat of privatization and they are subordinated to an alien system of appraisal in terms of commercial values. These public institutions have come under even greater erosion as a result of the credit crisis in the United Kingdom, where Cameron's Conservative Government has responded to the national debt with a policy of severe budget cuts and general austerity. If we take the issue of taxation in relation to social integration, in mundane and pedestrian terms, we might regard tax evasion as a basic denial of connectedness and responsibility. There is little in Alexander's account of the civil sphere about the economic dimensions of membership and solidarity from personal taxation to retirement and pensions. It is also characteristic of American social and political philosophy to regard the movement for civil rights as a movement for human rights, thereby neglecting the simple fact that the right to vote is the fundamental political right of citizenship. This absence is not however fatal to Alexander's theory, which could in principle accommodate these issues but it is an indication of the weakness of the theory of social repair in which cultural sociology appears to be incapable of including any significant analysis of what we might call the economics of membership.

Turning to the issue of religious differences, it is difficult to resolve religious disputes over incommensurable beliefs in secular society by procedures that could be mutually acceptable to both religion and state. Therefore, civil society remains unstable. The unspoken assumption of Alexander's study of the civil sphere and its politics is that the public remains a secular domain. What would happen if the holy city replaced the civil sphere? Can universalism be a sacred, rather than a profane domain and, if so, can it tolerate a struggle between competing gods? We can compare Alexander's account of the success of the American public sphere in absorbing different value systems and different social movements with a recent publication by Robert Putnam and David Campbell, *American Grace. How Religion Divides and Unites Us*.[34] It is well known that religion has played a major role in American public life, much more so than in Europe. We also know that religion has been a source of deep divisions in American history. It was thought that the election of President Kennedy, who was a Roman

Catholic, represented an important turning point in the acceptance of Catholicism into the political elite. Through an examination of national survey data, Putnam and Campbell conclude that while denominational differences are still important they are not divisive. They write, 'A leading, perhaps even primary, reason that America manages to be both highly religious and highly diverse is that most Americans do not believe that those of a different religious faith are damned. Devotion plus diversity, minus damnation, equals comity.'[35] One might speculate that while the mainstream denominations no longer adhere to a determined and distinctive view of damnation, evangelicals might have more severe restrictions on who could enter into heaven, and yet the survey data (Faith Matters Survey 2007) shows that in fact 83 per cent of evangelical Protestants believed that a 'good person not of your faith can go to heaven'.

There are several responses that one could make to these findings. The first is that given the outcry against Muslims in America – such as the public hostility to the creation of a Muslim culture centre near the site of what was the Twin Towers – it would be reasonable to assume that Americans are not receptive to a Muslim presence in their cities. The other response to Putnam and Campbell might be that it is only because Americans are increasingly secular that the traditional theology of heaven and hell no longer impresses them. Further, there may be alternative sources of religious solidarity in the United States that holds Americans together, namely what the American sociologist Robert Bellah, borrowing a term from Rousseau, calls civil religion. This is a system of values and institutions, separate but connected to Christianity, that commemorate and celebrate American history – its foundation as the 'First New Nation', the trials and tribulations of the Civil War, its confrontations during the Cold War and its eventual triumph over Communism. This civil religion is shared by Americans as a common history of suffering and final triumph as a democratic nation.

Alexander is, of course, preoccupied with the legacy of Durkheim, who after all developed an implicit theory of the civil sphere in *Professional Ethics and Civic Morals*. Although Alexander very openly recognizes that the civil sphere is subject to contestation, he sees these in terms of particularistic cultural threats to the democratic ideal, rather than a constant battle between schism[36] driven by material interests and solidarity forged by common values. Durkheim was also deeply influenced by Rousseau and there is a strong connection therefore with Bellah's account of the civil religion and Alexander's view of the American public sphere as a site of social repair.

This discussion of Alexander, Bellah and Durkheim does however raise a conceptual issue about solidarity that we must elaborate. We need to distinguish two forms of solidarity that are often blurred and confused in social theory. In terms of micro-sociological analysis we need to refer to a form of solidarity that emerges more or less spontaneously from all human social interaction. These spontaneous eruptions of sociality may be fleeting and inconsequential when two strangers join in a conversation on their way to work in the subway, or they may be longer lasting such as the friendship between two lovers or the solidarity that takes place when a family sits down to an evening meal by the fireside. This type of solidarity might be defined as lower-case, spontaneous, voluntary and bottom-up. It is essentially the site of intimacy and friendship. This type of solidarity is very different from the collective membership and identity of individuals in the Hitler Youth Movement or the solidarity associated with nationalism or the solidarity of a Japanese corporation. These forms of solidarity we might call upper case, large scale, orchestrated and typically top down. This collective Solidarity is often involuntary and coercive; it punishes deviance and apostasy. Lower-case solidarity has a close connection with the idea of society as creation, since we think of inter-personal sociability as a phenomenon that is constantly renewed and regenerated through the mundane processes of exchange and interaction.

Communitarianism

We can also see the legacy of the Christian notion of communalism and charity in modern communitarianism. In its modern form, communitarianism has offered an important criticism of unbridled individualism and naked market forces, especially in the context of American society. Its doctrines have been successfully articulated by sociologists such as Amitai Etzioni and Philip Selznick, who believe fervently that the communal foundations of modern America have been severely shaken. The evidence for a social crisis was widespread: the decline of the family, rising divorce rates and moral confusion. There were also troublesome race riots and urban violence bringing the US Riot Commission at the end of the 1960s to conclude that there were two separate and unequal nations in America – the Black and the White. The social crisis was also indicated by the rise in the number of people (around 6 per cent) by 1990 who were either in prison, or caught up in the justice system (where they were on parole or probation).

Etzioni rejected both coercive strategies (such as greater law enforcement) and conservative policies (such as enhancing individual autonomy by reducing the role of the state) as responses to America's problems, defending through a large array of publications the project of communitarianism. His philosophy was that America – indeed any liberal democratic society – required a set of core values, but these are handed down from one generation to another and they cannot be simply invented. This notion was the basis for rejecting American individualism as a shared value, since it cannot in fact offer any common ground for action. In addition, while Etzioni advocated public debate about values, he rejected what he called the 'deliberative-rational' approach to these core values, because such an approach neglected the role of emotion and feeling as important aspects of the impact of such values in the lives of individuals.

Having rejected both coercive measures and rational deliberation, Etzioni argued that the necessary commitment and conviction behind such shared values could only arise from what he called the 'moral voice' behind or 'beyond sharing'.[37] This moral voice is both internal (the conviction of the individual) and external (the encouragement of consociates). Etzioni recognized that there are three circumstances or conditions under which people will comply, namely when they are 'coerced, paid or convinced'.[38] He came to the unsurprising conclusion that affective or moral conviction about an issue is the strongest ground for compliance. There is thus a powerful connection between 'affective attachment' and a 'moral voice'. Finally this moral voice is institutionalized in the law in a democratic society – 'law in a good society is first and foremost the continuation of morality by other means'.[39]

In this account of the communitarian society, we detect a continuation of Augustinian social theory. There is a tendency to equate 'society' and 'community'; there is a distrust of human nature which needs the constraint of the inner moral voice and the external regulation of law; there is the criticism of individualism as the hallmark of modernity; and there is a dichotomy therefore between the moral community and the market. Above all, there is the search for the 'golden rule' by which an unruly society might be transformed into the caring or loving community. It is through the moral voice that the negative forces of resentment and individualism might be kept at bay – at least to allow communities to rebuild and recover from anomie.

Roland Robertson has argued that the communitarian argument needs to be tested against the growth of globalization and he is sceptical of expressions such as 'the global village' which express a nostalgic view of community.[40] He notes correctly that attempts to extend Tönnies's idea of *Gemeinschaft* to the world community is confronted by many difficulties in which the ideas of both 'communuity' and 'communitarianism' have variable meaning. The invocation of 'community' can have very specific meanings as for example when Japan attempted to think of itself as a 'familial nation'. Few communitarians – including Etzioni – have tried to think of communitarianism in a global context and have consequently failed to address the moral issues around intercommunal conflicts over values, including the value of community itself.

Reassessing Solidarity: The Corrosion of Citizenship and the Demise of 'Sticky Societies'

Why, then, has society ousted solidarity? And is it feasible to contend, as do those like Etzioni (for whom 'community' is always a positive term), that the re-emergence of solidaristic societies is likely? One straightforward answer, which undeniably is politically pessimistic, is 'no'. Caught between societies of structure and creation, the whole project of solidarity has become increasingly drained of political substance in these early years of the twenty-first century, although it is also true that its various ideological variations appear incapable of coming to an end. One form of cultural politics where this has been especially evident is the debate over citizenship, particularly the complex ways in which economic globalization eats away at nationalist forms of belonging and citizenship rights. There is a general consensus that traditional forms of social citizenship are in considerable crisis, or at least in a radical transition to new forms. The legacy of Keynesian social welfare models has been radically challenged and changed by the globalization of neoliberal economic reforms initiated initially under Thatcherism in the UK and Reaganism in the USA. However these neoliberal models have, in fact, continued under or were implicitly sustained by the governments that followed them. The majority of Western governments of the centre left – such as Tony Blair's Labour government and its Third-Way policies – embraced lower personal taxation, less government intervention into economic activity, the privatization of public utilities and pensions, the outsourcing of economic activity and the like. These measures removed state support for many public functions that had been closely associated with social citizenship.

Two examples are instructive. The first and most important has been the global drift away from secure public support for pensions towards privatization. Many workers in European societies saw this development as a departure from collective solidarity and the consequence has been to undermine the trust and solidarity underpinning citizenship that had evolved in the post-war period. The second is the outsourcing of military activity. The two principal indications of the rise of citizenship were universal taxation and compulsory military service. The first condition is eroded by the reduction of personal taxation and the introduction of various tax breaks for the wealthy and the second condition is eroded by the privatization of the military and its outsourcing to private companies, such as Blackwater Worldwide. The difficulty of maintaining state regulation of such private security agencies was very clearly

demonstrated in Iraq. Although during the 2008 global financial crisis there have been some policy attempts to foster greater
regulation of financial institutions, it is unlikely that the recent
worldwide credit crunch will, in the long run, bring about a
return to Keynesian welfare states. Hence, we do not anticipate a
rebuilding of the social model of citizenship, nor the re-assertion
of solidaristic societies.

What social and economic conditions produced the neoliberal
experiment? One issue was the perception of falling profitabil-
ity in the 1960s onwards and hence lower labour costs in Asia
encouraged Western capitalist corporations to transfer production activity out of Europe and North America. The result was
to weaken the capacity of the trade unions to maintain wage
levels and in addition governments were able to bring in legislation to curtail the capacity of trade unions through strike activity
to secure wage increases. The history of modern Italy in which
the Left has been undermined, with the irresistible rise of Silvio
Berlusconi is a classical illustration of the disappearance of the
mass movement of workers.[41] However, as the consumer power
of the working population declined, it was necessary to stimulate
domestic consumption through a credit card revolution alongside
the deregulation of the banks and the creation of cheap mortgages
and easy credit. The decade-long boom in the housing market
was one obvious result, but the collapse of this housing boom is
now illustrated by the so-called 'ghost towns' of Ireland and Spain
where thousands of unoccupied units are now a major drag on the
banking and development sectors.

Talk about transformations in work throughout Western countries remains embarrassingly general in many recent studies, and
yet such changes are of core importance to grasping the decline of
sticky societies as we have defined the register of solidarity. During
the 1990s and into the 2000s, neoliberalism in the West has largely
transformed the nature of work through casualization, outsourcing,
part-time employment and flexible retirement. De-unionization
has been especially consequential in this connection. Consider, for
example, the sharp decline in union membership in the United
States in Figure 2.1, which sets out American union membership
from 1973 to 2008.

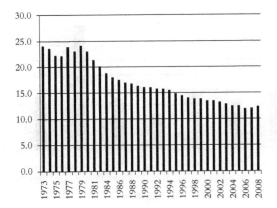

Data Source: Hirsch, B. and Macpherson, D. 2003, 'Union membership and coverage database from the current population survey', *Industrial and Labor Relations Review*, Vol. 56, No. 2, pp. 349–54.

Figure 2.1 Union Membership %, USA.

Alongside the United States, other countries throughout the West have witnessed similar rates of decline of 'unionicity'. Figure 2.2 provides graphic evidence of changes in labour conditions over the ten year period from 1993 to 2003, in which countries such as New Zealand saw an approximate decline of 35 per cent and Australia an approximate decline of 40 per cent in trade union membership.

At the level of social values, cultural meanings and communal solidarity, these changes to labour conditions have been well documented by sociologists such as Richard Sennett and Barbara Ehrenreich. The general picture is one of a growing phenomenon of impoverished employees or the working poor, whose wages are insufficient to support domestic households, marriage and successful social reproduction. In short, the solidaristic dream of a 'social safety net' provided through citizenship can no longer catch the growing tide of people falling out of union-protected, full-time employment and into poverty. Casualization of work, by contrast, tends to promote tendencies towards privatization. Privatization in this context is corrosive of solidarity because it disconnects people from the communal threads of the social: workers find that they

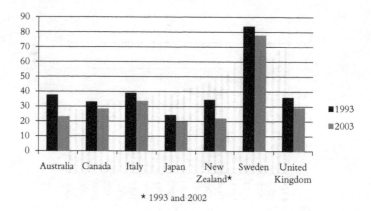

Data Sources: Visser, J 2006, 'Union membership statistics in 24 countries', Monthly Labour Review, January, pp. 38–49; Blanchflower, D. 2007, 'International Patterns of Union Membership', British Journal of Industrial Relations, Vol. 45, No. 1, pp. 1–28.

Figure 2.2 Union Membership %, Selected Countries.

have no union membership and enjoy very limited social prestige because the traditional notion of the 'dignity of labour' has been destroyed by monotonous and repetitious work practices.

Indeed, the global financial crisis of 2008–9 and its economic consequences through to 2012 and beyond perfectly illustrate the structural contradictions of capitalism which erode solidarity, caught as it is between the need for profits and investment on the one hand and the necessity of saving and investment on the other. The result of this contradiction has been to transform the active citizen of the traditional social model of welfare citizenship into the passive consumer citizen of late capitalism. This is illustrated by the fact that governments in America, Australia and Britain encouraged their citizens throughout 2009 to spend in order to save their societies from collapse, while at the same time the press were condemning the 'fat cats' of the financial world because their greed had destroyed the economy. The Asian economies were less exposed to these instabilities than was the case for the United States, Britain, Ireland and Iceland, but the crunch has only served to underline the importance of the Chinese economy to continu-

ing global economic growth. Western powers will be less likely
to raise criticisms of China's domestic policies as a result, and
countries like Australia and New Zealand which are resource-
rich societies may well find themselves drawn inexorably into
the Chinese tributary system. The rapid growth of China's naval
power and growing confrontations in the South China Sea and on
the disputed border between North and South Korea are probably the most obvious indications of both its new found economic
power and its emerging imperial ambitions.

Conclusion: From Community to Transnational Solidarity

The idea of society as solidarity emphasizes social relations which
are intricately interpersonal, dialogical and based on mutual understanding or consensus. In sociological terms, there is no tragic
conflict here between the individual and society, as there is in the
ultra–rationalistic, scientistic and totalizing worldview of society as
structure. Rather, the values of solidarity are entrenched in social
relations as a natural tendency towards unity. For Tönnies, at the
core of community lies Nature – or at least a vision of the enduring
relationships between people, land, production and community
that forged the medieval community that sits at the base of his view
of *Gemeinschaft*. Just as the sphere of solidarity springs from a pre-
existing intersubjective unity or natural unity, and thus contains
its ends in itself, so the universe of community, or *Gemeinschaft*, is
the unfolding of a spontaneously common spirit rooted in concord
or consensus. These and related conceptions of the centrality of
solidarity to society anchor emotional connection, friendship, love
and the search for peace at the heart of both individual experience
and social life, with a strong emphasis on the intricate dependence
of the individual upon others.

One important development that any theory of society must
now consider is of course the impact of the current phase of
globalization. We do not subscribe to the view that globalization is simply a product of recent social transformations, which
is often linked for example to the emergence of new information

technologies in some social theories.[42] For example the development of the Silk Road contributed to the spread of Buddhism into
Asia long before the rise of the West. It is the case however that
globalization has intensified in the late twentieth and early twenty-
first centuries. Visions of society – structure, solidarity and creation
– will need to incorporate ideas about the effects of globalizing
forces on social relations. George Simmel's idea of the social group
took little notice unsurprisingly of global developments – although
of course his essays on 'the stranger' and his book on money were
clearly compatible with a globalizing world. However in modern
sociology we must be far more attentive to the issues of how and
whether globalization stretches solidarity, transforming in its wake
local and rooted communities into thin and fluid social forms.
How are societies transforming the prism of the global?

In our own time of accelerated globalization, more intricate
processes of solidarity – embedded in transnational forms of
governance – replace the 'natural', trusting informality of traditional social relations. In contemporary social theory, the doctrine
of society as solidarity tends to gravitate towards the communicative, dialogical and civic arenas. For instance, Habermas's
deliberative conception of political democracy is redolent of
mature solidarity and deeply rooted care and concern for others.
Deep moral convictions are also fostered regarding the importance
of communal life in other solidaristic theories of society and politics, as we have seen in this chapter. What is interesting, in terms
of our specific concern with the theorization of the social, is the
ongoing power of the doctrine of communal solidarity. Finding
notions of structured society too rigid, too Hobbesian, to capture
the complexities of global civil society, contemporary approaches
to solidarity stress the communicative, discursive and reparative
aspects of contemporary social, cultural and political life.

But the rise and fall of upper-case Solidarity may mask another
story about the conviviality of everyday life. It is unsurprisingly
easy to be pessimistic about the erosion of upper-case Solidarity
that is illustrated by the weakening of citizenship, of national identity, of church membership and social capital. There is a general
view held by communitarians, by philosophers like MacIntyre
and by conservatives like Roger Scruton, that the large bonds that

held us together in the past are now devastated by individualism, secularism and the neoliberal economic experiment. This view of declining Solidarity obscures the equally important vitality of everyday interactive solidarity between friends and neighbours. This robustness of lower-case solidarity takes us into our final consideration, namely society as a stream of creative acts.

3
Society as Creation

If society as structure is too abstract and thin-blooded in its regulating of human affairs, and society as solidarity is too nostalgic in its sentimentalist hopes of bridging identity and difference, there is another register of discourse concerning the social that functions as a ground or prop for the constitution of human bonds from the ancient world to the modern day. This is a mode of thought at considerable remove from structure's obsession with a faceless collective, which as we have seen is played out in one or another dream of universality: the social system, the progress of humanity, the end of history. It is equally wary of the privileging of sentiment, sensibility, the affections and communality that we have charted in the moral discourse of society as solidarity. Rejecting calls for structure as an affront to the pure singularity of the individual, and dismissive of solidaristic demands for equality, at least in its upper-case and top-down manifestation, as a hidden form of social levelling, this alternative line of thought confronts head-on the troublesome questions of personal authenticity and innovations of identity within the realm of society as constituting and facilitating. Anyone who inspects recent European social theory and continental philosophy will surely be struck by the prominence of the idea of creation in political, cultural and philosophical debates. Ranging from the 'return to Simmel' in social theory to the structuration theory of Anthony Giddens, and from the philosophical world of Nietzschean tragedy to the psycho-analytical thought of Julia Kristeva and Cornelius Castoriadis, the problem of creation emerges centre stage within a whole range of vital political issues such as identity, sexuality, power and social transformation. In the face of the political deadlocks of society as structure, and against the backdrop of the contradictions of society as solidarity, we have now entered the terrain of the discourse of society as creation.

For the contemporary age, the appeal of creativity is radically ambivalent, split as it is between subjective innovation and cultural imposition, freedom and domination. If there is something sublime about creation it is not only because it is deliciously indeterminate, but because it can construct as well as destroy. 'Creation', writes Cornelius Castoriadis, 'does not necessarily – nor even generally – signify "good" creation or the creation of "positive values".'[1] On this view, while society as creation can give rise to Amnesty International and the United Nations, it can also give rise to Auschwitz and Pol Pot. We might say that social creativity is blind in the sense that its outcomes cannot be predicted. It follows from this that genuine human creation is about as far removed as one might find from the degraded discourse of 'creativity' that infects the contemporary popular culture of self-help, reality television and therapy movements. Creation thus is not co-terminous with creativity, or at least not that version of it propagated by cultural industries selling pathways to 'inner you' or the 'real you'. At the level of social theory, creation signifies – among other things – the indeterminate, the ambiguous, pure open-endedness. Society as creation, in its various discourses in social theory, is built on trans-actions with the social that exemplify artistry, innovation and the welcoming of change. But that is not all. Versions of society as creation detect an imaginative substratum at the very heart of social relations. The emphasis here is on curiosity, innovation, stimula-tion and exhilaration. In contrast to the controlled and competitive world of society as structure, with its hankering for order, rooted-ness and community, the frames of reference that make up society as creation emphasize sociality, particularism, communication and the aesthetic, with considerable toleration of ambivalence and contingency.

In earlier chapters we sought to connect the notion of structure with the rise of enclave societies, and the notion of solidarity with the rise of sticky societies. In this chapter we similarly engage in terminological innovation, through linking the notion of creation to the rise of what we term 'elastic societies'. The metaphor of social elasticity provides us with a valuable entrée into the nature of modern societies that are now far removed from the fixed and structured world of traditional societies, as well as societies that we have called 'sticky'. Whereas traditional societies were typically closely tied to the land, people now live in social systems that are only indirectly connected to physical space. Whereas traditional societies were bound by blood and soil, many contemporary social relations are carried out online. We propose thinking about such relations in terms of 'elasticity', which are social relations stretched over time and space. Traditional societies can be thought of as thick social relations, whereas the Internet social relationship is thin, transitory and elastic. The structures of modern societies are not made up entirely of functional institutions with a definite relation to each other and they do not necessarily connect to some specific landscape or geography. The structures of Internet connections are thin and extended or stretched out. Elasticity in this context has the additional property that is important for our social theory, namely that elastic is robust and difficult to crush or distort – it recoils to the touch. This is important because, while many critical theories take a nostalgic view of social relations, social elasticity allows us to think about contemporary Internet relationships as durable and not necessarily fragmented. Elasticity holds together across space. Modern social connections can hold individuals and groups in relations that are admittedly thin and possibly superficial (such as Twitter or Facebook), but can also be recognized as effective and functional. We should not decry modern systems of communication that can hold strangers together in elastic bonds. Political struggles in the Middle East and North Africa in the early part of 2011 were greatly facilitated by mobile phones that made possible political movements between disconnected individuals (often strangers) across time and space.

In our discussion of sticky societies in Chapter 2 we made a distinction between upper-case and lower-case examples. We propose a similar way of thinking about the metaphor of social elasticity. Upper case social Elasticity might refer to modern corporations that in a global world are stretched out over space and that favour highly flexible social arrangements (such as work teams) between groups that are constantly changing and re-organizing. The modern global corporation is constantly re-structuring and re-focusing the corporation's basic patterns of work. The modern corporation is in this sense an elastic network of activities. There is a second type of elasticity which is the micro-world of everyday interactions in which, with globalization, individuals are connected by thin but robust communication patterns. Labour migration is one of the most important features of modern economies; we can think of global diasporas as no longer merely confined to specific urban spaces, but rather as dispersed and localized nodes within a communication system involving exchanges of messages, remittances, services and so forth. Migrants live within this highly elastic social context.

In this chapter, therefore, we seek to think about modern societies in terms of creation and elasticity, thereby avoiding the trap of negative nostalgia in which, with the death of society, there is only fragmentation or a vacuum. By contrast, we see social relations being constantly rebuilt and refashioned – but not as solid structures or sticky primary groups. We see the social as re-fashioned by stretching over space and time in an array of thin but elastic connections.

What are the consequences of this mode of discourse for the way in which we have come to think about the production and politics of society? What possibility does this focus on creation generate for sociality, and what limitations does it introduce? And does the discourse of society as creation always function as the opposite of societies of structure as well as societies of solidarity, or is it supplementary? These are some of the issues we will consider in this chapter. We begin by looking at critiques of society in the discourse of sociology, exploring the ideas of 'the social' and structuration. The next section is devoted to the philosophical thought of Nietzsche. Following from this, we turn to consider a set of psychoanalytic debates concerning the dynamics of creation at the levels of self, society and culture. As in previous chapters, we then seek to situate this discourse on society – namely, the theory of creation – within more concrete instances of contemporary politics and culture. The second section of the chapter thus develops the argument that new forms of sociality associated with the impacts of globalization can be understood as an attempt to assert the discourse of creation over the demise of more traditional understandings of society as represented in the discourses of structure and solidarity. In making this argument, we consider recent debates over (1) digital cultures, specifically the rise of new information technologies and the Internet, and (2) cosmopolitanization in the wider frame of the global electronic economy.

Visions of Society as Creation

Society as creation is radically de-centred, indeterminate and free-flowing. From this angle, the creativity of the social works to reconcile novelty and necessity, individual and culture, autonomy and dependency. This would certainly seem true of Georg Simmel's use of the term 'the social' (*das Sozial*), which he presents as that which 'springing from the most diverse impulses, directed towards the most diverse objects, and aiming at the most diverse ends, constitutes "society"'.[2] The quotation marks around the term society are telling. Where the other founding fathers of sociology – Marx, Weber and Durkheim – conceived of the social as a totality, perhaps indeed as a stand-in for God, Simmel contends that society is only a secondary phenomenon compared to the interchanges that simultaneously link and separate people. Simmel pictures society as a web of interactions between individuals, of invisible threads of sociability. He thus pits the productive vitality of relations against the sacred precincts of individualism and universalism. As one contemporary commentator on Simmel remarks, 'the social amounts to relations between individuals. In Simmel's view, sociology should first and foremost be a study of relations and their forms. The individual itself is only an intersection, a crossroads.'[3]

To claim that there is nothing but relations is to argue, in effect, that 'society' must relinquish its traditional metaphysical groundings. At the very least it should abandon anything that smacks of reification, of treating society as an object that is relatively static. The social for Simmel is by contrast self-generative. To live life artfully is to engage the social neither securely nor casually; sociality is playfully detached, ironic, jealously focused on the future of unrealized possibilities. As such, there is an immediacy or vitality to interaction which can never be determined in advance by a totalized, institutionalized structure, assimilated to the preconscious dispositions and traditions of a social order, and so resists the claims of universalism. In contrast to the rigid determinancy of society as structure or the sensuous familiarity of society as identity, the social sphere for Simmel signifies artistry, play, creativity, potentiality, even eroticism. As Simmel writes of the interactive webs that bind: 'On every day, at every hour, such threads are spun, are allowed to fall, are taken up again, replaced by others, intertwined with others. Here lie the interactions . . . between the atoms of society which bear the whole tenacity and elasticity, the whole colourfulness and unity of this so evident and so puzzling life of society.'[4] The Simmelian notion of relation is itself, one might claim, deconstructive of both society and the individual. The individual is not the absolute, self-legislating agent that Enlightenment thought advances, but rather is traversed or shot through by specific sets of social relations.

If the human subject is fully dismantled through relationalism, however, the objective world would appear no less immune to such processual activities. Society for Simmel is at once condition and outcome of social forms, relations and connections. By opposing society to sociality, Simmel undoes in one stroke the orthodox sociological wisdom that society exists as totalized entity. Consequently in various writings, most notably 'What is Society?', and 'How is Society Possible?', Simmel wrestled with diverse conceptualizations of the social, and shifted the whole concept of 'society' from its universalistic to its relational sense. As Simmel remarks:

What is society as such? Society exists where several individuals (for one another, with one another or against one another) enter into interaction . . . In turn, this interaction always takes place from drives which are terminus a quo (e.g. love, hunger, impulse to play, etc.) or terminus ad quem (acquisition, defence, nourishment, instruction). The working together of these drives is the unity of human beings which we term society. We know empirically no other unities than interactions of several elements. The 'organism' is a unity and this because all its elements work together. Society is a unity because and insofar as all its individuals interact.[5]

There is a tension between what makes for the threads of fragmented sociality, and the labyrinth of social interaction itself. To say that the social exists where people enter into interaction is, at least for some critics, to reduce the study of society to that of individuals alone. This is the criticism that Simmel's work represents a psychological conception of society. It could be claimed, however, that a central conceptual dilemma of Simmel's corpus is how to investigate sociologically the affective or aesthetic foundations of social interaction. Indeed, this is precisely how Simmel responds to such a critique. 'If society is to be an autonomous object of an independent discipline', he writes, 'then it can only be so by virtue of the fact that, out of the sum total of individual elements which constitute it, a new entity emerges; otherwise, all problems of social science would only be those of individual psychology.'[6]

Simmel's German has proved difficult to translate into English. In his attempt to develop the new science of sociology in his *Sociology: Inquiries into the Construction of Social Forms*, he coined a new term, namely *Vergesellschaftung*, to express the process of what we might call 'sociation'.[7] Simmel's terminology here for 'society' was of course part of the legacy of the distinction between *Gemeinschaft* and *Gesellschaft*, but here Simmel is seeking to capture the movement of society in the tensions between forms (such as competition or domination) and contents (such as the human movitivation to be dominating). This idea of Simmel's was probably misleadingly translated as 'socialization', whereas in modern sociology we would typically use that term to refer to the processes by which people acquire values and norms and become part of the larger society. By contrast, when Simmel used *Vergesellschaft* he was thinking of the processes by which society is created.

We have seen that the register of creation embraces, among other things, Simmel's 'invisible threads', which simultaneously link and separate human agents and social structures. From what has been said so far, the theory of creation is inseparable from an account of the ways in which societies, or specific forms of social activities, are reproduced by the interactive webs of human actions and reactions. But it can be argued that society, or social structure, is not so much a thing in itself as a primary, if invisible, domain of social life. Nobody, after all, has ever clapped eyes on society writ large; like History or Fate, society is primarily discernible only in its instantiations – that is to say, in the concrete instances of social practice through which individuals pursue their everyday life. Such an understanding of the creative properties facilitating the structures of contemporary living have come to be called 'structuration theory', and over recent decades its contours have been persuasively developed by the British sociologist Anthony Giddens.[8] Rejecting both objectivistic accounts in which society determines human action and subjectivistic accounts in which a sum total of actions make up society, Giddens argues instead that action is structured in everyday social practices. To say that action is structured in everyday contexts is to say that the structural features of action are, through the very performance of social activity, thereby reproduced. This is what Giddens terms the 'duality of structure', in a formulation which positions human creation centre stage within social life: 'social structures are both constituted by human agency, and yet at the same time are the very medium of the constitution'.

If society cannot be separated from human agency, then neither can action be isolated from social reproduction. This is why Giddens rejects our inherited ways of thinking about society – especially objectivistic definitions of society which, he believes, deny the vitality and creativity of the social. As he develops this point in *The Constitution of Society*:

> We have to be very careful indeed with the concept of 'social system' and the associated notion of 'society'. They sound innocent terms, and

they are probably indispensable if used with appropriate measures of caution. 'Society' has a useful double meaning, which I have relied upon – signifying a bounded system, and social association in general. An emphasis upon regionalization helps to remind us that the degree of 'systemness' in social systems is very variable and that 'societies' rarely have easily specifiable boundaries – until, at least, we enter the modern world of nation-states. Functionlism and naturalism tend to encourage unthinking acceptance of societies as clearly delimited entities, and social systems as internally highly integrated unities . . . But 'societies' are very often not like this at all.[9]

By contrast to the bloodless standpoints of functionalism and naturalism, Giddens's structuration theory grants the agency of the individual, and the structural contexts in which a person is embedded, their proper due.

Every act of human agency is for Giddens inscribed in the structured features of social organization. Giddens contends that social structure, or 'society', is a constant product of our social activities – of our talk, our practices, our doings. Such a conception of social structure contrasts powerfully with more mainstream sociological accounts. Sociologists have tended to conceptualize structure in terms of institutional constraint, often in a quasi-hydraulical or mechanical fashion, such that structure is likened to the biological workings of the body or the girders of a building. Giddens strongly rejects functionalist, biological and empiricist analyses of structure. Following the 'linguistic turn' in twentieth-century social theory, Giddens draws critically upon structuralist and post-structuralist theory, specifically the relationship posited between language and speech in linguistics. He does this, not because society is structured like a language (as structuralists have argued), but because he believes that language can be taken as exemplifying core aspects of social life. Language, according to Giddens, has a virtual existence; it 'exists' outside time and space, and is only present in its instantiations as speech or writing. By contrast, speech presupposes a subject and exists in time/space intersections. In Giddens's reading of structural linguistics, the subject draws from the rules of language in order to produce a phrase or sentence, and in so doing contributes to the reproduction of that language as a whole.

Giddens draws extensively from such a conception of the structures of language in order to account for structures of action. His theorem is that agents draw from structures in order to perform and carry out social interactions, and in so doing contribute to the reproduction of institutions and structures. This analysis leads to a very specific conception of structure and social systems. 'Structure', writes Giddens,[10] 'has no existence independent of the knowledge that agents have about what they do in their day-to-day activity.'

Giddens's theoretical approach emphasizes that structures should be conceptualized as 'rules and resources': the application of rules which comprise structure may be regarded as generating differential access to social, economic, cultural and political resources. In *The Constitution of Society* Giddens argues that the sense of 'rule' most relevant to understanding social life is that which pertains to a mathematical formula – for instance, if the sequence is 2, 4, 6, 8, the formula is $x = n \times 2$. Understanding a formula, says Giddens, enables an agent to carry on in social life in a routine manner, to apply the rule in a range of different contexts. The same is true of bureaucratic rules, traffic rules, rules of football, rules of grammar, rules of social etiquette: to know a rule does not necessarily mean that one is able to explicitly formulate the principle, but it does mean that one can use the rule 'to go on' in social life. 'The rules and resources of social action', writes Giddens, 'are at the same time the means of systems reproduction' (1984: 19). Systems reproduction, as Giddens conceives it, is complex and contradictory, involving structures, systems, and institutions. Social systems, for Giddens, are not equivalent with structures. Social systems are regularized patterns of interaction; such systems are in turn structured by rules and resources. Institutions are understood by Giddens as involving different modalities in and through which structuration occurs. Political institutions, for example, involve the generation of commands over people in relation to issues of authorization, signification and legitimation; economic institutions, by contrast, involve the allocation of resources through processes of signification and legitimation.

This position – though Giddens does not explicitly argue the case – is resolutely an outcrop of the register of creation. The social world may not just automatically appear to be structured according to various kinds of routines and rules, but there is a sense in which resources of the social creatively enable the practical conduct of everyday life. Social rules and routines, amazingly, are learned and nurtured by us in a largely semi-conscious way. We know how to apply countless rules to the conduct of our social life – we know 'how to go on', as Giddens says – even though we may not be able to explicitly formulate those rules. Going out to 'the pub' in the UK, for instance, involves individuals in all sorts of conversational exchanges – from the mundane (with someone, say, serving behind the bar) to the deeply intimate (with, say, a sexual partner). What is interesting, when viewed through the lens of Giddens's structuration theory, is that people apply the 'rules' of social interaction fairly easily – though usually without being aware of doing so – to these practical situations. Individuals talk generalities, and sometime make jokes, when ordering their drinks from a bartender; the same individuals may subsequently talk earnestly, about deeply personal matters, only a few feet from the bar with a loved one. But try imagining what might happen if people got mixed up in these social contexts and applied the wrong rules. Talking about deeply personal problems, or emotional difficulties, is unlikely to win you many friends when ordering a drink at a pub, and certainly not the approval of others in line to purchase a drink. Similarly, talk of a general, banal nature is unlikely to go down well with someone very close if it is engaged in for too long. Fortunately, however, 'social rules' in the sense of which Giddens writes are are usually applied to the appropriate social situation. Rules, according to Giddens, are about knowing 'how to go on', how to apply the right rules to particular social contexts. And knowing 'how to go on' in social life is part and parcel of the creative repertoire of skilled human agents.

The work of the late French sociologist Pierre Bourdieu expresses certain parallels with Giddens's conceptualization of the structure and agency question – an overlapping which has now been extensively discussed in social theory.[11] While Bourdieu did not explicitly concern himself with the question 'what is society?', his epistemological reflections on 'objectivism' and 'subjectivism' give a clear indication of his underlining of the social. In terms of our tripartite scheme, we argue that Bourdieu has been deeply critical of structure and sceptical about creation. His opposition to structuralism is well known and began early in his career with his criticisms of the legacies of both Ferdinand de Saussure and Claude Levi-Strauss. Bourdieu has objected to the fact that both theorists treat the social actor as merely a passive vehicle of social or linguistic structures.

Bourdieu can be said to have approached society as a social game in which social actors compete and struggle with others over scarce material and symbolic goods. All social games are therefore games of power. The innovative aspects of Bourdieu's work is his treatment of the idea of 'following a rule'. In this respect, his work is similar to both British philosopher of language J. L. Austin and Austrian philosopher Ludwig Wittgenstein.[12] We normally think of rule-following as involving intentionality, and much of Bourdieu's own work supports such a view. Actors are knowledgeable and active; they can both follow and change rules, and subvert them. He argued that he wished to avoid the 'mechanistic tendencies of Saussure' while giving 'to practice an active inventive intention' (Bourdieu, 1990:13). While this is the case, rule following can also look habitual. For example in sport we do not stop to think about the rules, because we are too busy with the action. Bourdieu referred to this practical attitude as 'the sense of the game' (*le sens du jeu*). This regular and habitual disposition is what Bourdieu meant by 'habitus'. He famously defined habitus as 'the form of durable dispositions' that permits collective history, culture and social relations to be successfully reproduced. These dispositions are not subject to constant reflection; they are taken for granted because they are embodied.

The dispositions are the 'taste' that individuals have for various objects, ways of life, cultural forms and so on. They shape how the actor responds to and incorporates the social world. We prefer football to rugby because our habitus has formed dispositions for one type of sport over another. We prefer to read Agatha Christie rather than Shakespeare because of our habitus, and habitus is of course closely related to the social class, or class fraction, to which we belong. Social reality is a habitual world, but the decisive factor in our dispositions is related to our educational experiences and hence to social class. In *Distinction*, he demonstrated how different class fractions in France that are related to different educational backgrounds share a common habitus that determines what they prefer to consume. In sport, the working class prefer physical combative games such as wrestling, whereas upper classes prefer such sports as tennis and mountaineering. This account of taste appears to have a decisively deterministic character and it has led many sociologists to regard Bourdieu as, after all, a Marxist sociologist for whom cultural preferences are ultimately determined by class position.

Bourdieu's view of the social also raises acute questions about the position of the sociologist as scientist who is outside the game. In his defence of reflexive sociology, Bourdieu has sought to challenge the idea that the sociologist is an external and objective observer of reality. This notion of reflexivity has involved two steps. The first is to show that the scientist is also part of a particular social game and that their views of reality are also determined by their position in the field. In *Homo academicus*, he tried to demonstrate that different philosophical orientations and traditions were themselves determined by the educational trajectories of different social groups, and that even philosophical beliefs are related to the habitus of the philosopher. The result is to question the notion of objectivity. The second move is to show that the researcher is typically a parasitic reporter of interpretations given to him or her by participants in the field. These are both powerful arguments, but what then is the point of the social sciences, and are all accounts from the field equally valid?

Critics of Bourdieu have concluded that his sociological theories do not transcend the old problems of objective knowledge versus subjective understanding, and that the deterministic direction of his research means that the creativity of the social actor often appears to be overwhelmed by the force of habit. In terms of our scheme, it looks as if Bourdieu veers towards structure and away from creation. The question remains: what does Bourdieu think of the problem of solidarity? If the social game involves unending competition and conflict, where does cohesion come from? The answer must be that insofar as the social actors agree to play by the rules of the game, then the game can take place. And accepting the rules over time is no longer a conscious decision, but a habitual attitude. Solidarity occurs provided the actors in the social game do not question the rules and in particular they don't question their application. The point of this emphasis on habitus is to permit Bourdieu to avoid the notion of interest, and in particular to distinguish his position from the work of rational choice theory which treats strategy as a game of competing interests. In Bourdieu's (largely implicit) theory of society, 'habitus' stands in for 'interest'. We conclude however that Bourdieu's sociology gives a strong account of 'structure' and a weak notion of 'creation'.

Nietzsche

If the classical sociology of Simmel excoriates men and women to engage the unrealized possibilities of social interaction, the philosophy of Friedrich Nietzsche goes one step further in celebrating societal adventures of self-experiment and self-creation. Nietzsche's ethic is overtly aristocratic and he condemned modern society as a place where the herd might triumph over the individual, and he therefore bemoaned the loss of a world in which genuinely heroic acts and values could survive. Nietzsche's originality is to see not just structure or solidarity in the production of the social, but artistic creativity as well. In deconstructing the whole traditional opposition between autonomy and necessity, Nietzsche is out to show that our social practices – and especially the most refined, ordered and structured ones – can unfold only on the basis of a traumatizing violence, terror and self-aggression. 'Every small step on earth', writes Nietzsche, 'has been paid for by spiritual and physical torture . . . How much blood and cruelty lies at the bottom of all 'good things'!'[13] Nietzsche's view is that society is, at root, a history of conflict, suffering and domination. Life and self development are equally about struggle. Morality, as represented in the discourse of structure and solidarity, is merely the ideological inculcation of high-minded traditions and enfeebled customs – which in turn is denied and displaced by a vulgarized culture that goes about the business of promoting abstract moral norms and levelling standards in favour of social conformity and

the herd mentality. The so-called moral individual for Nietzsche is
actually no more and no less than the sadomasochistic recipient of
a barbarous social order.

Nietzsche's philosophy has been characterized as a 'politics of
the soul' in which he saw self-development as a heroic struggle to master the instinctual life to promote the health of the
individual.[14] Consequently Nietzsche's whole philosophy can be
seen as an exploration of the problem of individualism in modern
society where there is an overwhelming threat of standardization
and regulation. In this respect, we can treat Nietzsche as a social
thinker whose philosophy has a close relationship to the sociology
of Weber in the sense that Weber also saw society as subject to
an endless and ineluctable process of rationalization and struggles
against rationalization. In the 'iron cage' of modern society, we are
all reduced to mere cogs in a machine.[15]

Is Nietzsche's philosophy just another brand of subjectivism?
While Nietzsche was self-absorbed, his philosophy was aimed to
awaken people to the death of God and the need to revalue life. He
also craved for friendship, but his journey was necessarily lonely.
He recognized that 'society' was necessary for the great majority
of men. Given the death of God, we are of necessity forced to
think seriously about how we might live our lives without secure
boundaries and directives. For Nietzsche, the moral person has to
shape their lives according to their own values. Nietzsche literally
and metaphorically stands on the mountain top and calls people to
heroic acts of self-reconstruction.

The analysis of resentment runs through Nietzsche's entire philosophy; it certainly shaped his attitude to his own circumstances
and was central to his critiques of religion, nihilism and modernity.
Indeed, one might reasonably argue that it is the key concept in
his overall vision of the need for a creative revaluation of values
in modernity. On the face of it, Nietzsche is the least sociological
of the authors we analyse in this study. However, several contemporary interpretations of Nietzsche have stressed his relevance to
the ideas of social and political creation. These include William
Hennis's *Max Webers Fragstellung*,[16] Georg Stauth and Bryan
Turner's *Nietzsche's Dance*,[17] Daniel W. Conway's *Nietzsche and the
Political*,[18] and Keith Ansell-Pearson's *An Introduction to Nietzsche as*

Political Thinker.[19] This view of the social as the politically creative is also an important theme in Michel Foucault's *Society Must Be Defended.*[20] Despite the title of the book, Foucault declared that his major interest had been to focus on power as it becomes manifest in local practices and institutions. However, it emerged clearly in these lectures that his historical interest had been concerned to understand the rise of sovereign power and especially around royal power. Foucault commented that 'the elaboration of juridical thought was essentially centred around royal power ever since the Middle Ages . . . In the West, right is the right of the royal command.'[21] These lectures, while opening up new issues, can also be read as the summation of earlier work, for example in *Discipline and Punish.*[22] They also reveal the influence of Nietzsche in this understanding of the social as a space largely determined by creative unleashings – at once productive and destructive – of power.

One can readily see why Nietzsche's work might be attractive to modern political theory – he was concerned to analyse power, he was critical of the rise of the modern state, and he offers an 'ideological' critique. His critique has of course been recognized as a general attack on the standardization of modern society. His approach appears to be resistant to any easy translation into a specifically *sociological* language. There are sound reasons to agree with M. S. Silk and Joseph Peter Stern that his philosophy appears to be focused on the problem of the individual in modernity and the idea of an organized social community appears to be anathema to his critical thought:

> For all this talk of 'wholeness', Nietzsche is not seriously concerned to envisage a whole *society.* He envisages the whole *man,* but he shows insufficient interest in the social patterns which would facilitate and sustain his wholeness. The excessive individualism of his interpretation of Greek art is matchless by the nature of his concern for the creative individual and the social needs of his creative individuality at the expense of society's other members or functions.[23]

The task then is to tease out Nietzsche's revolutionary creed and his denunciation of modern nihilism, in order for an understanding of resentment and its social location as a foundation for a more systemic analysis of the conditions of resentment in modernity.

His view of life as struggle and at its most advanced a work of art provides us with a model of what genuine creation might entail – the aim of the heroic individual is to *create* a well-ordered soul in which we have achieved a balance over emotions and desires. Every experiment has to be undertaken and every avenue has to be explored if we are to become who we are. This is the real doctrine of the overman – not the Nazi fantasy of a superman. It is in many respects the realization of Aristotle's notion of excellence or virtue. While Nietzsche did not specifically address the theme of creation in any sustained fashion, he did concern himself a great deal with the creative self-fashionings arising from food, diet, exercise and, generally, what he called 'the little things' of everyday life.[24] The well-balanced soul also strived for balanced health. Clearly Nietzsche's ethic is aristocratic, and indeed it could be argued that his ideal of the well-ordered soul is too demanding and too energetic to offer any real or practical guidance. Yet it is worth remembering that Nietzsche assumed that this quest for personal excellence through struggle – and especially a struggle through which the individual would experience considerable suffering – was a road strewn with failures and disappointments. Nietzsche's overman provides a figure with whom we can make a distinction between life as mere survival and life as a creation – as an aesthetic achievement. In the end, he believed that what does not kill me in this struggle to create myself will give me strength.

Creation and Freedom: Freud, Castoriadis, Kristeva

Nietzsche's view of sociality deals, at one stroke, a massive blow to theories of society premised upon conceptions of either free will or voluntarism. In contrast to both visions of society as structure and society as solidarity, which rely in various ways upon a so-called free human subject who is morally responsible for their own actions, Nietzsche contends that the individual always acts out of the traumatizing weight of self-violence. This is the will of terror and self-oblivion. Those who think of social life primarily in terms of conscious or intentional practices, says Nietzsche, are merely engaged in ideological self-deception. The truth is that conventional morality merely mimics the repressive powers of law and social domination. For Nietzsche, the individual in fact bears the intolerable trauma of amnesia or repression at the very core of the self, and it is this aspect of his philosophy that subsequently comes to influence both Freud and later psychoanalytic conceptions of self and world.

Freud is an astonishingly radical theorist of human creativity, and his discovery of the repressed unconscious re-casts the human subject as at the core of the representational space of fantasy, drives and affect. Although he does not use the term directly in his writings, the problem of human creation is fundamental for Freud from beginning to end. In the light of his arrestingly original formulations on the individual as *split* between consciousness of self on the one hand and repressed desire on the other, the phenomenon of creation appears anew. After Freud, human creation is not so much a matter of personal creativity as it is an issue in its own right. Freud sees creation as reconciling desire and repression, libidinal energy and anxiety, representational flux and submissions to the superego. If creation is constraining as well as enabling, it is because it is implicated in suffering as well as autonomy. We might consider this power of the unconscious an essential wellspring of the creativity of the social, but this is not a conclusion that Freud himself ever reached. The irony is that while Freud devoted his life to uncovering the creative pathways of the unconscious imagination (and its intricate sub-systems and symptoms), he equally set his face against recognizing the constituting role of the imaginary order in society as such.[25]

Unconscious desire for Freud is an unfathomable, excessive force, at once definitive of our deepest emotional and erotic attachments and disruptive of everything we consciously strive to achieve. The unconscious, Freud wrote, is unaware of contradiction, time, or closure. Indeed, it is blissfully and remorselessly untroubled by the demands of reality. Fully subversive of the world of reason and commonsense, the unconscious is concerned only with the enactment of pleasure. 'The unconscious', as Freud remarks, 'is unable to do anything but wish.'[26] In the same manner that unconscious desire splits and disperses the human subject, rendering identity non-identical with itself, so too the boundaries of the object-world are cast within an imaginary space. The unconscious as a primal condition of subjectivity denotes a fundamental lack of distinction between self and other. From this point of view, the emergence of consciousness, as we shall see, is a painful and difficult departure from the unconscious realm of libidinal plenitude. In examining the conflicts and struggles that take place inside us, Freud was led to construct a picture of the human subject that radically transcends the Cartesian understanding of the ego as a fixed, indivisible and permanent whole. By a reliance on the metaphor of place, positing psychical not anatomical localities, Freud's dialectical interweaving of consciousness and the unconscious ruptured the certainty on which Western metaphysics had been premised: the rational and knowledgable subject, the Cartesian cogito, whose first truth, 'I think, therefore I am', had been shattered. Freud argues that consciousness is *discontinuous*, being overdetermined and dislocated by unconscious processes. On this view, the essence of being lies not in the cogito, but in the vicissitudes of desire. Yet this very 'discovery' of desire in the Freudian system is turned around with a vengeance upon the claims of philosophy: unconscious desire is not a deeper ground of subjectivity since, in many ways, desire has no 'essence'.

Sexual desire, on Freud's reckoning, knows no limit and forever circles back upon itself. It is a kind of self-reproducing system, albeit one beyond the conscious determinations of the individual subject. And yet, for all that, desire for Freud is deeply interwoven with biology, with the essential needs that make us what we are. The exemplary psychoanalytic case is the human infant sucking at its mother's breast. After the biological need for milk is satisfied, Freud notes, the desire for pleasure derived from sucking continues. The human infant hallucinates a phantasy of the pleasure derived from this original satisfaction. This is said to form a basis for subsequent psychical productions. 'The baby's obstinate persistence in sucking', writes Freud, 'gives evidence at an early stage of a need for satisfaction which, though it originates from and is instigated by the taking of nourishment, nevertheless strives to obtain pleasure independently of nourishment and for that reason may and should be termed *sexual*.'[27] In deriving pleasure from the 'erotogenic zone' of orality, a new libidinal relation with the *Other* (usually, but not necessarily, the biological mother) arises. Sexuality for Freud is coterminous with creation.

The creation of human sexuality of which Freud writes is, in most standard versions of psychoanalysis, understood to operate from the 'inside' of subjectivity, as a dramatization of the repressed unconscious. Thus, a sharp contrast is usually accorded to internal and external happenings, to the 'pleasure-ego' and the 'reality-ego'. In a strict sense, however, the unconscious for Freud transcends all such dualism, since the former is actually the imaginative substratum upon which subsequent divisions between self and other, internal and external, individual and society are constituted. This is less a full-blooded subjectivism than an attempt to give the slip to inherited forms of thought based upon dualism. To do this, Freud argues that the self develops in an imaginary register, rather than through the brute enforcement of a 'reality-ego'. By underscoring the imaginary dimensions of human creation, Freud posits that the ego is fabricated as a structure arising through multiple identifications with other persons. In his celebrated essay 'Mourning and melancholia',[28] as well as his subsequent topographical revisions in *The Ego and the Id*,[29] Freud argues that the loss of a loved person necessitates an introjection of the Other into the structure of the ego itself. Through the mechanism of narcissistic identification, the lost love is installed within the structure of the self as an act of self-preservation. In this way, the emotional investment in the lost object is sustained in a manner which fits with the demands of reality. As Freud comments:

> Each single one of the memories and situations of expectancy which demonstrate the libido's attachment to the lost object is met by the verdict of reality that the object no longer exists; and the ego, confronted as it were with the question whether it shall share this fate, is persuaded by the sum of the narcissistic satisfaction it derives from being alive to sever its attachment to the object that has been abolished.[30]

The abandonment of lost love sparks an unconscious anger actually intended for the object itself, yet now reversed upon the self in violent blows of self-punishment. It is, however, the synthetic aspects of grief – the internalization and, hence, psychical preservation of the object – that Freud highlights in conceptualizing self-development. 'When the ego', writes Freud, 'assumes the features of the object, it is forcing itself, so to speak, upon the id's loss by saying: "Look, you can love me too – I am so like the object."'[31] The constituted self through loss, Freud suggests in his late writings, leads to the notion of a *bodily ego*. The ego is given representation since the human subject identifies, through an interplay of projection and introjection, with the surfaces of the body. 'In seeing itself on the model of the body', as Richard Wollheim writes, 'the ego sees its activities on the model of bodily activity.'[32] This, it might be noted, is not a form of biological reductionism. For Freud, the body-ego concerns the psychical representation of the subject; it is 'a mental projection of the surface of the body'. Again, human creation in a multiplicity of psychical forms.

In the writings of Cornelius Castoriadis, perhaps the most theoretically sophisticated and sociologically minded of recent European inheritors of Freudianism, the domains of unconscious imagination in particular and human creation more generally are viewed as constitutive of social life itself. Indeed creation becomes in Castoriadis's hands the basis for a full-blown theory of the social; and yet this is a kind of imaginary foundation to society that is, paradoxically, non-foundational. For Castoriadis, the imaginary tribulations of the unconscious are utterly fresh, primary fabrications founded purely in themselves, erupting out of nothing and nowhere, and sprung *ex nihilo* from a disorderly chaos of representational flux. While recognizing that the psyche cannot produce everything out of itself, otherwise there would be no reason for the human subject to open itself to other persons and objects, Castoriadis claims it is meaningless to see psychic reality as simply a 'receptacle' of the external world. For there can be no social practice without a human subject; and with individuals there is psychic organization and emotional experience. Instead, the question of representation for Castoriadis centres on the capacity of the psyche itself to *instantiate* representations. Inherent in the Freudian problematic, he writes:

. . . we can say that the first delegation of the drive in the psyche is the affect, in particular that of displeasure. But we can find nothing in an affect, whether of pleasure or unpleasure, that could account for the form or the content of a representation; at the most the affect could induce the 'finality' of the representative process. *It is therefore necessary to postulate (even if this is only implicitly) that the psyche is the capacity to produce an 'initial' representation, the capacity of putting into image or making an image.* This may appear self-evident. But this image-making must at the same time relate to a drive, at a time when nothing ensures this relation. This may well be the point of condensation and accumulation for all the mysteries of the 'bonding' between the soul and the body.[33]

Castoriadis is thus perhaps the first major modern intellectual to place at the centre of his reflections on the social the abstract category of psychical representation itself, both at the levels of the individual ('radical imaginary') and society ('social imaginary'). The imaginary, contends Castoriadis, is not just a question of 'the creation of images in society' but rather of the productive energies of self-creation, which in turn generates social imaginary significations and the institutions of each particular society. What is radically imaginary about the psychic process of every individual is precisely the representational pleasure of the unconscious monad, initially closed in upon itself and subsequently forced to shift from self-generating solipsistic fantasy to the shared meanings of society. To the radical imaginary of the psychic monad corresponds the collective order of the 'social imaginary', an aesthetics of imagination that holds together the primary institutions of society (language, norms, customs and law) and the form of relation through which individuals and collectivities come to relate to such objects of representational and affective investment.

Where then does radical imagination originate? What is the condition of possibility for its eruption? Castoriadis reflects on the creative indeterminacy of the imagination thus:

I am not fixated on the 'scopic'; one of the gross inadequacies of Lacan's conception of the imagination is his fixation of the scopic. For me, if one is speaking of stages that are worked out, the *imagination* par excellence is the imagination of the musical composer (which is

what I wanted to be). Suddenly, figures surge forth which are not in
the least visual. They are essentially auditory and kinetic – for there
is also rhythm. There is a marvellous excerpt from a letter of Mozart
cited by Brigitte Massin, in which Mozart describes how he composes.
Like every self-respecting composer, he composes, obviously, in his
head. When deaf, Beethoven heard – imagined – in his head. A true
composer writes and hears chords, chordal progressions, as I, in closing
my eyes, can review some scene or imagine some scene, bringing into
mutual presence characters who have never really been present to each
other. Mozart explains that the piece composes itself in his head, and
he says the following hallucinatory thing: when the piece is finished, it
is all laid out simultaneously before him in its progression. He hears in
one moment the beginning, the middle, the end of the first movement
of the sonata. As Galileo says of God, the proofs we arduously traverse
step by step are laid out before Him *instantaneously*. That is an imagination. When Mozart says, I have the entire piece laid out in my head, it
is not that he sees the score, it is that he hears the totality of the piece.
That appears incomprehensible to us because our musical imagination
is rather poor: to be able to hear simultaneously the beginning of the
symphony in G minor and the minuet. Nor is there anything 'visual' in
the social imaginary. The social imaginary is not the creation of images
in society; it is not the fact that one paints the walls of towns. A fundamental creation of the social imaginary, the gods or rules of behaviour
are neither visible nor even audible but *signifiable*.[34]

Castoriadis's reflections on the imaginary principally concern,
one might say, the ways in which a world (at once emotional and
social) somehow or other comes to be ordered and organized from
groundlessness or chaos; about the creation of imagination from
'dull mass'; about creation and invention as a consequence of an
'explosion that digs into this mass a hole'. The constitution of these
imaginary determinations manifests the creativity that appertains
to the psyche as such, and that 'opens an interior space within it'.

It should be clear enough from Castoriadis's reflections on
the radical imagination of the unconscious that any traversal of
repressed desire – either in psychoanalysis or some more culturally
uplifting enterprise such as the arts – is unlikely to lead to the discovery of some 'pure', assured identity. In this sense, the lifting of

repression – at once social and sexual – cannot be equated with the celebration of authentic identities which are, somehow magically, true to themselves. The radical inventiveness of the unconscious imagination is just that: *pure creation*. And so, there can be no guarantees as to future pathways of identity, nor of society. But if this is so, then what would a politics of revolt look like? Julia Kristeva, one of Europe's most eloquent public intellectuals, has powerfully addressed this issue of the precariousness of human creativity in an age of advanced globalization. In her view, the contemporary world system inflicts novel, and dramatically escalating, forms of suffering on individuals and cultures; one consequence of this, she argues, has been that people have lost access to symbolic discourse and have retreated inwards. This turn to empty narcissistic satisfaction she describes as 'new maladies of the soul'; today more individuals than ever before have retreated to privatism, to a denial of community and public engagement. Such denial of the connection between the self and others reflects a deadening of public discourse, a jamming of dialogue.

In several works, notably *Black Sun*,[35] *New Maladies of the Soul*,[36] and *Crisis of the European Subject*,[37] Kristeva analyses the psychic crisis of contemporary culture – the jamming of autonomous creative thought, as it were – with reference to the themes of depression, mourning and melancholia. In depression, says Kristeva, there is an emotional disinvestment from the symbolic power of language and intersubjectivity. The depressed person, overwhelmed by sadness (often as a result of lost love), suffers from a paralysis of symbolic activity. In effect, language fails to fill in or substitute for what has been lost at the level of the psyche. The loss of loved ones, the loss of identity, the loss of pasts: as the depressed person loses all interest in the surrounding world, in language itself, psychic energy shifts to a more primitive mode of functioning, to a maternal, drive-related form of experience. In short, depression produces a trauma of symbolic identification, a trauma that unleashes the power of semiotic energy. In the force field of the semiotic – silences, rhythms, changes in intonation, semantic shifts – Kristeva finds a means to connect the unspoken experience of the depressed person to established meaning, thereby permitting for a psychic re-organization of the self.

Kristeva does not think that the semiotic or affective realm can simply replace symbolic or rational law; but she does hold that rationality in itself is insufficient for genuine social creation. The cultural field thus holds especial significance for grasping the free play of creation in her writings. Societies are of course routinely viewed as peculiarly culturalist, rather than only as normative systems of rationalized action. But what is culturalist about the social field for Kristeva is not that it penetrates to the core of preconscious dispositions and practical forms of knowledge, but that it is deeply interwoven with the deeper affective textures of lived experience. In *Crisis of the European Subject*, Kristeva argues that contemporary multicultural societies are typically mixtures of normative structures and rationalized identities on the one hand, and affective and unconscious significations on the other. This she does in the book by considering the social textures of Europe. 'Europeans are cultured', writes Kristeva, 'in the sense that culture is their critical conscience; it suffices to think of Cartesian doubt, the freethinking of the Enlightenment, Hegelian negativity, Marx's thought, Freud's unconscious, not to mention Zola's *J'accuse* and formal revolts such as Bauhaus and surrealism, Artaud and Stockhausen, Picasso, Pollock and Francis Bacon. The great moments of twentieth-century art and culture are moments of formal and metaphysical revolt.' Kristeva has, for some time now, been widely hailed as a genuinely courageous intellectual rebel, and also an energetic campaigner for women's rights. The terrain on which Kristeva thinks societal rebellion can best be grasped, however, is that of psychoanalysis. Kristeva's recent work develops, through a psychoanalytic lens, a series of reflections on the spread of global political apathy ('shouldn't we just be content with entertainment culture, show culture and complacent commentary?'), and contrasts this with a more radical impulse, an intensively politicized imagination (what she terms 'the necessity of a culture of revolt in a society that is alive and developing, not stagnating').

Symbol, scene, play, pleasure and text: these are the central psychical and aesthetic forms in and through which the society of revolt is produced. Revolt is historical for Kristeva insofar as it is all about the twists and turns of *society as creative unfolding*. Tracing the historical trajectories of rebellious ideologies (from socialism to existentialism), Kristeva maps how the radical political impulse has time and again veered off in either utopic or utilitarian directions. So it is that Kristeva traces the notion of revolt as a series of reversals, curves, upheavals and unfoldings, calling upon various European intellectuals of great distinction along the way to fathom what guarantees our independence and our creative abilities.

In attempting to solve the riddle of contradictions between societal reproduction and cultural revolt, Kristeva draws from her highly influential notion of *semiotic displacement of symbolic forms*, a notion she thinks fundamental to the analysis of identity and society alike. In an earlier pathbreaking work, *Revolution in Poetic Language*, Kristeva contrasted the French psychoanalyst Jacques Lacan's account of the symbolic order – the social and sexual system of patriarchal Law – with those multiple psychic forces she terms 'semiotic'.[38] The semiotic, according to Kristeva, is primarily pro-linguistic – semiotic processes include libidinal energies and bodily rhythms experienced by the child which arise in the pre-Oedipal stage of infancy. For Kristeva, these pre-Oedipal forms undergo repression with entry to the social and cultural processes of the symbolic order. That is to say, the flux of semiotic experience is channelled into the relatively stable domain of symbolization and language. However, Kristeva contends that the repression of the semiotic is by no means complete; the semiotic remains present in the unconscious and cannot be shut off from culture. And it is precisely this lurking of the semiotic, the bubbling away of pre-Oedipal affective forces, which provides a creative substratum to the functioning of the social.

Creation, one might argue, is at once particular and general, or subjective and universal. Kristeva[39] situates the creative form of unconscious fantasy thus:

> The unconscious or preconscious fantasy is present in all psychic activities and behaviours, so much so that the fantasy is an 'active presence of fantasy scenes'. Such a fantasy is, strictly speaking, bound up with motivity, taste and food aversions, the sharpness of the perception (particularly the visual perception) of the primal scene, the image of the body, voice-song-and-speech, sporting activities, concert-show-and-film attendance, educational and intellectual activities, neurotic

symptoms and, in the end, the entire organization of the personality. Not only is the totality of psychic life *impregnated* with fantasies, but in the child whom Klein listened to and analysed, the fantasy – that is, the fantasy that preceded repression – is *united* with psychic life, because this fantasy and this life, 'the representative of the earliest impulses of desire and aggressiveness, are expressed in and dealt with by *mental processes far removed from words* and conscious relational thinking'.[40]

Kristeva's reflections are in one sense primarily concerned with the presence of fantasy and unconscious work, all to do with the imagination of sensational life. The psychic work of representation is a universal feature 'present in all psychic activities and behaviours', by no means restricted to the therapeutic relationship, nor to particular aspects of mental functioning, such as the standard psychoanalytic menu of day-dreaming or erotic imaginings. Rather, it is our ordinary experiences – from sporting activities to the practicalities of learning and education – that are saturated with this originary imagination. All psychic activity, says Kristeva, is 'impregnated with fantasies'.

What is clear in Kristeva's account of fantasy is that this imaginary domain is inextricably interwoven with the motions of pleasure and unpleasure, the most primitive impulses of desire and aggressiveness which bring a world of subjectivity into being in the first place. Freud astutely captured the theatrical dynamics of sensational life in terms of the logics of dreaming; and it is these affective processes (the dream-work) which for Kristeva dominate the mental apparatus from start to finish. Kristeva conceptualizes what she refers to as the 'proto-fantasy' as a kind of oscillation of the imagination, with the human subject internally divided, split between infantile narcissism and the other's lack. Strictly speaking, if representation is an 'active presence of fantasy scenes', this is because desire, for Kristeva as for Lacan, is the desire of the Other. To desire the Other is a kind of fashioning, an imagining of what the Other dreams, an imitating, an identification with the Other's desire. Notwithstanding that it is the inescapability of imaginary misrecognition that leaves the human subject to impute an imaginary fullness to the Other's desire which, in fact, pertains only to the representation (that is, the imaginary plenitude that the subject itself desires), the point is there would be no meaning, not to say anything of the possibility for self-knowledge, without these imaginative fashionings.

None of these psychoanalytical insights in Kristeva's work are separable from her politics. The semiotic as a domain of the repressed unconscious is, politically speaking, subversive of the symbolic order, primarily since this architecture of affect is rooted in a pre-patriarchal connection to others. This is clearly of key importance to the political drafting of identity; Kristeva's point is that the semiotic functions equally to disturb and disrupt social order. In political terms, Kristeva's work takes as its target the globalization of culture, which amounts in effect to a history of the drastically shrinking world under the forces of transnational capitalism. Culture is in a broad sense for Kristeva the very stuff of politics, and one of her central claims is that a sense of cultural belonging or identity has begun to stall in the face of globalizing social forces. Her political critique focuses on how worldwide social transformations – and particularly European cultural shifts – are becoming more and more suited to the success of the far Right and a general climate of hostility to immigration, and less and less open to voices speaking up for cultural difference, moderation or reason. While it may not be exactly clear which particular globalizing forces Kristeva has in mind, it is evident that she writes among other things as an intellectual exile, anxious over the consequences of recent NATO operations and of transnational political attempts in the wake of 9/11 to legislate the winners from the losers of globalization.

Kristeva's primary purpose is to return to European national identities a sense of what is missing or lacking from much of the recent excited talk on globalization. She is out to probe the unwitting ways in which globalism, and particularly the insidious cultural influence of Americanization, inaugurates new levels of emotional denial and the repression of desire. To this end, her social theory is full of sinuous reflection on the transformative power of grief, mourning and melancholia in public political life, coupled with a detailed examination of cultural memory and the power of imagination. In Kristeva's culturalist version of psychoanalysis, nations, just like individuals, must work through grief and trauma. In the same manner that depressed individuals lose interest in the surrounding world, so too nations may become disconnected from their historical past. From this angle, Kristeva argues that the newly constituted European citizen will surely fall short of the political ideals governing the process of globalization unless nations undertake the difficult task of working through specific cultural pathologies, from neonationalism to the cult of militarism. This, one might consider, is something of a tall order. But Kristeva makes an urgent plea for citizens to try to 'think the horror' of their specific cultural pasts and national histories. Drawing from her own past, Kristeva reflects on the Bulgarian Orthodox Christian tradition, speculating whether Eastern conceptions of identity and culture might offer an emotional corrective or political supplement to the rationalistic excesses of West European life.

Mapping the Contours of Creation: The Examples of Digital Culture and Cosmopolitanization

So what are the key changes that are transforming contemporary societies in these early years of the twenty-first century which arise from the register of creation? New information technologies and the rise of digital culture undoubtedly must feature significantly here, but in terms of assessing societies of creation the emergence of digital media culture is a very uneven phenomenon and, even then, is only part of the story. Contemporary societies are also undergoing major changes of a political, cultural and legal kind, and in this connection the cosmopolitanization of societal dynamics at national, regional and global levels must also figure prominently. In the remainder of this chapter, we develop a provisional and partial account of both the spread of digital culture and cosmopolitanization which, while focusing on particular aspects of these phenomena, emphasizes the broader societal elements of creation and cultural innovation. We address throughout the key problem of defining the contours of genuine societal creation, and of how this register not only enters into dialogue, tension and conflict with societies of structure and societies of solidarity but also of how societies of creation contribute to broad social transformations which are reshaping the contemporary world.

Creative Communities of Digitalization

Contemporary media and cultural studies – especially that sector of it shaped by post-structuralist and postmodern theory – has advanced the argument that the world is increasingly remade with utopic consequences as a result of new information technologies and digital communications media.[41] As a result, there has been a shift in sociological terminology away from 'societies' or 'co-present socialities' and towards the notion of *mediated socialities*. In an age of global media institutions, 24/7 digital communication and the Internet, new information technologies play a particularly significant role in the development of contemporary societies. For communication media, all the way from mobile telephony and email to video-conferencing and Second Life, are today a central means by which people interact with each other and experience 'other' points of view within the wider contours of the social. There are, as a result, novel mixtures or hybrids of presence and absence, of mobility and fixation – as 'Others' who are 'at a distance' arrive on our screens, computers and mobile phones. Viewed from this perspective, the rising dominance of mediated interaction in the early years of the twenty-first century is held to have changed the very psychological and political forms of subjecthood and personal identity. This is a transformation away from the self as a coherent, centred entity, as dramatized in the Enlightenment moment of modernity, and towards a disjointed subjectivity profoundly dispersed and decentred within the post-Enlightenment contours of postmodernity. There is, it might be noted, a profound political irony in this estimate of mediated socialities emanating from media and cultural studies. On the one hand, the individual subject is allegedly rendered more and more fragmented in the process of engaging with mediated messages and a postmodern media culture of MTV, reality television programmes and Internet chat-rooms. On the other hand, it is through immersion in a mediated hall of mirrors that the subject experiences its own dissolution simply in order to realize a new sense of freedom in the act of celebrating a globally mediated world of complexity. This is why much recent media and cultural studies talks so admiringly of plurality, dispersal, ambiguity and ambivalence.

All of this began innocently enough, at least as far as assessing transformations of society goes. It is now over fifteen years since American sociologist Sherry Turkle declared, in her best-selling *Life on the Screen* that mediated simulation allows people to try on and out alternative identities and ways of being in society.[42] Perhaps Turkle's reflections struck a chord, especially with Americans held in thrall to the lures of self-reinvention, because she based a good deal of what she had to say on the then newly emerging phenomenon of 'Netsex'. In the cyberspace of 'anything goes', people can change gender, sexual orientation, race, ethnicity, status, class – in short, the Net-self is one that outstrips the situated self. This argument was, according to Turkle, more than just fanciful theory; she based what she had to say on countless interviews with people experimenting with Internet socialities. Thus, for Turkle, Netsex was intrinsically episodic and fragmentary: at the click of a mouse a person could shift from flirtation to cross-dressing, from fetishism to sadomasochism. Communication media and especially the Internet accordingly promised to bulk large in all transformations of the social, and for the most part this was unequivocally welcomed. Still, at this point of the debate over communication media, it was difficult to grasp what fell within the province of 'society' and what did not. New communications media were social – that much was agreed – but there was also the dawning realization that the Internet and digital culture outstripped the local, or even national, operations of 'society'. It was thus to fall to a more full-blooded postmodern version of cultural and media studies to make explicit the link between electronically mediated experiences on the one hand and the demise of society as a territorially fixed, bounded entity on the other. By a curious twist, cultural and media studies scholars turned to the theoretical texts of post-structuralists (Michel Foucault, Jacques Derrida, Jean-François Lyotard, Gilles Deleuze and Jean Baudrillard among others) to make the argument that electronically mediated communications 'lock' individuals into increasingly self-referential linguistic positions of computer writing. This was a vision of computer writing in the service of the post-societal. Not only were traditional signifiers of social interaction rendered redundant – from voice and skin to sex and gender – but the very idea of one's embeddedness in society (with a specific history, particular culture and distinct politics) was brought undone.

The strife between national societies, political domination and the decentring effects of computer writing on individuals is summarized by American historian Mark Poster thus:

> With computer writing, spacing is subordinated to a new wrapping of the text: writing could take place anywhere and the electrification of the mark (gramme) calls into question its materiality. With the mark losing its rootedness in space, so its temporality becomes complicated. Computer writing, instantaneously available over the globe, inserts itself into a nonlinear temporality that unsettles the relation to the writing subject . . . Computer writing institutes a factory of postmodern subjectivity, a machine for constituting non-identical subjects, an inscription of an other of Western culture into its most cherished manifestation.[43]

Societies were becoming mediated through and through, and this also spelt the arrival of the post-societal. Exactly what the arrival of the post-societal meant to people on the ground – to those carrying their laptops and dialling their mobiles – wasn't exactly easy to see from the standpoint of a cultural and media studies obsessed with post-structuralist and deconstructionist modes of thought. Even so, the notion of the social taken to braking point by the speed of communications was developed a good deal further in cultural and media studies, with some talking of the death of the social in the aftermath of cyberspace and others praising the arrival of post-societal configurations of identity with the advent of digitally simulated environments.[44]

Fortunately, many could see that experimentations with media culture and new technologies were still usually societally based. One might spend several hours in an Internet chat-room playing around with various reversals of identity, but eventually the time would come to take a break and return to the daily realities of work, credit-card bills or outstanding tax matters. The issue then was not so much a matter of Internet-based sociality versus traditional society, since social interaction and virtuality were interlaced in complex, contradictory ways. Even so, the political conflict erupting between digital socialities and territorial society was increasingly evident for all to see, especially with the dramatic rise of the commercialization of sexuality and the globalization of porn as relayed through the medium of the Internet. But there were also other ways in which social scientists and public intellectuals sought to analyse the types of social relations to which communication media gave rise. We have touched in the previous chapter on the solidaristic argument closely associated with Jürgen Habermas that the civil sphere created by bourgeois society has been severely compromised by the commercialization of the media, the concentration of media ownership, and the consequent trivialization of information circulating to the public. This Habermasian interpretation of communication is part of a larger contemporary debate in which it is asserted that the whole edifice of 'the social' has been challenged and eroded by neoliberal economic orthodoxy which privileged markets over society, praised individual entrepreneurship over community responsibility, and installed a radical policy of down-sizing, privatizing and out-sourcing that stripped social life of its foundations. The critical response to the crisis in the financial markets suggests that faith in the neoliberal creed has been severely damaged, that financial gurus in Wall Street and the City have been roundly condemned for their destructive greed and that a return to some form of Keynesianism might help to rebuild the social fabric. The other argument is that Internet networks and their creative communities of virtuality are creating new global communities within which the citizen can become an actor within a new public sphere. There is as a result a critical vision of the economy that talks about 'the financialization of capitalism' in which industrial production has been replaced by the growth of the banking sctor and global financial services, creating a new financial elite with little or no local connections. It is claimed that, while the great industrial families of capitalism such as the Carnegies and Rothschilds had attachments to society through charities, the new elites are free floating cosmopolitans with little or no moral sense.

They are represented on screen by Gordon Gekko and in real life by Bernie Madoff.

If the fiscal crisis was the traumatically destructive outcome of fiscal creativity such as 'collateral debt obligations' and the carry trade in currencies, others see creative opportunities in new social movements and the communication systems that make them possible. The American political economist Daniel Drache is among those who wish to speak up for the creativity of virtual socialities. In *Defiant Publics*, he argues, against Habermas's pessimistic view that the re-feudalization of the public sphere means that the bureaucracy has trapped the citizen in a client relationship, claiming instead that the new communication technologies have extended and enhanced the access points to public discourse.[45] Popular protests against authoritarian governments in Tunisia, Egypt, Bahrain and Jordan in 2011 might be obvious examples of when attempts to close down the Internet did little to stem the flow of opposition. Just as print was constitutive of modern forms of national identity, so the hypertext has given rise to the global citizen who is connected to other citizens through networked public spaces. The global citizen according to Drache is disgruntled (with the Washington Consensus, globalization, predatory corporations, unregulated free trade and rampant consumerism), but the disenchantment is producing greater criticism, debate and protest. Hence, his emphasis on new forms of public defiance attempts to capture the creative opportunities emerging from the media. Disgruntled voters are punishing neoliberal governments and programs, because they have produced disastrous results in terms of rising food prices, income inequality, callous consumerism and unbridled individualism. These deregulated economies gave rise to Enron, Worldcom, the Hollinger newspaper empire, the credit crunch of 2008–10, the Madoff Ponzi scheme and a cascade of mortgage foreclosures in the United States. In response these alienated voters are, according to Drache, also electing coalition governments that can put a brake on privatization. This conclusion appears to be merely wishful thinking since the major response to the crisis has been to cut back on government spending on welfare programmes, an emphasis on austerity and economic policies which encourage the privatization of utilities – for example the proposal in the United Kingdom to breakup the postal service.

Globalization has as a result produced major contradictions of the social. Economic globalization has produced increasing social inequality, and cultural globalization has produced McDonaldization and Disneyland resulting in a certain degree of cultural standardization and trivialization. The globalization of the labour market saw a rise in illegal migration, the exploitation of domestic workers and sex-trafficking. On the other hand, however, communications technologies have produced a globalization that can also help to construct new publics and vibrant forms of debate and participation. These socialities involve very different publics from the past, because they are to a large extent post-national, often ephemeral and de-territorialized. The global citizen now belongs to groups who organize and communicate beyond the fixed boundaries of the state. In a period when trust in major institutions – corporations, states and professional bodies – is declining sharply, citizens have found new ways of being together through file-sharing, blogging and texting. Furthermore the digital divide is contracting with the declining cost of technology and as a result of programs such as One Laptop per Child. The network society has grown at a startling pace. In the G8 countries the number of people using the Internet exploded from 7.3 million in 1993 to 297 million by 2001, and in the same period the number of Internet users in the G20 rose from 430,000 people to 25 million. By the year 2007, there were one billion people on line. Alongside this network society, NGOs have also increased dramatically. Since 1950 the number of NGOs which are active internationally (that is with memberships in three or more countries) has grown from 1,000 to 25,000. These provide some of the framework of dissent and debate.

Dissent is now orchestrated around four large themes or clusters of engagement. The first concerns the issue of social inclusion and it is directed towards the homeless, the migrant without the correct documents, the stateless refugees and asylum seekers, and the mass of people who are drifting and disrupted. The second cluster of engagement concerns trust and human security, and it embraces the large army of activists who are committed to cosmopolitanism and multiculturalism. The institutional expression of these interests is to be found in Medecins Sans Frontières, OneWorld, ActionAid and the Global Development Network. While these organizations prioritize the local, they are committed to building communities on a global scale. The third configuration of concern is for individual freedom. This is a libertarian cluster concerned with questions of recognition and the protection of minorities. While they are libertarian, they also recognize the importance of state involvement in protecting minority rights. This dimension is represented by such activist groups as ACT UP, Global Aids Alliance and Global Alliance Project (GAP). The final cluster is around the project of building political community. These are the micro-activists who develop networks and enhance the social power of the public such as Habitat for Humanity that provides homes for the homeless and supports low-income groups. These micro-activists organize highly visible campaigns from the cancellation of Third World Debt to protecting workers in the sex trade. The result of these combinations of clusters is that modern dissent is ideologically fluid and no longer tied to orthodox Marxism or doctrinaire socialism. In addition, dissenters move easily and rapidly between clusters and social movements. These dissenting groups effectively use modern communication technology to mobilize globally in cycles of political rebellion and nonconformity that cut across age, gender and class barriers. The mentality of the disgruntled citizen is primarily one of skepticism, thereby expressing disbelief in official information and public pronouncements, and the Internet through Google and Wikipedia allows the citizen to counter and contradict official stories and justifications. In fact these new social movements typically reject the label 'anti-globalization' movements which merely serve to belittle or tarnish their protests. As the American social theorist Tom Mertes observes these movements which emerged out of opposition to neoliberal economic strategies prefer to define themselves as 'global justice movements' or 'global solidarity movements' or 'alter-globalization movements'.[46] The term 'anti-globalization' was used in defence of economic globalization to label all opposition groups as irrational, ignorant or anarchist.

Contemporary media analysts are primarily concerned with new communicative publics that extend beyond the state and with new forms of citizenship that emerge with global publics. However, the difficulty here is that publics were also built in the past by nation states creating public utilities (drainage systems, sewerage, roads, street lighting, public toilets, bridges and public buildings) through the taxation of its citizens. Will the modern state with a shrinking taxation base be able to maintain existing public works and to build new utilities? In the United States while the Congressional Budget Office projects that within the next decade the federal debt will equal 90 per cent of GDP, the IMF claims that by 2015 the debt will equal the total GDP. The result will be years of austerity. This crisis has many roots but they include the decision of President Bush to slash personal taxation, the costs of foreign wars and changes in the funding of Medicare.[47]

One problem with the modern state is that, in following neo-liberal economics, most of our public utilities are now in need of costly repair and with privatization many public utilities have by definition simply ceased to be public. In many British cities, the Victorian investments in drainage, sewerage and water supply were in need of significant investment and as a result they were sold off to private companies. The other problem is that a massive amount of taxation goes into military expenditure and governments have used the defence budget as a means of job creation. It is estimated that over the next fifteen to twenty-five years the US government will spend $238 billion on the National Missile Defence System in a society where 47 million citizens have no health care protection. It is thus not clear how the role of the state in creating 'things public' can be reconciled with the spontaneous creation of publics through the Internet. In short how do we reconcile the need for taxation and accountable governments with the sprawling mobile communities that lie beyond the state?

Perhaps confusing creation with creativity, critics like Drache also appear too optimistic in their evaluations of the social. He says, for example, that 'gamblers, porn surfers, trolls, spammers and lurkers represent the dark side of the net' and 'experts certainly agree that the Internet has facilitated the gratification of baser human impulses. Pedophilia, non-consensual sexual violence, fraud, blackmail . . . have contributed to a new awareness about the dangers of virtual interaction.'[48] Is the dark side actually larger than the light side? Does the information wall of spam and junk mail compete successfully with useful information? Have modern societies become simply large entertainment parks? Of course nobody can give an entirely plausible answer to this question, but we do need to know what safeguards can be built into the new publics to protect them from the dark side. Perhaps more importantly we need to recognize that the web facilitates democracy because it also permits the mobilization of fascism, racism and other extreme ideologies. It is not clear whether the protests sweeping the Arab world in 2011 will in fact be the basis for a peaceful democratic transition or whether the social disruptions will result in a return to military government.

We argue there are three major ways (no doubt others can be isolated) in which digital, virtual, Web-based socialities enter into the reconstitution of society and bring about novel social patterns. These are (1) virtual fluidity, (2) mobile connectivity and (3) virtual wars. Our contention is that such virtual socialities are complex and contradictory, simultaneously enabling and constraining forms of innovative, creative social action.

Firstly, virtual socialities are predominantly *fluid* in form, and involve complex mixtures of subjects, machines, switching systems, wi-fi, telephone lines, software programmes, hypertext and images. 'Cyberspace communications', writes the American sociologist William Bogard, 'in a word, are strange – at the push of a button, territories dissolve, oppositions of distant and close, motion and stasis, inside and outside, collapse; identities are marginalized and simulated, and collectivities lose their borders'.[49] It is difficult to describe the bond between virtual interlocutors as an interpersonal relationship (although it is surely that in a sense), since the communicative flows of virtuality comprise networks and links which are hugely unpredictable, mixed and open-ended. It is also, at times, a strangely 'identity-free' domain – as traditional markers of sex, gender, race, ethnicity, class and social status sink to zero. If it is hard to apply virtual socialities to conventional moral discourse of rights, duties and obligations, it is because there is something curiously fantasmatic about 'life on the screen' which – in blurring boundaries between self and others – proves recalcitrant to structured social life. This is not to say that the relationship

between the Internet and society is one of complete novelty, nor
that the registers of structure and solidarity are not of relevance for
conceptualizing how virtual socialities unfold in the twenty-first
century. As the Spanish sociologist Manuel Castells contends in
The Internet Galaxy, people use the Internet to accommodate their
lifestyles, their identities and their interests.[50] Moreover Castells
argues that the more people use the Internet, the more socially
interactive they are likely to be 'offline'. The Internet for Castells
multiplies, rather than subtracts, sociability. Against this backdrop
it is important to note the dramatic rises in worldwide Internet use
from the 1990s onwards (see Tables 3.1 and 3.2 below), especially
in the broader context of a 'digital divide' between those countries
that facilitate individuals and communities to extend their lives
through Internet access and those that limit such developments and
opportunities.

What is especially interesting about these figures is that the end
of 1998 marked the first time that the USA did not make up over
half of the world's Internet users. There were 101,035,725 worldwide users outside the USA, and 84,587,000 American users. The
previous year, at the end of 1996, there were only 58,926,825
users outside the USA, while there were 60,000,000 American
users. Also, the end of 2004 marked the first time non-G8 countries' Internet users outnumbered their G8 counterparts. There
were 466,182,359 users in the former category, and 443,149,558
users in the latter. The end of 2005 marked the surpassing of one
billion Internet users worldwide, with 1,020,677,714 users. Only
three years later, by the end of 2008, there were over one billion
Internet users outside the G8, with 1,013,363,601 users.

This is perhaps why the Internet itself is a signal example of how
creation, contingency and contradiction become intricately interwoven today, for the Net facilitates a constant process of openness
– which simultaneously enables and limits sociabilities of various
kinds. Despite attempts to regulate and control the Internet in
countries such as China and Vietnam, Internet communication is
vital to economic activities and hence states can never close down
or seriously monitor the flow of communication. The recent
development of WikiLeaks also demonstrates the opposite – states
both democratic and authoritarian can be exposed by modern

Table 3.1 Internet Users: G8 versus the World.

G8 Members	1990	1993	1996	1999	2002	2005	2008
Canada	100,000	340,000	2,000,000	11,000,000	19,287,884	21,942,404	25,086,000
France	30,000	340,000	1,504,000	5,370,000	18,057,000	26,154,000	42,315,424
Germany	100,000	375,000	2,500,000	17,100,000	40,143,248	53,470,848	61,973,096
Italy	10,000	70,000	585,000	8,200,000	16,145,312	19,741,136	24,991,542
Japan	25,000	500,000	5,500,000	27,060,000	59,220,000	85,290,000	95,978,992
Russia	N/A	20,000	400,000	1,500,000	6,000,000	21,800,000	45,250,000
UK	50,000	300,000	2,400,000	12,500,000	33,542,500	39,993,048	46,683,900
USA	2,000,000	6,000,000	45,000,000	102,000,000	172,834,272	205,766,896	230,630,000
TOTALS							
G8	2,315,000	7,945,000	59,889,000	184,730,000	365,230,216	474,158,332	572,908,954
Non-G8	325,100	2,124,000	13,930,369	94,441,473	308,200,599	546,519,382	1,013,363,601
World	2,640,100	10,069,000	73,819,369	279,171,473	673,430,815	1,020,677,714	1,586,272,555

Compiled from: International Telecommunication Union, World Telecommunication/ICT
Development Report and database, accessed via http://data.worldbank.org/

Table 3.2 Percentage Increase of Internet Users: G8 versus the World.

	1990–3%	1993–6 %	1996–9 %	1999–2002 %	2002–5 %	2005–8 %
G8	243.20	653.79	208.45	97.71	29.82	20.83
Non-G8	553.34	555.86	577.95	226.34	77.33	85.42
World	281.39	633.14	278.18	141.22	51.56	55.41

Compiled from: International Telecommunication Union, World Telecommunication/
ICT Development Report and database, accessed via http://data.worldbank.org/

media. Dating from the late 1970s, the Internet emerged as a communications system of the American intelligence services. But as a result of innovations made by American scientific networks and from counter-cultural kinds of networked experimentation, the Internet in turn became available to global public access. The British philosopher Sadie Plant describes the fluid, self-organizing character of the Internet thus:

> No central hub or command structure has constructed it. . . . It has installed none of the hardware on which it works, simply hitching a largely free ride on existing computers, networks, switching systems, telephone lines. This was one of the first systems to present itself as a multiplicitous, bottom-up, piecemeal, self-organizing network which . . . could be seen to be emerging without any centralized control.[51]

Secondly, the social today is reconfigured as a result of what one of us has elsewhere termed 'mobile connectivity'.[52] The notion of mobile connectivity refers to the self's liberation from fixed places or locations in terms of mediated communications with others. It also captures the sense of dispersal or drift that 'life on the move' carries for both self-identity and social relations in our age of Web 2.0. A signal example in this connection is the mobile phone, and especially the more recent emergence of 'smartphones'. 'Mobile phones', writes sociologist Barry Wellman, 'afford a fundamental liberation from place.'[53] The intricate interconnections between online mobility and novel patterns of social relationships are graphically brought into focus if we consider the rise of social networking sites – which it has been estimated accounts for

Table 3.3 Worldwide Internet and Mobile Phone Users.

	1998	2003	2008
Internet users	185,622,725	782,673,940	1,586,272,555
Internet users (per 100 people)	3.2	12.5	23.9
Mobile Cellular Subscriptions	318,171,123	1,415,068,352	4,030,530,838

Data Source: World Bank Statistics, http://data.worldbank.org/topic/infrastructure

approximately 22 per cent of all time spent online by people today. In the case of Facebook, for example, there are now over a half a billion accounts, and of these over 200 million Facebook users access their accounts using a mobile device. Moreover, Facebook users that access the site using a mobile device are twice as active on Facebook than non-mobile users. Thus it can be plausibly argued that, against the institutionalized backdrop of wireless technology, international roaming and spatial fluidity, the person today is reconfigured as the portal. Mobiles, laptops, palmtops and other digital devices provide the wireless communications-based platform from which individuals can design their own networks and connections. The worldwide spread of powerful, interdependent, communications-based systems forms a virtual infrastructure, or what the Austrian sociologist Karin Knorr Cetina terms 'flow architectures', for the intensive mobilization of social relations – see Table 3.3. This intensive mobilization of social practices involves novel, post-societal forms of relationships, intimacies, sexualities, identities, careers and families.

Thirdly, as a result of the digitization of information connected with the Internet, we are today witnessing the full-blown emergence of cyber-battlefields and *virtual wars*. The cyber-hackers or 'hacktivists' in this new kind of emerging warfare espouse a manifesto which is predominantly anti-American, anti-corporations, anti-censorship and anti-copyright – fitting as it does with a 'new artificial life-form of the global telecommunications Matrix'. Sociologically, the central significance of this matrix is (1) it is informationalized and networked, and (2) its circuits and audiences are located in transnational spaces.

The emergence of networked warfare, or what Arquilla and Ronfeldt term 'netwars', is evidenced by the anonymous community of hacktivists launching cyber-attacks on US corporations that sought to close down WikiLeaks in 2010. The WikiLeaks controversy arose from the site's release of confidential US government cables, and of American political and corporate attempts to close down WikiLeaks. The emergence of network virtual warfare arose following the arrest of WikiLeaks founder Julian Assange, with 'Operation Payback' unfolding as a series of cyber-attacks on websites, such as Amazon, Visa and Mastercard. Operation Payback, as various media commentators have noted, was non-linear, asymmetrical and Internet-assembled. But it was also highly politically specific, seeking to pit an amorphous army of cyberhackers against the US government and some of the largest corporations in the world. Further, as branded by the UK's Guardian newspaper, Operation Payback 'seemed to be the first sustained clash between the established order and the organic, grassroots culture of the Net'.[54]

Another instance of societies of creation entering into conflict with societies of structure? From one angle, this may seem self-evident. Yet it is hard not to suspect that the parcelling out of creation and structure does not neatly divide into any such traditional political dualism. The WikiLeaks backlash undoubtedly was part of an information war, and significantly its virtual weaponry was not bound to a local or a national space. But its contextualization unfolded, and remained operationalized, in human society and history. As such, the technically experimental and politically exploratory form of the WikiLeaks cyberwar unravelled within and across various registers of the social: structure, solidarity and creation.

In sum, digital culture and new information technologies demonstrate some strikingly powerful social forms of creation. Computing, software systems, databases of information, smartphones, social networking sites such as Facebook and Twitter, Internet telephony and video applications such as Skype and Telepresence, and personal digitized information libraries such as iTunes and iPhoto: all of these digitized informational forms involve novel patterns of the social which comprise (1) fluid, open-ended, multi-dimensional and non-linear systems; and (2) modes of mediated socialities in which presence is created through the 'absence of the Other'. Further, these new modes of presence and absence are intricately interwoven with novel compressions of time-space – such as the nanosecond instantaneity of mobile and Internet communications. However while the virtual infra-structures of digital culture promote new forms of subjecthood and novel patterns of the social (or 'post-societal socialities'), these new scapes, networks and fluids remain unpredictable. That is to say, 'life on the screen' is full of the unexpected: systems fail, signals fade, communications fragment. Moreover, the complex, contradictory oscillating of presence and absence which charac-terizes mediated socialities cannot in advance guarantee forms of social interaction (however post-societal in orientation) that are genuinely creative. Digital culture, we have suggested, combines creation and repetition in unexpected ways. Hence, the mediated socialities of digital culture are not, by definition, autonomous processes of creation; equally they are inscribed in social-historical forms of structured socialities and solidaristic socialities, and this in turn can produce unexpected couplings and dependencies within and across the registers of structure, solidarity and creation.

Cosmopolitanization as Creation: Globalism, Transnational Assemblages and Religion

Just as communication in the era of the Internet involves an encounter with new forms of sociality and creativity, so does politics. We refer to the recent explosion of intellectual debates concerning epochal social transformations (from global warming and climate change to the global financial crisis arising in 2008) and associated claims regarding growing global complexity and intensification of cosmopolitan processes and practices in respect of international law, social justice and the consolidation of trans-national institutions and forms of governance. Cosmopolitanism, its terrains and trajectories, has become an object of intense debate in the social sciences and humanities over recent years; there is now an extensive literature, ranging from social theory to social measurement, dealing with its settings, fields, practices, processes, attitudes and mindsets.[55] Perhaps the central conflict documented in these social-theoretical debates concerns the political conflict between cosmopolitanism and parochial attitudes, which in effect translates as a broader tension between ethics and politics. Our contention will be that when we are speaking of cosmopolitanization – not the political ideal of cosmopolitanism, but rather cosmopolitan social practices which are geared to 'the Other' – we are speaking of the growing creativity and complexity of average lives and not of the ethical splendour of isolated political acts. We further contend that the sociological analysis of cosmopolitanization should encompass both cosmopolitan and anti-cosmopolitan social practices – in order to grasp adequately how societies of creation intersect with societies of structure and solidarity.

Against the ethical backdrop of high-toned talk of international law, right, duty, obligation and principle, it is perhaps easy enough to forget that the debate over cosmopolitanism exploded onto the intellectual scene in the early 2000s as a consequence of various global transformations. That is to say, the complex, contradictory conflict dynamics stemming from globalization has given rise to the living of life in a milieu of blurring national distinctions and cultural ambiguities. Ulrich Beck, in seeking to shift the debate away from the politics of cosmopolitanism and towards the sociology of cosmopolitanization, writes that 'national institutions alone are unable to cope with the challenges of regulating global capitalism and responding to new global risks'.[56] Cosmopolitanization thus means acceptance not only of cultural mixture, but of transnational social and political complexity. For Beck, it is not just that globalization results in a displacement or deconstruction of the nation-state, for the central point is that there is also no global state or transnational governance organization capable of regulating global capitalism and the globalization of risk. As such, Beck argues that cosmopolitanization 'is an extraordinarily intricate terrain, composed, among other things, of co-ordinated national mechanisms, bilateral and multilateral agreements, inter-, trans- and supranational institutions, transnational corporations, private charity foundations, and civil society groups'.

In his major sociological statements on the field of cosmopolitanization, *Cosmopolitan Vision* and *Power in the Global Age*, Beck
distinguishes two kinds of relation between politics and power
in our time of transnational interdependencies.[57] There is what
he terms the 'national outlook', or 'methodological nationalism', which holds that politics should be principally concerned
with the assertion of sovereignty, the policing of local or regional
borders and the maintenance of exclusive identities. The national
outlook, says Beck, is premised upon a full-blooded essentialist
sociology that squares the circle between national and universal
society, squeezing to the sidelines incommensurability in people's
attitudes, beliefs, values and orientations. By contrast, Beck speaks
of the emergence of 'cosmopolitanization', or 'methodological cosmopolitanism', by which he means to underscore internal
processes of transformation affecting societies across the globe.
Cosmopolitanism for Beck involves a positive pluralization of
national borders, a deterritorialized society, a mushrooming of globalism from within the nation-state. From international students
and transmigrants to multinational global businesses and transnational criminal networks, Beck sees the influence everywhere of an
ever-expanding cosmopolitanization.

The sociological significance of Beck's vision of cosmopolitanization is striking, and his research certainly offers suggestive
mappings of the extent to which the world has moved more
deeply in a cosmopolitan direction – with transnational forms
of governance now intricately institutionalized across the globe.
What remains troubling, however, is the lack of political specificity
to Beck's analysis, which at times threatens to sag into ideological
naivety. For in rhapsodizing this century's brave new cosmopolitanism, Beck sometimes appears unaware of its more virulent
forms. If cosmopolitanism combines cultural openness with a cava-
lier disregard of place, this is because it is arguably a manifestation
of the mentality of global elites. On this view, cosmopolitanism
functions as the ideology of advanced capitalism. It allows white
Westerners to jet around the globe, effortlessly living transnational
lifestyles, crossing national borders (in real and virtual time) almost
as easily as money flows between multinational corporations. This
supposedly universal and classless doctrine, however, screens from

view those excluded from the privileges and wealth of global capitalism. Though Beck himself is by no means suggesting that cosmopolitanism is a purely affirmative category (he writes, for example, of 'contradictory tendencies'), the question remains whether the sociology is not too insular and, concomitantly, of whether cosmopolitanization is as genuinely creative as is passed off in some versions of recent social theory. For example, what of the millions of refugees, trans-migrants and asylum seekers who are less well off than the global cosmopolitans of many recent social theories? Undoubtedly the world is becoming increasingly transnational, especially for those in the expensive cities of the West. But the point is that for the vast swathe of humanity, from rural Chinese peasants to women and children in Central Asia, the transnational capitalist system does not usually bring about positive cosmopolitan consequences.

This point connects with other political difficulties to which Beck may be insufficiently attentive. Beck's language for capturing cosmopolitanization – ranging, as it does, across terminological innovations such as 'individualization', 'reflexivity' and 'cosmopolitan nationalism' – is conceptually sophisticated and complex. Such labours of the theoretician, however, still fail to get around the fact that there are those who have access to cosmopolitan culture on the cheap, just as there are those excluded from its benefits. The relevant conflict here is between economies of transnationalism and the politics of cosmopolitanism. Beck's sociology betrays an incipient idealism in its heavily cosmopolitan bias. Tellingly, he passes over in silence the whole issue of how transnationalism and cosmopolitanism intertwine, and sometimes conflates the two. Some cruder versions of cosmopolitanism go further, and involve an intellectual sleight-of-hand by passing off transnational activities as always and everywhere leading to processes of cosmopolitanization. To suggest that someone watching satellite TV necessarily also moves within the culture of cosmopolitanism may sound peculiarly idealist, patronizing or politically naive. It is also notable that many recent treatments of cosmopolitanization are relentlessly focused on Western or indeed European political developments. While there is nothing necessarily wrong with this, it is surely a defect of recent, grand theorizations of global cosmopolitanism that there are scarcely any detailed discussions of, say, Africa, East and South Asia nor the Islamic diaspora.

One might contrast this strain of German sociological thinking on cosmopolitanization of societal dynamics in the most global sense with other, more specific forms of cosmopolitan preoccupation in the field of religion – all the way from Marcus Tullius Cicero and Immanuel Kant to Jacques Derrida and Charles Taylor. If religion represents, among other things, both a replication of and resistance to the world of market capitalism, then contemporary cultural ideologies infusing religion become intriguingly transformed in our own time of cosmopolitanism. In this sense, it is primarily through seeking to extend the language of cosmopolitanism – through a more detailed acquaintance with notions of religiousity, natural law or the radical openness of hospitality – that a more informed assessment of the creativity and complexity of processes of cosmopolitanization might best be pursued.

Religion is always operationalized in the context of the socio-symbolic order, which in turn raises fundamental issues about inter-cultural understanding. The American political scientist Samuel Huntington's thesis of 'the clash of civilizations' has shaped much of the academic debate about inter-cultural understanding for over a decade. Yet, in retrospect, Palestinian-American postcolonial theorist Edward Saïd's criticisms of Orientalism,[58] and more especially his *Representations of the Intellectual*,[59] offered some prospect that intellectuals could cross boundaries between cultures, and forge a pathway towards mutual respect and understanding. In the post 9/11 world, Huntington's bleak analysis of the development of micro fault line conflicts and macro core state conflicts has captured the mood of foreign policy in the West in the era of the 'war on terror'. Huntington of course believes that the major division is between the Christian West and the Muslim world. More recently, Huntington has even more openly spoken about 'the age of Muslim Wars' and widespread Muslim grievance and hostility towards the United States. Any attempt to engage with Islamic civilization is now seen as a 'war for Muslim minds'.[60]

The ethical imperative for mutual dialogue, recognition and care is, arguably, as old as humanity itself. Inter-civilizational contact inevitably creates a sense of the otherness or alterity of different societies, cultures and civilizations. Any society or group with a more or less coherent cultural boundary will tend to have an exclusionary notion of the outside and hence otherness; the more exclusive the notion of ethnic membership, the more intense the notion of an outside. It is perhaps inevitable therefore in any discussion of cosmopolitanism that we would want to start an inquiry with the ancient world. The growing diversity of the ancient city is plausibly held to be the origins not only of cosmopolitanism but of politics as such. However, the most articulate statement of secular cosmopolitanism came from Stoicism, especially from the third phase of Roman Stoicism in the works of Seneca, Epictetus and Marcus Aurelius. In this phase, Stoicism held that while national or local attachments were 'natural', they were morally underdeveloped and hence emotional attachments to a place should be replaced by rational concern for the world. The Stoics aimed for a sameness of emotional attachment in which virtue is best exercised within a world-state or *oikoumene*. For these Stoic *cosmopolitai* social distinctions based on particular characteristics of ethnicity and gender are irrelevant and the political aim of a rational community would be to embrace the idea of a common humanity. Rejecting 'blood' as a basis for community, they emphasized human *nous* (mind) as the rational basis of membership. We might find it paradoxical that the Stoics accepted Roman imperial rule as the basis for a world society of citizens. Roman rule could be morally sustained if it was just and enlightened, for example if it extended the natural law over the barbarian customs of subordinated peoples.

Three important issues arise from this brief recognition of the importance of Stoicism in the origins of cosmopolitanism. The first is that cosmopolitanism has a strong association with secularism or at least with the idea of a rational Natural Law in which divine intervention is either unnecessary or inconsistent with reason. Cicero's sceptical arguments about religion in *On the Nature of the Gods* is characteristic of Stoic secularism. Secondly, Stoicism emphasized universal principles over local and particular attachments, but thirdly this acceptance of universalism was based on the actual growth of Roman imperial power.

There is a close connection between Stoicism and the most powerful modern expression of cosmopolitanism, namely Immanuel Kant's ideas of a 'perpetual peace'. In this famous essay where he elaborated early ideas from the *Rechtslehre*, Kant defended two ideas – a defence of the moral necessity of world government and a set of guidelines for existing governments to make world government a practical objective.[61] Representative government is necessary since democracies are less like to wage war on their neighbours, and hence Kant also in *The Metaphysical Elements of Justice* provided arguments against slavery, serfdom and imperialism, thereby departing from the Stoic legacy.[62] Kant also rejected the arguments of Stoicism and the Epicureans who sought to reconcile virtue and happiness; for Kant, doing our duty is always hard, and may well conflict with our personal desire for happiness.[63]

Nevertheless there does appear to be a coherent secular cosmopolitanism from Cicero to Kant which stresses the need for universal government, world citizenship, secularism and the rule of reason. Kant's hostility to fanaticism in both morals and religion expresses a Stoical scepticism against passionately held opinions. In Kant's account of Enlightenment in the essay 'What is Enlightenment?' he gives the famous definition of moral autonomy and maturity as 'man's release from his self-incurred tutelage' and argues that the motto of the Enlightenment must be to have the courage to use your own reason. Kant's rational version of Protestantism recognized ironically that as a 'moral faith' Christianity must be self-defeating since dependence on reason alone must rule out child-like dependence on a personal saviour and hence there was no need for revelation.

For postmodern culture and global culture, however, relations between identity and difference are significantly recast. In our own time, globalization compresses the spatial relations between societies and hence the problem of alterity is magnified by modern systems of global communication, transportation and migration. Thus a paradoxical relationship exists between the growing hybridity, interconnectedness and interdependency of the world and the problem of exclusionary alterity. This divisive question of alterity has been closely associated with the emergence of world religions, the development of imperial powers, and the history of colonialism and postcolonialism. Hence the question of cosmopolitanism and the Other has become a central issue in modern politics with the crisis of secularism and a dominant topic of philosophy in the work of figures such as Emmanuel Levinas, Charles Taylor, Kwame Appiah, Martha Nussbaum and Ulrich Beck.

The contemporary ethical debates about how to address the question of the Other have their origins in Hegel's theory of recognition. The master–slave dialectic suggests that neither slave nor master can achieve authentic recognition, and hence, without some degree of social equality no ethical community – a system of rights and obligations – can function. Rights presuppose relatively free, autonomous and self-conscious agents capable of rational choice. Recognition is required if people are to be mutually acceptable as moral agents, but life is unequal. Economic scarcity undercuts the roots of solidarity (community) without which conscious, rational agency is difficult. A variety of modern writers, in particular the American philosopher Charles Taylor have appealed to recognition ethics as the base line for the enjoyment of rights in multicultural societies. Without recognition of minority rights, no liberal democratic society can function. The growth of human rights is a major index of the growth of juridical globalization, and recognition of the rights of others is an ethical precondition for global governance. In the work of the French philosopher Jacques Derrida, ethics is hospitality.

With the collapse of the ancient world, the question of alterity was particularly acute in the context of the Abrahamic religions of Judaism, Christianity and Islam. Because Yahweh was a jealous God, there was a sacred covenant between God and the tribes of Israel, which excluded those who worshipped idols and false gods. In Christianity, a universalistic orientation that recognized the Other was contained in Paul's letters to the Galatians and Romans, which rejected circumcision as a condition of salvation. Because the uncircumcized were among the righteous, the message of Jesus had, at least in Pauline theology, a global significance. However, Christian theology treated Islam as a false religion, and the West Christians came to imagine Islam as an irrational, stagnant and licentious sect – thus the origins of what social critic Edward Saïd described as Orientalism. The modern Western view of Islam has concentrated on the apostasy laws, the treatment of women, the absence of freedom of conscience, the presence of punitive criminal law systems as defining characteristics of Islam. How can we start a conversation of recognition in such circumstances?

Recognition of the Other can be formulated through ethical cosmopolitanism but it is difficult to formulate a normative account of cosmopolitanism without assuming (1) 'our' moral superiority over the provincial nature of other cultures (2) the military and technological superiority of our civilization and (3) some level of condescension towards the Other. In short 'our' cosmopolitanism, even when well intentioned, may be inescapably elitist and offered from a position of superior power. The problem is how to formulate a positive form of cosmopolitanism without elitism and moral superiority. Furthermore, how can mutual recognition be achieved when there may be so to speak competing versions of cosmopolitanism. This issue has been raised powerfully by Sheldon Pollock in his account of (voluntary) Sanskrit and (compulsory) Latin cosmopolitanism. In other work, one of us has attempted to defend the idea of cosmopolitan virtue as involving recognition, respect and care for cultural diversity. However what is crucial to cosmopolitanism is ironically namely the capacity to distance oneself from one's own culture and to reflect critically on one's own civilizational standpoint.

We should distinguish between a number of separate meanings of the Other, otherness and alterity. The concept of the Other has been important in phenomenology and psychoanalysis, where the self as a subject presupposes the existence of a non-self or other. In existentialism, the Other often assumes an antagonistic relationship with the self. Because the individual resides in a world of other subjectivities, there exists a mode of existence that is referred to as 'being-for-others'. In the work of the French Jewish philosopher Emmanuel Levinas, the Other plays a positive role in questioning the confidence and assurance of the subject. The face of the Other challenges us to take responsibility for the Other, and hence otherness creates the conditions that make ethics possible. This philosophical analysis of the role of the Other in ethical discourse has an important and obvious relationship to nationalism, ethnic cleansing and globalization. With the collapse of the Soviet Union between 1989 and 1992, there has been a resurgence of ethnic identity as the basis of national communities, and ethnic violence has replaced class conflict as the major arena of political confrontation. The disintegration of Yugoslavia and the 1992 crisis in Bosnia were tragic illustrations of the importance of ethnicity in international conflicts. Where globalization has weakened the nation state and promoted identity politics, alterity can play a violent role in ethnic conflict.

The universalism of Christianity and Islam was compromised by their involvement in the institution of slavery and the ideology of racial supremacy. The introduction of slavery in the Americas, the Protestant underpinning of the South African apartheid system, and the subordination of indigenous peoples in America and Australia by the doctrine that these colonies were empty lands, created a powerful imperialist legacy in which other races were treated as uncivilized, if not inhuman. The great land rush between 1650 and 1900 destroyed indigenous communities around the world, but colonization also converted aboriginal people into objects of Western science, especially cultural anthropology and colonial medicine. Nineteenth-century anthropology, an exploration of the alterity of indigenous cultures, developed parasitically on the back of British colonial administrators, medical doctors and Christian missionaries. In the same period, social Darwinism – often expressed, in shorthand, as 'survival of the fittest' – came to serve as a convenient doctrine of the racial superiority of the white man within a hierarchy of racial orders. Twentieth-century struggles against colonialism restored some dignity to the subjects of Western colonialism, but the Martinique-Algerian psychiatrist and philosopher Frantz Fanon demonstrated in *Black Skin, White Masks* (1952) that, while blacks must be liberated from their inferiority complex, whites must be liberated from their superiority complex.[64]

In the aftermath of the attacks on the United States in 2001, the social tensions between the West and Islam have been intensified. Political Islam has, in the post-Cold War period, replaced Communism as the imaginary enemy of liberal capitalism. Samuel Huntington argues that there is a religious fault line dividing Islam and the West producing a 'clash of civilizations'.[65] Huntington's thesis follows Carl Schmitt's *The Concept of the Political* as a struggle between friend and foe. Huntington's thesis dividing the world into us and them is controversial, especially since the majority of conflicts since 1989 have been within rather than between religious traditions.[66] Conflict between Protestants and Catholics in Northern Ireland is the typical example of the politics of alterity.

Conclusion: Creation as a Form of Social Life

From Simmel to Castoriadis, the society of creation is figured as a kind of artfulness, a realm of potentially autonomous interaction free of social conventions or cultural solidarity. Sociability is invention, creativity, playfulness, eroticism, open-endedness. One might make the same point for identity and subjectivity: in this frame of reference there is emphasis on the self-realization of critical reflection, artful communication and emotional literacy over social roles, and of a moral responsibility over public opinion. Society as creation thus does away with foundations; it is a realm without structure; it needs no guide book, and presents social life as a world of vulnerabilities, torments, imaginings, differences and indeed hauntings. Such a response to the crisis of social values, need it be said, is unlikely to generate much sympathy from the world of institutionalized politics, with its relentless bureaucratic stress on ordered predictabilities. There is, however, still a political edge here, and this is that society as creation represents a *dissident cultural form*, one which contributes to the radical political imagination, pointing to a world beyond Left or Right, beyond competition or solidarity, as well as to the critique of notions that individual subjectivity and social relations automatically correspond.

Conclusion

In 2009, media worldwide reported the brutal gang rape of a teenager at a school dance in California. What attracted the attention of global media to this sexual assault was not only the extremely violent nature of the rape, but that witnesses both watched and filmed the assault on mobile phones. There was an outcry of public horror, and in reaction various media commentators wrote of the catastrophic condition of a society held in thrall to new information technologies, and especially of its grossly diseased moral sentiments. That people could stand by and film such a horrific attack signalled not only the sickness of society writ large, but also its destructive nihilism.

A police officer involved in the case likened the attack to a horror movie, commenting 'I can't believe not one person felt compelled to help her.'[1] Such cross-referencing to Hollywood horror was perhaps culled from the memory bank of popular culture, since actress Jodie Forster had won an Oscar for her portrayal of a woman raped while others looked on and did nothing to help in the 1988 film *The Accused*. Yet the public horror in this case concerned not only the failure of others to act and report the attack. Rather, what was especially shocking was that word of the sexual assault had spread by text messages around the school dance, and that a crowd of more than twenty people came to watch the sexual assault – with some filming on mobile phones, and some joining in the assault itself.

The police officer's questioning of why witnesses did not feel compelled to help this young girl is a form of lay interrogation into our shared social conditions relating to mutual obligations, moral sentiments and ethical behaviour. Yet curiously his comment also deflects attention from what these witnesses did, in fact, feel compelled to do. That is to say, while a young girl was severely beaten, repeatedly raped and dehumanized, a group of people crowded around and chose to film the attack on mobile phones. While police subsequently arrested several men in connection with the rape, onlookers of the assault were immune to prosecution for failure to phone 911 and report the attack under Californian state law. Police checks were later conducted to see if any of the filmed footage had been posted on Internet sites such as YouTube or Facebook.

As regards the critique of society and the social, what can be gleaned from this horrific attack on a young, defenceless teenager? The main critique, in both social science and public political debate, is that society is on the verge of collapse. The contemporary age, so it would seem, involves what one might call a transition from order to disorder, from stability to chaos, from sociability to unsociability. This is the critical sensibility that society in the twenty-first century is irrevocably damaged, rudderless, immoral, terroristic and, indeed, evil.

However the theory of society we have expounded in this book demonstrates the limitations of such judgements, and in particular the idea that there is some irreversible wedge between society and sociability, the social and the sublime. There are of course many instances of socialities of destruction and evil, ranging from the brutalities of gang rape to the carnage of political genocide. To acknowledge the social powers of destruction and the death-drive, however, is not necessarily to hold that we have entered a new a-social condition. Rather, this book has sought to outline a theory of the complexity of the social moving beyond final determinations or categorizations of society. The upshot of this is that sociology can acknowledge the deleterious impacts of destructive socialities without supposing that they are everywhere supreme. Again, this is largely because social life rests upon a profound contextualization – ideologies, technologies, assemblages or networks – for its production, reproduction and transformation. In respect of the brutal gang rape of a teenager we have been examining, this means – among other things – that people will differ on the question of social circumstances, conditions and consequences surrounding the attack. For example, such was the shock in the community of Richmond following the attack that various local calls for a re-assertion of structured society were heard. This commentary ranged from editorial observation in the *San Francisco Chronicle*, in which it was argued the attack was carried out by 'a roving pack of vicious animals, and in a civilized society, vicious animals are put down',[2] to demands for vigilante justice against the attackers and bystanders. By contrast, others responded in terms of the societal logics of solidarity, with demands for increased community support of its citizens. This ranged from new school volunteer groups to demands for improved communal security (such as the installation of surveillance cameras and increased lighting within the local school). Still others responded differently, arguing for novel kinds of social innovation and societal creativity – such as the broadening of legal criteria when failure to report a crime results in criminal prosecution.[3]

In a broader context, the debate about whether our sympathy for the suffering of others has any relationship to our physical proximity to the victim is long standing. Is pity determined by our relationship to the victim, for example, a kinship relationship? Indeed it was perfectly captured in the New Testament parable of the Good Samaritan where the man who has been robbed receives help, not from the religious authorities, but from a stranger. The story, which has become the universal model of charity, raises in an acute form questions about the obligations we may or may not have to strangers and the expectations that victims may have for help. The parable pinpoints the problem of an unequal exchange relationship. Should we feel pity towards the poor and should the poor feel a sense of gratitude towards those who are benevolent? It also, as we have considered this issue earlier in this study, brings into focus the probability that the

deeply injured may well feel resentment against those who offer
them pity.

These questions constitute the central topic of an influential
work by the French sociologist Luc Boltanski on suffering at a
distance.[4] The problem of suffering is to some extent inextricably
bound up with vision. The Good Samaritan sees the suffering
of the man at the roadside and hence suffering tends inevitably
to raise the moral problem of the visibility of suffering and the
prospect that we might enjoy a benefit from the sight of suffering
because we feel grateful that we are not also victims. This question of spectatorship has been an important theme in the study
of suffering from Adam Smith in the *Theory of Moral Sentiments*
and in Rousseau's *Émile* and *Confessions*. As we have noted in our
previous reflections on Rousseau, Goffman and MacIntyre, the
metaphor of society as theatre was the setting for much specula-
tion about sentiments. If society is not just a metaphorical theatre,
but an actual spectacle then the problem of suffering becomes an
acutely modern issue.

In this final section of our study of society, we have played with
yet another metaphor – society as elastic. Following Boltanski's
account, the media in modern society have made the spectacle of
suffering a regular aspect of our daily consumption of news and
information. Whereas the Good Samaritan sees the actual suffering of the man who he passes on the roadside, we watching our
daily serving of TV news witness any amount of human suffering
– famines in Africa, bloodshed in Libya, flood victims in Australia
and Brazil, or bombings in Iraq. There is one argument of course
that as a result we have become deaf to the cries of the unfortunate
because we are saturated by examples of human misery. In addition, we are less affected psychologically by 'distant suffering' to
quote the title of Boltanski's book. In a situation where we are
burdened by the miseries of the past (such as the Holocaust of the
European Jews) and by the future problems of the planet (such
as the consequences of global warming for the Pacific islanders),
how can we find space for pity? Boltanski argues that our moral
obligations should be concentrated not on accusations about past
suffering or justifications for actions oriented towards the future,
but solidly concentrated on a 'politics of the present'.

One underlying problem in this debate is therefore the very elasticity of society and consequently the thinness of any sense of obligation to the present in terms of time and space. In the elastic society, our social obligations are thin and cool rather than, as in a sticky society, thick and hot.

Overall our argument is that sociabilities, socialities and the social are not incommensurable realms in the twenty-first century, forever fractured by catastrophic narratives of the collapse of society. There are instead different viewpoints or idioms on the institutional stitching of 'societies' and 'individuals', of 'macro' and 'micro' levels of analysis. There are various trajectories or movements of the social in this connection, which we have mapped in terms of the tripartite logics of structure, solidarity and creation. There is, however, surely little doubt that horrific social events in the twenty-first century – such as the Californian gang rape of an innocent schoolgirl in 2009 – are stretching sociological categories of understanding to breaking point. For this brutal attack is one – and sadly only one among many recent sexual attacks involving new information technologies[5] – in which the idioms of structure, solidarity and creation can only be cast in the negative. That is to say, each of these ideologies or registers can only respond to such horrific social events with an array of general claims as to the 'absence' or 'lack' of structuring properties – loss of structure; erosion of solidarity; or, corrosion of creative social action. The appeal to idioms of structure, solidarity and creation thus occurs only to indict social practices for what they are missing. There is, it should be emphasized, no automatic connection between loss of solidarity and brutal acts, since honour killings of daughters by fathers (for example in rural Pakistan or in a town in the British Midlands) appears to be a function of solidarity – perhaps too much solidarity in which disobedience is punished with violence.

Throughout this book we have, among other things, reviewed the complex, contradictory ways in which current global transformations – from the global electronic economy to new information technologies – undermine the ideological powers of the registers of structure, solidarity and creation. For example, the category of society as structure, or upper-case society, has been brought low in our own time of multicultural communities, cultural hybridization and postmodern relativism. In Chapter 1, we examined various political forms through which re-assertions of society as structure are today enunciated, principally in relation to the war on terror and the advent of processes of enclavement. Similarly with the idiom of society as solidarity, our argument has been that recent global transformations have undermined what we call 'sticky societies' – that is, societies in which there is sufficient societal glue to over-ride conflicting interests around economic or political power. Sticky societies are ones in which citizens are held together by the thick ties of locality, language and culture. Changes that have to a large measure been brought about by globalization have dissolved the sticky ties of national communities leaving individuals free to migrate (within the constraints imposed by the global bureaucracy around the management of work permits and visas). The massive movement of rural workers out of the countryside into the mega-cities of East Asia and Southeast Asia, for example, has done much to undermine the family system and filial piety, but it has also left an atomized, exploited and disconnected urban population of workers. Keeping this floating population of rural migrants in full-time employment is a major task facing countries as different as Malaysia and China.[6]

Against this sociological backdrop, we thus conclude the book by considering some possible trajectories of society and the social in the twenty-first century that challenge or outstrip the registers of structure, solidarity and creation. Our aim is to make, albeit in a partial and provisional fashion, some contributions to the further development of a social science of social futures. We thus now describe some such possible futures – no doubt more abound – for societies in the coming century.

Feral Societies

One emergent condition and future trajectory for the social in the twenty-first century is that which we term, elaborating upon recent research in political science, 'feral societies'. This notion of society as feralization refers in general terms to the disorientating, destructive personal and social impacts of globalism, transnationalism and neoliberalism. More specifically, feral society is closely connected to the rise of civil conflicts, crime and incivility. If contemporary societies cannot find adequate solutions to political issues around multiculturalism, ageing populations, declining tax basis, youth unemployment and social solidarity, it is perhaps not hard to imagine that the mega-cities of North America, Europe, Asia and elsewhere will become ungovernable. With the erosion of the public sphere, the decline of social welfare, the growth in various forms of poverty (the working poor, the underemployed and the unemployable) and the disappearance of welfare safety nets, there is an increasing prospect of urban unrest. In this emerging scenario of sporadic urban violence, the feralization of cities in particular is an area where state power is ineffective in the slums, and the state has failed to protect its citizens.[7]

In this connection, modern cities are frequently the sites of urban insurgency which seeks to incapacitate governments by the use of sheer violence. Insurgents typically recruit from university students and middle-class intellectuals, and typically operate on a local or national scale. The Symbionese Liberation Army and the Red Army Faction are characteristic illustrations, but modern insurgencies have become more global seeking funding from global terrorist organizations, often bringing neighbouring states into the conflict. The terrorist attack on Mumbai illustrates the changing nature of such insurgency strategies. New techniques also became familiar in the 1990s, namely the car bomb and suicide bombing. While civilian casualties are often the consequence of urban violence, terrorist attacks aim to disrupt the essential functions of a city by destroying its communication, transport and energy systems. In Nigeria and Mexico, terrorists target basic utilities and supplies, especially oil and gas supplies. With globalization, there is now a level of incivility in many states, and political scientists have referred to the emergence of 'feral cities' to capture the decay of urban spaces With urban decay and the growth of no-go areas in modern cities, the creation of safe zones or security enclaves is one obvious response to these dilemmas.

Modern societies are vulnerable to attack, and becoming more so. Population density, urban propinquity, modern transport systems, the global distribution of small arms and explosives, the anonymity of city life, and the presence of large, typically alienated, diasporic communities has produced a social environment that is difficult to police and is exposed to terrorism from small terrorist groups with devolved authority structures. The war zones in Iraq, Afghanistan, Chechnya, Somalia and the Sudan are examples of such instability in the Third World, but attacks on cities are perhaps better illustrations of the social fragility we are describing: the attack on Mumbai, 7/11 in London, the Madrid bombings and, of course, the attack on the Twin Towers in New York. The response to this terrorist threat has been to enhance the process of securitization, to intensify border controls and to extend the surveillance of populations. Although Western cities have experienced civil unrest and terrorist attacks, the urban instability in the developing world is obviously far more acute and persistent. Karachi is an instructive example. The city has grown from 450,000 in 1947 to an estimated eighteen million today; it suffers from a mixture of ethnic conflict between Pushtun and Mohajir communities, organized crime, a weak state and sectarian conflict. We can summarize this development of new forms of violence and social responses under the heading of the feral society. The instabilities of feral society appear to be connected with demography – the growth of large cohorts of unemployed and unemployable young men in societies that are being transformed by both general consumerism and widespread corruption. Their lack of resources as disprivileged youth is highlighted by the wealth around them resulting in a generalized resentment.

Although urban violence and civil disturbance has been associated with Third World or developing societies, the riots that shook London in August 2011 illustrate the vulnerability of any large city in the West. The causes of these riots have important political implications and hence there was an inconclusive debate about what had caused them. While the coalition government argued that they were examples of criminality pure and simple, the Labour opposition, while not denying the facts of criminality, argued that they were a response to the austerity measures of the government in response to the economic crisis. The Prime Minister David

Cameron claimed the riots were examples of moral failure in Britain, resulting from broken families and inadequate discipline.

The rioters were drawn from a wide cross-section of British society. They included students, social workers, unemployed kids from ethnic minorities and organized criminal gangs. As a result simple explanations of the riots will not capture the complexity of their composition. They were seen to be a rational if negative response to the austerity package of the government and a failure of family discipline. They were seen to be examples of mindless fun, because the rioters were seen to be enjoying themselves. They were also seen to be irrational. One rioter had stolen one bottle of water, for which he received a police sentence. There was general criticism of the failure of the police to control the crowds and make arrests. In summary the riots were seen to be the result of boredom on the part of young people, the widespread availability of alcohol in British cities, unemployment and low educational achievement and broken families and lack of discipline. Psychologists argued that bystanders were simply caught up in the exuberance of crowd behaviour.

However, three aspects of the riots were instructive. The disturbances did not take place in the affluent areas of London and Birmingham, but in the disprivileged inner-urban areas from which the rioters came. The disturbances were targeted at their own communities. Some commentators in the media compared the mentality of the rioters to the dystopian figures in Anthony Burgess's *A Clockwork Orange*. Secondly, they were targeted at stores carrying cell phones, sports wear and television sets, and were as a consequence described in the press as 'shopping riots'. Finally, they were also organized by the use of Twitter. These riots therefore illustrate our argument about the nature of modern societies. Although modern sociality lacks any strong sense of social solidarity or an absence of stickiness, they nevertheless exhibit a certain creativity through the use of electronic communication technology. Of course creativity can be either positive – assembling networks for the disabled – or negative – facilitating the organization of urban riots.

Although there were several deaths resulting from the riots, we do not want to exaggerate their significance. Criminologists in Britain have pointed out that, contrary to the views of Mr Cameron, offending is at a historically low level in Britain. Our argument is that the riots illustrate the vulnerability of modern society in which an incident – in the London riots the shooting of a man by the police – can result in widespread rioting and looting across many cities. It also illustrates the fact that urban instability is not confined to Mumbai or Karachi, but extends to cities such as London, Paris and Los Angeles. The problem of the feral society is a global issue.

Entertainment Societies

Another emergent condition and future trajectory for the social in the twenty-first century is that which we term 'entertainment societies'. In *The Sense and Non-Sense of Revolt*, Julia Kristeva traces the decline of European cultures of revolt and critical counter-cultures, and writes of the growing supremacy of 'the culture of entertainment, the culture of performance, the culture of the show'.[8] Contemporary entertainment culture, for Kristeva, is inextricably linked to the surge of consumer society. The seemingly unstoppable globalization of consumerism goes hand in hand with a massive surge in online entertainments and mediated spectacles, all of which support complacent forms of individualism and identity. Moreover, Kristeva argues that even the socially excluded (the unemployed, the poor in the projects, foreigners) are increasingly fed on a cultural diet of mediated entertainments, which seductively pass off the lived texture of daily life as autonomous and free.

Various social theorists have tried to understand the global transformations associated with the rise of entertainment societies. Zygmunt Bauman describes in detail the wholesale shift from 'societies of production' to 'societies of consumption'. Manuel Castells writes of the spectacular growth of an 'Internet galaxy', in which lives are lived against the backdrop of complex informational networks. The American author and feminist Barbara Ehrenreich talks of the socio-economic arrival of a precarious life centred on low wages, insecurity of employment and under-employment.

But there are other sociological factors that should also be briefly considered when critiquing the rise of entertainment societies. Whereas classical liberalism assumed that the employed person, uninhibited by the state and directly involved in the market, would be an active and autonomous agent, the contemporary citizen emerges instead as merely a consumer disconnected from civil society, living passively in a consumer society. On this view, modern citizens consume politics rather than acting out political life through an information network; moreover, their connections with the market are no longer mediated by trade unions or artisans associations, because their working lives are likely to be based on casual and short-term employment in global corporations. Facebook arguably thus becomes society for the 'entertained consumer', and this is potentially the case for increasing numbers of people today.[9] As regards the theme of disconnection from civil society for those addicted to the online, entertainment society, recent scientific studies reported by *The New York Times* underscore that the ability to concentrate over long periods of time is undermined by the 'twitterization' of communication – that is, beyond short bursts of information people feel bored.[10]

There is an important political context to this rise of the entertainment society as well. In the UK throughout the 1990s there was considerable interest in the notion of the consumer-citizen, especially from the Blair New Labour government. This idea was presented as a new principle by which service delivery in the public sector could be greatly improved by competition and by an emphasis on freedom of choice. Citizens would no longer be mere recipients of services delivered by large opaque bureaucratic institutions; they would instead exercise choice in such key areas as education and health. In fact, this idea went back to the 1979 government of Prime Minister Margaret Thatcher, who wanted to roll back the state and give more power to the individual. With the rise of public choice theory, the aim was to make state bureaucracies more efficient and more accountable. These laudable aims were combined with a hostility to 'the scrounger' and praise for 'the entrepreneurial spirit'.[11] Faced with the global financial crisis which spread across the world in 2008, the notion of active consumption has acquired a largely hollow meaning with rising credit-card indebtedness, a liquidity crisis, a failure of major financial institutions, high unemployment and growing income inequality. As a result, the consumer-citizen has increasingly been viewed as merely the passive observer of a society that maintains social order and stimulates the economy through large-scale spectacles such as the World Cup, American Idol and the Olympic Games. These spectacles are themselves often engineered or promoted by politicians who have themselves become media celebrities. These social and economic changes provide the sociological justification for defining the modern world in terms of 'entertainment societies'.

Catastrophic Societies

In *Our Final Century?* the British cosmologist and astrophysicist Martin Rees argues that the chances of humanity surviving the twenty-first century are only 50/50.[12] Reviewing new threats of destruction in the biological, environmental and nuclear spheres, Rees writes dramatically of cosmic collisions, deadly viruses, nanobots and bioterrorism – all of which might destroy planet earth. A study in the possible pathways of a dying culture, *Our Final Century?* might at first glance strike readers as a combination of scientific futurology and science fiction. However, it is perhaps worth noting that Sir Martin Rees's scientific credentials are impeccable: he is Astronomer Royal as well as President of the UK's Royal Society. Yet his voice is only one (albeit highly distinguished) of a growing choir warning of disasters which threaten our societies and their possible futures.

In this connection, John Urry speaks of a 'new catastrophism' in both academic and public thinking about the future of societies.[13] This kind of thinking about societal catastrophe trades in both current epochal transformations (global warming, climate change, environmental disasters) and fantasy experiments as regards the emergence of a 'new dark age'. As Urry writes, 'the twentieth century in the rich North was a short period in human history; and there are no guarantees that the increasing prosperity, wealth, movement, knowledge and connectivity of that period (in the rich North) will continue and certainly not necessarily in anything like the same form'.

Building upon Urry's 'new catastrophism', we argue that grasping the possible trajectories of catastrophic societies depends on a sense of discontinuity and indeed radical rupture, on limits in progress, economic wealth and the good life, as well as on a society rich in resources. In *Collapse: How Societies Choose to Fail or Survive*, the American scientist Jared Diamond underscores the fundamental significance of environmental problems to the disintegration of societal orders.[14] From the collapse of the Maya in Mesoamerica to societal stagnation in modern Montana, Diamond identifies eight environmental drivers common to societal disasters:

1. deforestation and habitat destruction;
2. soil problems;
3. water management problems;
4. over-hunting;
5. over-fishing;
6. effects of introduced species on native species;
7. human population growth;
8. the increased per-capita impact of people.

For Diamond, when populations outstrip the carrying capacities of their environment (especially energy resources) societies fail.

In what follows, we note some of the central drivers conditioning catastrophic societies. Firstly, and most potentially catastrophically, there are the hugely destructive consequences of global warming and climate change. While political analyses of climate change have taken different forms (and while the scientific evidence for climate change is questioned by many), the large bulk of this research has emphasized that globally catastrophic processes are at work. From one angle, this is hardly surprising. As global temperatures in the twenty-first century are expected by the international scientific community to rise by four to seven degrees celsius, rather than the previously predicted two to three degrees, it is increasingly evident to many that we are fast approaching a 'tipping point' which spells the demise of high-carbon societies. The Stern Review states that increasing greenhouse gases in the earth's atmosphere will result in dramatic changes in sea and land temperatures worldwide, droughts, heatwaves, tropical cyclones and other extreme weather events. In terms of the global order, the catastrophe for societies is that climate change will cost millions of lives in ecological disasters and associated wars. Especially consequential here are the complex relations between climate change and global inequalities. Developing societies, and the poorest people who inhabit them, are especially vulnerable to climate change; there is much research which powerfully underscores that climate change will worsen the socio-economic tensions that already derive from global inequalities, that developing societies will bear the brunt of climate change disasters, and that this will in turn carry further destructive consequences for the global social order.

Secondly, there is the issue of energy security on a global scale and its multiple catastrophic consequences for contemporary societies. The peaking of oil supplies, dated as far back by some experts as 1970, is especially consequential for the future of manufacturing, agricultural processes and urbanization. Put simply, there will not be enough oil, or gas supplies, to fuel worldwide systems of production and consumption. For, in addition to high levels of energy consumption of Western countries, both the Chinese and Indian economies (termed by some commentators 'Chindia') have witnessed dramatic increases in their consumption of oil and gas. Add to this the geopolitical instabilities of various oil-producing countries, of continued surges and shocks in oil prices, and it is evident that there is gigantic potential for an increased number of failed societies. Reflecting on both climate change and energy security as a springboard for future global threats, Anthony Giddens writes: 'Our civilization could self-destruct – no doubt about it – and with awesome consequences, given its global reach. Doomsday is no longer a religious concept, a day of spiritual reckoning, but a possibility imminent in our society and economy. If unchecked, climate change alone could produce enormous human suffering. So also could the drying up of the energy resources upon which so many of our capacities are built. There remains the possibility of large-scale conflicts, perhaps involving the use of weapons of mass destruction.'[15]

Finally, there are emergent global threats to society resulting from concerns over food and water security. This last point is, in some ways, directly connected to issues of climate change and energy security. This is because food production depends very largely upon hydrocarbon fuels (from crop maintenance to harvesting and processing to transportation). Thus against the backdrop of oil reserves running out, 'food could be priced out of the reach of the majority of our population. Hunger could become commonplace in every corner of the world, including your own neighbourhood.' And yet food and water security also loom as global threats to the future of societies because of the very significant increases in world population: the planet is currently expanding by approximately 900 million people per decade, and is expected to reach 9.1 billion persons by 2050. In this worldwide context, water is likely to become an ever more scarce resource. Indeed, some commentators now speak of 'peak ecological water', in which it is estimated that only 0.007 per cent of the planet's water is available for human consumption. Much will depend on the development of global governance and transnational policy measures for responding to issues of food and water security, but it seems clear enough that severe water shortages and significant rising food costs have the potential to unleash deep societal problems.

Postscript: Social Futures

Historians and sociologists tend to disagree about what is 'new'. While historians emphasize continuity, sociologists focus on changes and transitions. In this study of the evolution of the concept of society, we have sought to strike a balance between recognizing the continuities, while respecting the emergence of new issues and ideas. The idea of society as community probably has its origins in the Christian notion of the Church, the body of Christ. Nevertheless the medieval Church did not have TV evangelism or mega-churches or Internet sites. In this study of social relations and especially in the idea of social elasticity – of thin, spaceless and cool connectivity – we think we are looking at emerging social orders that have few or no precursors.

In this eruption of new and creative social relations, there can be clearly many examples of how traditional practices can survive and merge with the new. Let us take a Chinese example. In traditional Chinese culture, the dead ancestors were respected and celebrated by relatives who, on visiting the graves of their dead kinfolk, would burn paper objects representing meat, fruit or wine. A large industry creating money sprang up in China around the belief that the ancestors would need money in the after-life. As a sign of modernity *wantchinatimes* reported on 7 April 2011, that the Chinese are now burning paper copies of iPhone, iPad and other technological gadgets on the assumption that the ancestors will want to communicate with these in the after world. These 'underworld gifts' can be taken to represent the elasticity of the Chinese spirit world and to show the strange combination of the ancient and the contemporary.

In our view the growth of instant communication has produced entirely new opportunities for the construction of global networks and social structures that have no connections with the historical societies of the past. We have charted both the dangers and the opportunities that are emerging under the heading of social creation. The dangers are obvious. There are strong indications that many cities in Mexico, in Central Africa and in South Asia are becoming feral cityscapes. As the cost of modern weaponry declines, terrorism will spread through much of the urban world. Bombings in recent years in London, Madrid and Mumbai are illustrations of how small and decentralized terrorist gangs can inflict significant civilian casualties through the use of microtechnology. The mobile phone is a basic necessity of localized violence. The result is a paradoxical world where terrorism rides on the back of the fluidity and elasticity of modern societies and at the same time, in response to globalization, social enclaves spring up around the world – through the creation of privatized armies and police forces; the mobilization of privatized security services; the multiplication of permits, work cards, visas and passports; and by the simple device of building walls to encircle both national and domestic spaces. The enclave society and globalization are twin processes of social change. While such violence may appear to be a mere continuity from a historian's perspective – the assassins and the thugs were creatures of ancient civilizations – the Twin Towers tragedy has taken air-borne urban violence to a new level of civilian destruction.

There is another change we can anticipate. Many of the ideas about society we have examined in this book – such as the notions about civil society, the private/public division, secularization, voluntary association and the distinction between community and association – were products of particular transformations in the West. Most of these ideas were associated with the growth of autonomous cities, bourgeois liberties, democratic representation and so forth. These ideas then spread around the world with the growth of Western imperialism, global trade and modernization. Liberal ideas and sociological theories entered Japan and China in the late nineteenth century as Herbert Spencer's vision of the individual and the state were taken up by intellectuals committed to the modernization of their societies. With the defeat of Japan, American ideas about democratic institutions were imposed through constitutional change. Marxist ideas about revolutionary transformations of the social were embraced in Cambodia and Vietnam, often of course merging with national ideas about social forms. It is unlikely that this transfer of ideas about the social will continue to be one way. With the current economic crisis in the West and the apparent unstoppable growth of the so-called BRICs (Brazil, Russia, India and China), this transfer of Western liberalism will change significantly.

Many sociologists believe that globalization offers new opportunities for cosmopolitanism. With globalization, it is assumed that the new opportunities for dialogue may give rise to a post-national consciousness. One obvious example is the rise of human rights not simply as a legal structure but as a moral vision of the world or, in the words of the American historian Samuel Moyn, 'the last utopia'.[16] Human rights hold out the cosmopolitan hope that we can avoid the horrors of genocide by the creation for example of international courts. These developments are consistent with our notion of social creation – the constant ongoing construction of new social relations and institutions. But we also see inevitable counter-movements in the contemporary growth of nationalism in response to worldwide labour migration; for example, restrictions on the movement of peoples through migration are being increased in societies as diverse as the United States, Denmark, the United Kingdom, Italy and Finland. Enclavement appears to be the constant companion of social elasticity.

It is difficult to be optimistic about the rise of a shared global consciousness. What appears more likely is global civil instability. The causes of social unrest include: steeply rising food prices as more and more vegetable material (soybean, grain and cassava) are used to produce fuel; high unemployment among young men who with low educational achievement cannot compete in the global labour market; the negative social consequences of global warming and environmental degradation; the disruption brought about by global disease from HIV to SARS and H1N1; and the political instability of so-called 'new wars' brought about by warlords and drug barons.

We might view this as a neo-Malthusian future in which the contradiction between the reduction in arable land available to produce food and the growth in the global population is eventually solved by new technologies. If we imagine as a science-fiction experiment a situation in which humans will no longer enjoy 'natural foods' but live off synthetically produced edible crops and that available land could be simply increased by building platforms to create sea-borne societies, then one could imagine the flourishing of new societies. However as many have argued (such as Fukuyama) this combination of circumstances would produce a post-human world and 'society' would once more be radically transformed.

Notes

Preface

1 See Turner, B. S. (ed.) 2009, *The Routledge International Handbook of Globalization Studies*, Routledge, London and New York; Lemert, C., Elliott, A., Chaffee, D. and Hsu E. (eds) 2010, *Globalization*, Routledge, London and New York.

2 Beck, U. 1997, *The Reinvention of Politics*, Polity, Cambridge.

Introduction

1 Parsons, T. 1951, *The Social System*, Free Press, Glencoe, Illinois.

2 Small, A. W. 1912, 'General sociology', *The American Journal of Sociology*, Vol. 18, No. 2, pp. 200–14.

3 Williams, R. 1976, *Keywords: A Vocabulary of Culture and Society*, Fontana, London, pp. 243–7.

4 See Lemert, C. 2004, *Sociology After the Crisis*, 2nd edition, Paradigm, Boulder; and also 2004, *The Structural Lie: Small Clues to Global Things*, Paradigm, Boulder.

5 Keay, D. 1987, 'Aids, education and the year 2000!', *Women's Own*, October 31.

6 Tönnies, F. 1963, *Community and Society*, Harper and Row, New York, p. 161

7 Ibid., p. 162.

8 Parsons, T. 2007, *American Society: Toward a Theory of Societal Community*, ed. Giuseppe Sciortino, Paradigm, Boulder.

9 Durkheim, É. 1964, *The Division of Labour in Society*, Free Press, Glencoe, Illinois, pp. 146–7.

10 Nisbet, R. 1993, 'Society', in William Outhwaite (ed.) *The Blackwell Companion of Modern Social Thought,* Blackwell, Oxford, pp. 640–2.

11 Dewey, J. 1927, *The Public and its Problems*, Holt, New York.

12 See Turner, B. S. 2004, *The New Medical Sociology: Social Forms of Health and Illness*, W. W. Norton, New York.

13 Lockwood, D. 1992, *Solidarity and Schism: 'The Problem of Disorder' in Durkheimian and Marxist Sociology,* Clarendon Press, Oxford, p.10. Same page for following quotation.

14 Outhwaite, W. 2006, *The Future of Society*, Blackwell, Oxford.

15 Touraine, A. 2000, *Can We Live Together? Equality and Difference,* Polity, Cambridge.

16 Ibid., p.194.

17 See Luhmann, N. 1997, 'Globalization or world society: How to conceive of modern society', *International Review of Sociology* 7(1): 67–80.

18 Gane, N. 2004, *The Future of Social Theory*, Continuum, London, p. 2.

1 Society as Structure

1 Hegel, G. 1896, *The Philosophy of Right*, Bell, London, section 261.

2 Marx, K. 1974, 'Critique of Hegel's doctrine of the state', in *Karl Marx: Early Writings*, trans. G. Benton and R. Livingstone, Penguin, Harmondsworth, pp. 57–198.

3 Lefort, C. *Les Formes de l'histoire*, cited in Thompson, J. B. 1984, *Studies in the Theory of Ideology*, Polity, Cambridge, p. 25.

4 Marx, K. 1975, *Karl Marx: Early Writings*, trans. G. Benton and R. Livingstone, Penguin, Harmondsworth, p. 234.

5 Eagleton, T. 2000, *The Idea of Culture*, Blackwell, Oxford, p. 55.

6 Durkheim, E. 1964, *Division of Labor in Society*, trans. G. Simpson, Free Press, New York, p. 226.

7 See Lemert, C. 2004, *Durkheim's Ghosts*, Cambridge University Press, Cambridge.

8 Berlin, I. 2003, *Freedom and its Betrayal*, Princeton University Press, Princeton, p. 49.

9 Nisbet, R. 1967, *The Sociological Tradition*, Heinemann Educational Books, London.

10 Parsons, T. 1991, *The Social System*, Routledge, London.

11 On the importance of Weber on Parsons, see Wearne, B. C. 1989, *The Theory and Scholarship of Talcott Parsons*, Cambridge University Press, Cambridge.

12 Among the key texts are Giddens, A. (ed.) 1986, *Durkheim on Politics and the State*, Polity, Cambridge; Lacroix, B. 1981, *Durkheim et le politique*, Presses de l'Universite de Montreal, Montreal; Pearce, F. 1989, *The Radical Durkheim*, Unwin Hyman, London.

13 Durkheim, E. 1992, *Professional Ethics and Civic Morals*, B. S. Turner (ed.), Routledge, London.

14 Miller, W. W. 2002, 'Morality and ethics', in W. S. F. Pickering (ed.), *Durkheim Today*, Berghahn Books, New York, p. 59.

15 Alexander, J. 1992, 'General theory in the postpositivist mode', in S. Seidman and D. Wagner (eds), *Postmodernism and Social Theory*, Blackwell, Oxford, p. 327.

16 Nisbet, R. 1966, *The Sociological Tradition*, Basic Books, New York.

17 This section is largely drawn from arguments set out in Turner, B. S. 1987, 'A note on nostalgia', *Theory, Culture and Society*, Vol. 4, No. 1, pp. 147–56.

18 See Mennell, S. 1985, *All Manners of Food, Eating and Taste in England and France from the Middle Ages to the Present*, Blackwell, Oxford.

19 See Elliott, A. 2004, *Social Theory Since Freud*, Routledge, London.

20 See Abercrombie, N., Hill S. and Turner B. S. 1980, *The Dominant Ideology Thesis*, George Allen and Unwin, London.

21 See among others MacIntyre, A. 1953, *Marxism: An Interpretation*, SCM Press, London; MacIntyre, A. 1962, 'A mistake about causality in social science' in P. Laslett and W. G. Runciman (eds) *Philosophy Politics and Society*, Basil Blackwell, Oxford, pp. 48–70; MacIntyre, A. 1967, *Secularization and Moral Change*, Oxford University Press, Oxford; MacIntyre, A. 1998, *A Short History of Ethics: A History of Moral Philosophy from the Homeric Age to the Twentieth Century*, Routledge and Kegan Paul, London.

22 See Alexander, J. 2006, *The Civil Sphere*, Oxford University Press, Oxford.

23 Inwood, M. 1992, *A Hegel Dictionary*, Blackwell, Oxford.

24 Weber cited in Radkau, 2009, p. 414.

25 Habermas, J. 1991, *The Structural Transformation of the Public Sphere*, trans. Thomas Burger with the assistance of Frederick Lawrence, MIT Press, Cambridge, Massachusetts.

26 Durkheim, É. 1964, *The Elementary Forms of the Religious Life*, Free Press, New York.

27 Hervieu-Leger, D. 2000, *Religion as a Chain of Memory*, Polity, Cambridge.

28 Aspects of this argument first appeared in Turner B. S 2011, *Religion and the Modern World: Citizenship, Secularization and the State*, Cambridge University Press, Cambridge.

   MacIntyre's vision of the past has been criticized as simply romantic while others have said that patriarchy was an important feature of the society that MacIntyre would have to defend. More damaging still is the argument from Nussbaum, M. 1989, 'Recoiling from reason', *New York Review of Books* 36(9), that his account of classical Greece and in particular his interpretation of Aristotle cannot be sustained. She contends that Aristotle saw the good, not arising from a single cultural source, but from many points and places. In short, Aristotle's vision was cosmopolitan – or at least not as narrow as MacIntyre suggests.

29 Our position here is largely informed by the research of David Held, who contends that globalism does not erode the national state as much as reconfigure it. See Held, D. 2004, *Global Covenant*, Polity, Cambridge.

30 Torpey, J. 2000, *The Invention of the Passport: Surveillance, Citizenship and the State*, Cambridge University Press, Cambridge.

31 Sassen, S. 1999, *Guests and Aliens*, The New Press, New York.

32 Turner, B. S. 2007, 'The Enclave Society: Towards a sociology of immobility', *European Journal of Social Theory*, Vol. 10, No. 2, pp. 287–303.

33 See Agamben, G. 1998, *Homo Sacer: Sovereign Power and Bare Life*, Stanford University Press, Stanford, California.

34 Mazower, M. 1999, *Dark Continent: Europe's Twentieth Century*, Penguin Books, London, p. 97.

35 Foucault, M. 1989, *Madness and Civilization*, Routledge, London.

36 Turner, B. S. 2006, 'Social capital, trust and offensive behaviour', in

A. von Hirsch and A.P. Semester (eds), *Incivilities: Regulating Offensive Behaviour*, Hart, Oxford, pp. 219–38.

37 See Butler, J. 2006, *Precarious Life: The Powers of Mourning and Violence*, Verso, London.

38 Bourdieu, P. 2000, *The Weight of the World: Social Suffering in Contemporary Society*, Polity, Cambridge.

2 Society as Solidarity

1 Hutcheson, F., 1897, *An Inquiry Concerning Moral Good and Evil*, in Selby-Bigge, L. A., *British Moralists*, Vol. 1, p. 17.

2 Ferguson, A. 1767, *An Essay on the History of Civil Society*, Dublin, p. 53.

3 See Bellah, R. N. 1999, 'Max Weber and world-denying love: a look at the historical sociology of religion', *Journal of the American Academy of Religion*, Vol. 67, No. 2, pp. 277–304.

4 Habermas, J. 2001, *The Postnational Constellation: Political Essays*, Polity, Cambridge, p. 21.

5 Alexander, J. 2001, 'The long and winding road: Civil repair of intimate injustice', *Sociological Theory*, Vol. 19, No. 3, pp. 371–400.

6 Habermas, J. 2001, *The Postnational Constellation: Political Essays*, Polity, Cambridge, p. 21.

7 Adair-Toteff, C. 1995, 'Ferdinand Tönnies: Utopian visionary', *Sociological Theory*, Vol. 13, No. 1, p. 61.

8 See Tönnies, F. 1920, *Karl Marx: Leben and Lehre*, Verlag, Berlin; Curtius, K. 1921, *Karl Marx: Life and Teachings*, Michigan State University, East Lansing.

9 Nietzsche, F. W. 1997, *Daybreak: Thoughts on the Prejudices of Morality*, M. Clark and B. Leite (eds), Cambridge University Press, Cambridge, pp. 48–9.

10 Taubes, J. 2004, *The Political Theology of Paul*, trans. D. Hollander, Stanford University Press, Stanford, California, p. 79.

11 Nietzsche, F. W. 2007, *Twilight of the Idols, with The Antichrist and Ecce Homo*, Wordsworth Editions Limited, Hertfordshire, p. 36.

12 Rose, G. 1993, *Judaism and Modernity: Philosophical Essays*, Blackwell, Oxford.

13 Ibid., p. 94.

14 Nietzsche, F. W. 1997, *Daybreak: Thoughts on the Prejudices of Morality*, M. Clark and B. Leite (eds), Cambridge University Press, Cambridge, p. 39.

15 Rose, G. 1993 *Judaism and Modernity: Philosophical Essays*, Blackwell, Oxford, p. 105.

16 Badiou, A. 2003, *Saint Paul: The Foundation of Universalism*, Stanford University Press, Stanford, California.

17 Taubes, 2004, *The Political Theology of Paul*.

18 Connolly, W. 1988, *Political Theory and Modernity*, Blackwell, Oxford, p. 161.

19 MacIntyre, A. 1967, *Secularization and Moral Change*, Oxford University Press, Oxford.

20 Held, D. 1980, *Introduction to Critical Theory: Horkheimer to Habermas*, University of California Press, Berkeley, California, p. 261.

21 Inwood, M. 1992, *A Hegel Dictionary*, Blackwell, Oxford, 1992.

22 Rojek, C. and Turner, B. S. 2001, *Society and Culture: Principles of Scarcity and Solidarity*, Sage, London.

23 Habermas, 2001, *The Postnational Constellation*.

24 Pensky, M. 1999, 'Jürgen Habermas and the antimonies of the intellectual', in *Habermas: A Critical Reader*, P. Dews (ed.), Blackwell, Oxford, p. 222.

25 Alexander, J. 2006, *The Civil Sphere*, Oxford University Press, New York and Oxford.

26 Rawls, J. 1999, *The Law of Peoples*, Harvard University Press, Cambridge, Massachusetts.

27 Ibid., p. 31.

28 Putnam, R. 2000, *Bowling Alone*, Simon and Schuster, New York.

29 Alexander, 2006, *The Civil Society*.

30 Ibid., p. 286.

31 Glazer, N. 1997, *We Are All Multiculturalists Now*, Harvard University Press, Cambridge, Massachusetts.

32 Steinberg, S. 1995, *Turning Back: The Retreat from Racial Justice in American Thought and Policy*, Beacon Press, Boston.

33 Alexander, 2006, *The Civil Society*.

34 Putnam, R. and Campbell, D. 2010, *American Grace: How Religion Divides and Unites Us*, Simon and Schuster, New York.

35 Ibid., p. 540.

36 Lockwood, D. 1992, *Solidarity and Schism: 'The Problem of Disorder' in Durkheimian and Marxist Sociology*, Clarendon Press, Oxford.

37 Etzioni, A. 1996, *The New Golden Rule: Community and Morality in a Democratic Society*, Basic Books, New York, p. 119.

38 Ibid., p. 122.

39 Ibid., p. 143.

40 Roberston, R. 1966, 'Values and globalization: Communitarianism and globality' in Luiz E. Soares (ed.) *Cultural Pluralism, Identity, and Globalization* UNESCO/ISSC/EDUCAM, pp. 73–96.

41 Anderson, Perry. 2002, 'Land Without Prejudice', *London Review of Books* 24 (6): 6–13.

42 For a more complex historical casting of globalism see Lemert, C., Elliott, A., Chaffee, D. and Hsu, E. (eds) 2010, *Globalization*, Routledge, London and New York.

3 Society as Creation

1 Castoriadis, C. 1991, *Philosophy, Politics, Autonomy*, Oxford University Press, Oxford, p. 3.

2 Simmel, G. 1896, 'Superiority and Subordination as Subject-Matter of Sociology', *American Journal of Sociology*, No. 2, p. 167.

3 Pyyhtinen, O. 2010, *Simmel and 'the Social'*, Palgrave, Basingstoke, p. 39.

4 Simmel, G. 1992, 'Soziologie der Sinne', cited in D. Frisby, *Simmel and Since*, Routledge, London, p. 14.

5 Simmel, G. 1992, 'Sociology Lectures', cited in D. Frisby, *Simmel and Since*, Routledge, London, p. 11.

6 Simmel, G. 1992, 'Zur Methodik der Sozialwissenschaft', cited in D. Frisby, *Simmel and Since*, Routledge, London, pp. 12–13.

7 Simmel, G. 2009, *Sociology. Inquiries into the Construction of Social Forms*, Brill, Leiden and Boston.

8 For more detailed treatments of Giddens's theory of structuration see Thompson, J. B. 1984, *Studies in the Theory of Ideology*, Polity, Cambridge, Chapter 5; and Elliott, A. 2003, *Critical Visions: New Directions in Social Theory*, Rowman and Littlefield, New York, Chapter 2.

9 Giddens, A. 1984, *The Constitution of Society*, Polity, Cambridge, pp. xxvi–xxvii.

10 Ibid., p. 26.

11 See Lemert, C. 2004, *Sociology After the Crisis*, 2nd edn, Paradigm Press, Boulder.

12 See Shusterman, R. (ed.) 1999, *Bourdieu: A Critical Reader,* Oxford, Blackwell.

13 Nietzsche, F. 1989, *On the Genealogy of Morals*, Vintage, London, pp. 498 and 550.

14 Thiele, L. P. 1990, *Friedrich Nietzsche and the Politics of the Soul: A Study of Heroic Individualism*, Princeton University Press, Princeton, N. J.

15 Turner, B. S. 1996, *For Weber: Essays on the Sociology of Fate*, Sage, London.

16 Hennis, W. 1987, *Max Webers Fragstellung: Studien zur Biographie des Werks*, Mohr, Tübingen.

17 Stauth, G. and Turner, B. S. 1998, *Nietzsche's Dance: Resentment, Reciprocity and Resistance in Social Life*, Blackwell, Oxford.

18 Conway, D. W. 1997, *Nietzsche and the Political*, Routledge, London.

19 Ansell-Pearson, K. 1994, *An Introduction to Nietzsche as Political Thinker: The Perfect Nihilist*, Cambridge University Press, Cambridge.

20 Foucault, M. 2003, *Society Must Be Defended*, Penguin, London.

21 Ibid., p. 25.

22 Foucault, M. 1995, *Discipline and Punish: The Birth of the Prison*, Vintage, New York.

23 Silk, M. S. and Stern, J. P. 1983, *Nietzsche on Tragedy*, Cambridge University Press, Cambridge, p. 284.

24 Stauth and Turner, 1998, *Nietzsche's Dance.*

25 See Elliott, A. 1999, *Social Theory and Psychoanalysis in Transition*, 2nd edn, Free Association Books, London, Chapter 1.

26 Freud writes that unconscious processes 'are not ordered temporally, are not altered by the passage of time; they have no reference to time at all'. 'The unconscious', *SE,* XIV, p.187.

27 Freud, S. 1940, *An Outline of Psycho-Analysis*, SE, XXIII, p.154.

28 Freud, S. 1917, 'Mourning and Melancholia', in *The Standard Edition of the Complete Psychological Works of Sigmund Freud*, The Hogarth Press, London, Vol. 14, pp. 239–60.

29 Freud, S. 1923, *The Ego and the Id*, in *The Standard Edition of the Complete Psychological Works of Sigmund Freud*, The Hogarth Press, London, Vol. 19, pp. 12–66.

30 Freud, S. 1917, 'Mourning and melancholia', p. 255.

31 Freud, S. 1923, *The Ego and the Id*, p. 30.

32 Wollheim, R. 1971, *Freud*, Fontana, London, p. 189.

33 Castoriadis, C. 1987, *The Imaginary Institution of Society*, Polity, Cambridge, p. 282.

34 Ibid., pp. 182–3.

35 Kristeva, J. 1989, *Black Sun: Depression and Melancholia*, Columbia University Press, New York.

36 Kristeva, J. 1993, *New Maladies of the Soul*, Columbia University Press, New York.

37 Kristeva, J. 2000, *Crisis of the European Subject*, Other Press, New York.

38 Kristeva, J. 1984, *Revolution in Poetic Language*, Columbia University Press, New York.

39 Kristeva, now Professor of Linguistics at the University of Paris VII, did her psychoanalytic training with Lacan. Already in her earliest theoretical work, however, she indicated a determination to move beyond the conceptual terrain of Lacanianism narrowly defined. For example, her doctoral dissertation, which was subsequently published as her first book, *Revolution in Poetic Language*, blends linguistics and psychoanalytical theory to advance a novel account of how pre-verbal experience – infantile, maternal, poetic – enters into, shapes, distorts and disrupts language through processes of art, literature and psychoanalysis. In her more recent work, which I trace throughout this book, Kristeva has turned away from Lacan and back to classical Freudianism, and especially toward Kleinian psychoanalysis. (See Smith, 1998; Elliott, 2003.)

40 Kristeva, J. 2001, *Melanie Klein*, Columbia Univeristy Press, New York, p. 140.

41 See, for example, Creeber, G. and Martin, R. 2008, *Digital Cultures: Understanding New Media*, Open University Press, Maidenhead; and Gere, C. 2009, *Digital Culture*, Reaktion Books, London.

42 Turkle, S. 1995, *Life on the Screen: Identity in the Age of the Internet*, Simon and Schuster, New York.

43 Poster, M. 1990, *The Mode of Information*, Polity, Cambridge, p. 128.

44 For a full-blown postmodern reckoning of how new information technologies facilitate the arrival of post-societal identities, see the collection ed. Holmes, D. 1997, *Virtual Politics: Identity and Community in Cyberspace*, Sage, London.

45 Drache, D. 2008, *Defiant Publics: The Unprecedented Reach of the Global Citizen*, Polity, Cambridge.

46 Mertes, T. 2010, 'Anti-globalization movements: From critiques to alternatives', in Turner, B. S. (ed.) *The Routledge International Handbook of Globalization Studies,* Routledge, London, pp. 77–95.

47 See Altman, R. C. and Haass, R. N. 2010, 'American profligacy and the American power: The consequences of fiscal irresponsibility', *Foreign Affairs* 89(6): 25–34.

48 Drache, 2008, *Defiant Publics.*

49 Bogard, W. 2000, 'Simmel in cyberspace: Strangeness and distance in postmodern communications', *Space and Culture*, No. 4, Vol. 5, pp. 23–46. The reference here is to p. 28.

50 Castells, M. 2001, *The Internet Galaxy: Reflections on the Internet, Business, and Society*, Oxford University Press, New York.

51 Plant, S. 1997, *Zeroes and Ones*, Fourth Estate, London, p. 49.

52 Elliott, A. and Urry, J. 2010, *Mobile Lives*, Routledge, New York, p. 30ff.

53 Wellman, B. 2001, 'Physical space and cyberplace: The rise of personalized networking', *International Journal of Urban and Regional Research*, No. 25, Vol. 2, p. 238.

54 Townsend, M. et al. 2010, 'WikiLeaks backlash: The first global cyber war has begun, claim hackers', **Guardian**, 10 December, viewed 12 December 2010, http://www.guardian.co.uk/media/2010/dec/11/wikileaks-backlash-cyber-war

55 Though there are too many contributions to detail, a useful starting point is Appiah, K. A. 2006, *Cosmopolitanism: Ethics in a World of Strangers*, W. W. Norton, New York; and Held, D. 2010, *Cosmopolitanism: Ideals, Realities and Deficits*, Polity, Cambridge.

56 Beck, U. and Grande, E. 2010, 'Varieties of second modernity: The cosmopolitan turn in social and political theory and research', *British Journal of Sociology*, Vol. 61, No. 3, p. 410. The following reference in this paragraph is also to this page.

57 Beck, U. 2006, *Cosmopolitan Vision*, Polity, Cambridge; Beck, U. 2005, *Power in the Global Age*, Polity, Cambridge.

58 Saïd, E. 1978, *Orientalism*, Pantheon, New York.

59 Saïd, E. 1994, *Representations of the Intellectual*, Vintage, New York.

60 Huntingdon, S. P. 2002, 'The Age of Muslim Wars', *Newsweek*, 3 January 2002.

61 Murphy, J. G. 1994, *Kant: The Philosophy of Right*, Mercer University Press, Macon, Georgia.

62 Kant, I. 1965, *The Metaphysical Elements of Justice*, Bobbs-Merrill, Indianapolis.

63 Neiman, S. 1994, *The Unity of Reason: Rereading Kant*, Oxford University Press, Oxford.

64 Fanon, F. 1952, *Black Skin, White Masks*, Grove, New York.

65 Huntington, S. P. 1996, *The Clash of Civilizations and the Remaking of World Order*, Touchstone, New York.

66 Schmitt, C. 1996, *The Concept of the Political*, Chicago University Press, Chicago.

Conclusion

1 See Thompson, P. 2009, 'Girl, 15, gang raped outside school dance while witnesses film horror attack', *Daily Mail Online*, 27 October, viewed 15 December 2010, http://www.dailymail.co.uk/news/worldnews/article-1223366/Girl-15–gang-raped-outside-school-dance-U-S-witnesses-film-horror-attack.html

2 Johnson, C. 2009, 'Primitive attack inspires primal reactions', *San Francisco Chronicle*, 30 October, viewed 15 December 2010, http://articles.sfgate.com/2009–10–30/bay-area/17186229_1_juveniles-bulletproof-vests-vicious

3 See details at http://en.wikipedia.org/wiki/2009_Richmond_High_School_gang_rape

4 Boltanski, L. 1999, *Distant Suffering. Morality, Media and Politics*, Cambridge University Press, Cambridge.

5 See Powell, A. 2009, 'New technologies, unauthorized visual images and sexual assault', *Australian Institute of Family Studies*, ACSSA Aware, No. 23, pp. 6–12.

6 See King, V. T. 2008, *The Sociology of Southeast Asia: Transformations in a developing region*, NIAS Press, Singapore.

7 Sullivan, J. P. and Elkus, A. 2009, 'Preventing another Mumbai: Building a police operational art', *CTC Sentinel*, 2(6), pp. 4–7.

8 Kristeva, J. 2000, *The Sense and Non-Sense of Revolt*, Columbia University Press, New York, p. 6.

9 See *http://www.facebook.com/press/info.php?statistics*

10 Ritchtel, M. 2010 'Attached to Technology and Paying a Price', *The*

New York Times, 6 June, viewed 15 December 2010, http://www.nytimes.com/2010/06/07/technology/07brain.html

11 Clarke, J., Newman, J., Smith, N., Vidler, E. and Westmarland, L. 2007, *Creating Citizen-Consumers: Changing Publics and Changing Public Services*, Sage, London.

12 Rees, M. 2003, *Our Final Century? Will the Human Race Survive the Twenty-First Century*, Heinemann, London.

13 Urry, J. 2011, *Climate Change and Society*, Polity, Cambridge.

14 Diamond, J. 2005, *Collapse: How Societies Choose to Fail or Survive*, Viking, New York.

15 Giddens, A. 2010, *The Politics of Climate Change*, Polity, Cambridge, p. 228.

16 Moyn, S. 2010, *The Last Utopia: Human Rights in History,* The Belknap Press of Harvard University Press, Cambridge MA.

Index

action, 16, 107, 109
activist groups, 134–5
Adorno, Theodor, 29
Afghanistan, 55, 161
Africa, 169
Agamben, Giorgio, 59, 60–1
ageing population, 59–60
agency, 39–40, 107, 108, 150
Albrow, Martin, 26
Alexander, Jeffrey, 44–5, 68, 70, 82–90
alienation, 8
alterity, 148, 149–52
   see also the Other
Americanization, 127
Amnesty International, x
anomie, 39
Ansell-Pearson, Keith, 114–15
anthropology, 152
anti-globalism, ix, xi, 135
Anti-Social Behaviour Act (2003), 60
'anti-society' critics, 2, 5–7
Appiah, Kwame, 150
Aquinas, Thomas, 48, 78
Arab Spring, 27, 137

Arendt, Hannah, 6–7, 9–10
Aristotle, 9, 50, 80, 116, 175n28
art, 124
Artaud, Antonin, 124
asceticism, 77
Asia, 146, 159, 169
Assange, Julian, 142
association, 10, 11–12, 13, 49, 50, 71
associations, 13, 83–4, 85
asylum seekers, 134, 146
Aurelius, Marcus, 148
Austin, J. L., 111
Australia, 95, 96, 97

Bacon, Francis, 4, 124
Badiou, Alain, 73
Bahrain, 133
'bare life', 61
Baudrillard, Jean, 4, 5, 7, 130
Bauman, Zygmunt, 14, 163
Beck, Ulrich, ix, 5–6, 14, 144–6, 150
Bell, Daniel, 52
Bellah, Robert, 89, 90
Benjamin, Walter, 52

Bensman, Joseph, 4
Bentham, Jeremy, 31
Berlin, Isaiah, 35, 40, 45
Berlusconi, Silvio, 94
Blair, Tony, 93, 164
bodily ego, 120
Bogard, William, 137
Boltanski, Luc, 157
borders, 56
Bosnia, 152
Bourdieu, Pierre, 110–13
Brazil, 170
brotherly love, 72–3
Buddhism, 98
bureaucracy, 33
Burgess, Anthony, 162
Bush, George W., 56, 136

Cambodia, 170
Cameron, David, 86, 88, 161–2, 163
Campbell, David, 88–9
Canada, 96, 139
capitalism, ix, 1, 7, 25, 29
    Alexander's 'civil sphere', 83
    as 'civilizing force', 33
    contradictions of, 96
    cosmopolitanization, 145
    cost to human happiness, 34
    destructive forces of, 68
    Durkheim's critique of, 46
    economic theory, 32
    erosion of national societies by, 54
    'financialization' of, 132–3
    globalization of culture, 127
    regulation of global, 144
    society as solidarity, 16
    spread of global, 9
    state/civil society relationship, 79
    Tönnies on, 71–2
    Weber's analysis of, 41
Castells, Manuel, 138, 163
Castoriadis, Cornelius, 101, 120–3,
    153
catastrophic societies, 165–8

Cetina, Karin Knorr, 141
charity, 156
Chechnya, 161
Chicago School, 52
children, 71
China, 96–7, 138, 159, 167, 169, 170
Christianity
    alterity, 150
    Bulgarian Orthodox, 128
    'clash of civilizations' thesis, 147
    communitarianism, 90
    fundamentalist, 62–4
    influence of, 78
    Kant on, 149
    medieval Church, 168
    Nietzsche's critique of, 74–5, 77
    Northern Ireland conflict, 153
    nostalgia, 46
    slavery, 152
    solidarity, 69, 72–4
    United States, 88–9
Cicero, Marcus Tullius, 147, 148, 149
cities, 35, 52, 160
citizenship, 53, 87
    Augustinian theology, 72
    cultural politics, 93
    global, 23, 24
    new forms of, 135–6
civic repair, 70, 82, 83, 85, 88, 90
civil religion, 40, 89, 90
Civil Rights movement, 85–6
civil society, 13, 49–50, 52–3, 87
    Alexander's 'civil sphere', 82–90
    cosmopolitanization, 144
    democratic participation, 25
    disconnection from, 164
    European, 80
    global, 98
    solidarity, 70
    state relationship, 36–7, 38, 79
'civil sphere', 82–90
'clash of civilizations' thesis, 24, 42,
    147, 152–3
class, 66, 78, 111–12

climate change, 166–7, 168
Clinton, Bill, 64
collective conscience, 12
collective will formation, 80, 81
colonialism, 33, 149–50, 152
commodification, 27, 51
communalism, 24, 26, 50–1
Communism, 68–9
communitarianism, x, 70, 73, 90–2,
    98
community, 13, 22, 49, 168
    association and, 50
    communitarianism, 92
    rift between society and, 10–11, 80
    sacred roots of, 51
    solidarity, 17–18, 65, 69, 70–1, 97
    see also Gesellschaft
companionship, 80
compassion, 68
competition, 16, 17
computer writing, 130–1
Comte, Auguste, 22
concentration camps, 60
conflict
    'clash of civilizations' thesis, 42, 147,
        152–3
    'feral societies', 160
    large scale, 167–8
    Marx, 21, 42
    Nietzsche, 113
    Northern Ireland, 153
    religious, 88–9
    virtual wars, 141–2
    see also war
conflict sociology, 23
conservatism, 6, 30, 40–1, 86
    American, 55
    Christian fundamentalism, 62–4
    influence on sociology, 45–6
consumer-citizens, 164–5
consumerism, 51, 133, 161, 163–4
Conway, Daniel W., 114
Cooley, Charles, 42
corporate culture, 19

cosmopolitanism, 30, 46, 80, 81
    activism, 134–5
    cosmopolitanization, 104, 128,
        143–53
    European, 82
    globalization, 170
creation, viii, 15, 18–19, 20–2, 100–53,
    159, 170–1
    Bourdieu, 110–13
    Castoriadis, 120–3
    cosmopolitanization, 128, 143–53
    creativity distinction, 101
    digital culture, 128, 129–43
    Freud, 117–20
    Giddens, 107–10
    Kristeva, 123–8
    Nietzsche, 113–16
    response to gang rape case, 156, 158
    Simmel, 104–7
    solidarity, 90
creativity, 101, 117, 162
crime, 160, 161–3
critical theory, 46–7, 51
cultural hybridization, 158–9
cultural studies, 129, 130, 131
culture
    cosmopolitanism, 151
    globalization, 23–4, 127
    habitus, 111
    Kristeva on, 124, 127, 128

'death of the social', 6, 13, 15, 17, 103,
    131
debt, 136
Deleuze, Gilles, 130
democracy, 24–5, 28
    Alexander's 'civil sphere', 84
    Internet, 137
    radicalization of, 80
    solidarity, 67, 98
democratization, 81
'demodernization', 25
Denmark, 171
depression, 123, 128

deregulation, 54, 133
Derrida, Jacques, 130, 147, 150
desire, 117, 118, 126–7
determinism, 9
de-unionization, 94–6
developing countries, 167
Dewey, John, 13
Diamond, Jared, 166
diasporas, 61–2, 103
digital culture, 128, 129–43
discursive will formation, 50, 80
dissent, 134–5
diversity, 23, 24
Drache, Daniel, 133, 136
duality of structure, 107
Durkheim, Émile, 1, 13
  'civil sphere', 89–90
  consensus, 21
  critique of Spencer, 31
  critique of Tönnies, 12, 14
  definition of society, 3
  division of labour, 8
  individual/society relationship, 38,
    41
  influence on MacIntyre, 51
  reciprocity, 29
  regulation, 46
  revival of interest in, 42
  role of the state, 22, 32, 42–4
  the social, 104
  social norms, 30
  society as structure, 16, 39–45
  'systemness', 19

Eagleton, Terry, 38
economic transformations, 10
economics, 32
ego, 118, 119, 120
Egypt, 28, 133
Ehrenreich, Barbara, 95, 163
elasticity, x, 102–3, 157–8, 169, 171
embourgeoisement, 66
Emerson, Ralph Waldo, 3
emotivism, 49

enclavement, 56–61, 169–70, 171
energy security, 167–8
Engels, Friedrich, 71
Enlightenment, 23, 34, 40, 42, 105,
  124, 129, 149
entertainment societies, 163–5
environmental problems, 166–8
Epictetus, 148
equality, 23, 24, 26, 100
ethnic cleansing, 151–2
ethnicity *see* race and ethnicity
ethnocentrism, 35
ethnomethodology, 23
Etzioni, Amitai, 91–2
eugenics, 59, 60
Europe
  civil society, 80
  cosmopolitanism, 82
  critiques of multiculturalism, 86
  Kristeva on, 124, 127, 128
  society as structure, 33, 52–3

Facebook, 28, 141, 142, 155, 164
fairness, 65
the Fall, 49, 50
Falwell, Jerry, 63
the family, 63–4, 71
Fanon, Frantz, 152
fantasy, 125–6
fear, 58–9
feminism, 7, 63, 85
'feral societies', 159–63, 169
Ferguson, Adam, 68
festivals, 48
Figgis, J. N., 13
financial crisis, ix–x, 94, 96, 132,
  133–4, 164–5, 170
Finland, 171
fluidity, virtual, 137–40
food security, 168, 171
Foucault, Michel, 47–8, 60, 115, 130
France, 24, 30, 67, 139
Frankfurt School, 47
freedom, 13, 35, 36, 39, 45, 116

Freud, Sigmund, 117–20, 124, 126
friendship, 18, 50, 71, 97
Frost, Robert, 4
Fukuyama, Francis, 171
functionalism, 22–3, 108

Gane, Nicholas, 27
gang rape case, 154–5, 156, 158
Gemeinschaft, 11, 17, 49, 69, 70–2, 92, 97
George, Stefan, 34
Germany, 33, 139
Gesellschaft, 11, 49, 50, 70, 72, 79–80
Giddens, Anthony, 4, 13, 26, 101, 107–10, 167
Glazer, Nathan, 86
global citizenship, 23, 24
global warming *see* climate change
globalization, ix–x, 2, 7, 9, 23–4, 169–70
 alterity, 151–2
 of communication, 27–8
 consumerism, 163
 cosmopolitanism, 144
 of crime and disease, 58
 cultural standardization, 134
 economic, 56, 93, 134, 135
 erosion of collective culture, 51
 'feral societies', 160
 impact on 'sticky societies', 159
 juridical, 150
 Kristeva on, 127, 128
 multilayered governance, 81
 Outhwaite on, 26–7
 pornography, 132
 society as creation, 104
 society as structure, 30, 53–5
 threats to solidarity, 66
 transnational solidarity, 97–8
 weakening of the nation-state, 80
Goffman, Erving, 1, 13, 157
Good Samaritan parable, 156, 157
Gouldner, Alvin, 1
governmentality, 57

Greece, ancient, 9–10, 48, 73, 76, 79, 175n28
Greenpeace, x
Guantanamo Bay, 59, 60–1

Habermas, Jürgen, 50, 132
 re-feudalization of the public sphere, 133
 solidarity, 65, 68, 69–70, 79–82, 98
habitus, 111–13
'hacktivists', 141
Hegel, Georg
 civil society, 49
 Marx's critique of, 37
 recognition, 150
 solidarity, 65
 state/civil society relationship, 36
Held, David, 175n29
Hennis, William, 114
herd mentality, 113–14
'high society', 8
Hitler, Adolf, 18, 59
homosexuality, 63, 64
honour killings, 158
human nature, 67, 76, 92
human rights, x, 88, 150, 170
Huntington, Samuel, 24, 147, 152–3
Hutcheson, Francis, 66
hyperreality, 5, 7

Iceland, 96
idealism, 66, 146
identity
 citizenship, 53
 common, 10, 20
 cultural, 8, 36
 divisive forces of, 24
 entertainment societies, 163
 ethnic, 152
 Kristeva on, 125, 127, 128
 politics of, 23
 postmodern culture, 149
 post-societal configurations of, 131
 society as creation, 101, 153

virtual socialities, 137
see also the self
ideological tropes, 10
ideology, 37–8
imagination, 19, 120, 121–3, 126–7
incarceration, 57, 91
India, 167, 170
individualism, 31, 44, 99
    capitalism and market relations, 16,
        17
    Christian theological critique of, 73,
        78
    communitarian critique of, 91,
        92
    'cult of', 43
    Durkheim, 12, 39–40, 46
    entertainment societies, 163
    modern societies, 51
    neoliberal, 133
    Nietzsche, 114, 115
    resistance to, 49, 51
    Simmel, 104
    social consequences of, 84
    society as structure, 69
    solidarity, 67
industrialization, 8–9, 33, 68
inequality, 68, 78, 133, 165, 167
institutions, 5, 83, 84, 87–8, 109, 121
interactionism, 20, 23
Internet, xi, 1, 9, 104, 128, 129–43
    'dark side', 136–7
    elasticity, 102
    growth in number of users, 134,
        138, 139, 140, 141
    'Internet galaxy' concept, 163
    'mobile connectivity', 140–1
    virtual fluidity, 137–40
    virtual wars, 141–2
introjection, 119, 120
Iraq, 55, 161
Ireland, 94, 96
Islam, 24, 26, 89, 147, 150–1, 152–3
Israel, 85
Italy, 84, 94, 96, 139, 171

Japan, 33, 96, 139, 170
Jasmine Revolution, x
Jordan, 28, 133
Judaism, 46, 73, 75, 150
justice, 83

Kant, Immanuel, 34, 45, 147, 149
Karachi, 161
Kennedy, John F., 88–9
Klein, Melanie, 126
Kristeva, Julia, 4, 13, 101, 123–8, 163,
    180n39
Kristol, Irving, 52

labour
    de-unionization, 94–6
    migrant, 61–2, 103, 134, 159, 171
Lacan, Jacques, 121, 125, 126, 180n39
language, 108–9, 123, 125
the Left, 6, 7, 46, 58, 94
Lemert, Charles, 5
Levinas, Emmanuel, 150, 151
Levi-Strauss, Claude, 111
Lewinsky, Monica, 64
liberalism, 6, 7, 23, 30, 45, 164
    critique of British, 31
    critiques of Rousseau, 35, 36
    multiculturalism, 86
    transfer of Western, 170
libertarianism, 135
'linguistic turn', 108
Lockwood, David, 21
London riots (2011), 161–3
loss, 119, 120, 123
love, 67, 68, 69, 97
    brotherly, 72–3
Luhmann, Niklas, 26
Lyotard, Jean-François, 130

MacIntyre, Alasdair, 48–9, 50, 51, 77–8,
    98–9, 157, 175n28
Madoff, Bernie, 133
Make Poverty History, x
Malaysia, 159

'Manchester School', 31, 43, 67
Marcuse, Herbert, 48
market relations, 16, 17
Marx, Karl, 1, 124
    capitalist division of labour, 29
    conflict, 21, 42
    definition of society, 3
    economic action, 32
    emancipated society, 38
    influence on Tönnies, 71
    the social, 104
    state/civil society relationship, 36–7
Marxism, 46, 50, 80, 135, 170
master-slave dialectic, 150
McDonaldization, 51, 134
media
    commercialization of, 132
    'mediated socialities', 129
    rise of the mass media, 79
    transnational, 80
media studies, 129, 130, 131
'mediated socialities', 129–30, 143
melancholia, 123, 127
Merkel, Angela, 86
Mertes, Tom, 135
methodological nationalism, ix, 145
Mexico, 160, 169
micro-activists, 135
migration, xi, 23, 56, 86, 146
    globalization, 159
    illegal, 134
    labour, 61–2, 103, 134, 159, 171
militarism, xi, 12, 33, 128
military expenditure, 136
military outsourcing, 93–4
Miller, W. Watts, 44
Mills, C. Wright, 1
minority rights, 135, 150
'mobile connectivity', 140–1, 142
modernism, 38
modernity, ix, 11, 13, 43
    critics of, 78
    Durkheim on, 12
    Nietzsche on, 114

society associated with, 23
    Touraine on, 24, 25
modernization, 8–9, 34, 79–80
Moral Majority, 18, 63
'moral voice', 91–2
morality, 16, 39, 45
    Christian theology, 77
    Nietzsche, 74, 113–14
    solidarity, 67, 68
    virtual socialities, 137
mourning, 123, 127
Moyn, Samuel, 170
Mozart, Wolfgang Amadeus, 122
multiculturalism, xi, 7, 86–7, 158–9
    activism, 134–5
    cultural differences, 61
    Kristeva on, 124
    recognition ethics, 26, 150
multinational corporations, 14, 66,
        103, 145
Murdoch, Rupert, 25

'national outlook', 145
nationalism, 18, 53, 90, 151–2, 171
nation-building, 53
naturalism, 67, 69, 108
neoconservatism, 6, 46, 86
neoliberalism, ix, 93–4, 99, 132
    'feral societies', 160
    opposition to, 133, 135
    privatization, 136
    society as structure, 54, 55
    threats to solidarity, 66
'Netsex', 130
networks
    global, 24
    Internet, 27
    social elasticity, x
    social networking sites, 140–1,
        142
    virtual, 137, 140
    voluntary, x–xi
New Christian Right, 63
New Zealand, 95, 96, 97

News Corporation, 25
newspapers, 79
NGOs *see* non-governmental
    organizations
Nietzsche, Friedrich, 17, 74–7, 101
    creation, 113–16
    death of God, 47
    influence of Christianity on, 78
    self-violence, 116–17
Nigeria, 160
nihilism, 77, 78, 114, 115
Nisbet, Robert, 12–13, 40–1, 45
non-governmental organizations
    (NGOs), 134
norms, 29–30
Northern Ireland, 153
nostalgia, 6, 12, 27, 46–51, 103
Nussbaum, Martha, 150, 175n28

Obama, Barack, 64
objectivism, 110, 112
Operation Payback, 142
organicism, 17, 67, 69, 70, 71
Orientalism, 150–1
the Other, 35, 144, 150
    Kristeva on, 126
    'mediated socialities', 129
    recognition of, 151
    solidarity with, 67
Outhwaite, William, 22, 24, 26–7
outsourcing, 93, 94, 132

Paine, Thomas, 4
Palin, Sarah, 64
parallel communities, 61–2
Parsons, Talcott, 1, 2, 4, 11–12, 13, 29,
    41–2
patriarchy, 7
Patriot Act, 60
Pearce, Frank, 46
peasant culture, 48
pensions, 93
Pensky, Max, 82
phenomenology, 151

Picasso, Pablo, 124
Plant, Sadie, 140
Poland, 68–9
Polanyi, Karl, 47
politics
    Alexander's 'civil sphere', 85
    citizenship, 93
    communitarianism, 70
    consumer society, 164
    cosmopolitanism, 143–4, 145
    cultural, 66
    Kristeva, 124–5, 127
    'of the present', 157
    society as creation, 153
    see also democracy
Pollock, Jackson, 124
Pollock, Sheldon, 151
population growth, xi, 35, 166, 171
pornography, 64, 132
Poster, Mark, 131
post-feminism, 7
postmodernism, 2, 9, 24, 149
    corporate culture, 19
    digital culture, 129, 130
'postnational constellations', 68,
    69–70
post-structuralism, 7, 108, 129, 130,
    131
poverty, 68, 160
power, 16, 101, 111, 115
privatism, 123
privatization, 54, 93, 95–6, 132, 133–4,
    136, 169
projection, 120
protests, x, 133, 137
the psyche, 120–1, 122, 123
psychoanalysis
    Castoriadis, 122
    Freud, 117–20
    Kristeva, 124, 125–8, 180n39
    the other, 151
public choice theory, 164
public sphere, 79, 80
Putnam, Robert, 6, 84, 88–9

Rabelais, François, 48
race and ethnicity, 85–7, 91, 152
    see also multiculturalism
radical conservatism, 46–7
radical imaginary, 121–2
rape case, 154–5, 156, 158
rationalization, 114
Rawls, John, 83
Reagan, Ronald, 46, 66, 93
reason, 149
reciprocity, 32, 41, 50, 80
recognition ethics, 26, 151
Rees, Martin, 165
reflexivity, 112
refugees, 134, 146
regulation, 39, 46, 47
    financial, 94
    global flows, 55, 56–8
relativism, 51, 158–9
religion
    alterity, 149
    'civil', 40, 89, 90
    'clash of civilizations' thesis, 42,
        152–3
    commercialization of, 27
    cosmopolitanism, 147
    fundamentalist, 18, 62–4
    Nietzsche's critique of, 114
    religious values, 41
    secularization, 47
    solidarity, 69
    Stoicism, 148
    United States, 88–9
    see also Christianity; Islam; Judaism
repression, 122–3, 125, 126
republicanism, 24
resentment, 17, 74, 77, 92, 114–16,
    156–7, 161
ressentiment, 75–6
revolt, 124–5
the Right, 6, 26, 46, 127
    Christian fundamentalist, 62–4
rights
    Hegel on, 36

Marx on, 37
minority, 135, 150
recognition, 150
role of the state, 43
universal, 23
virtual socialities, 137
Robertson, Roland, 26, 92
Roman Empire, 73, 148
romanticism, 34, 43
Rose, Gillian, 74–5
Rosenberg, Bernard, 4
Rousseau, Jean-Jacques
    civil religion, 40, 89
    conservatism, 41
    freedom, 35
    influence on Durkheim, 45, 90
    political theory, 25
    social contract, 47
    spectatorship, 157
rules, 109, 110, 111, 112–13
Rumsfeld, Donald, 61
Russia, 139, 170

the sacred, 9, 47, 51
Saïd, Edward, 147, 150–1
Saint-Simon, Henri de, 22, 40
Sarkozy, Nicolas, 86
Sassen, Saskia, 56
Saussure, Ferdinand, 111
scandals, 133
Schmitt, Carl, 53, 153
Scruton, Roger, 98–9
seclusion, 59, 62
secularism, 47, 99, 148, 149, 150
the self
    decentred, 129
    Freudian theory, 117, 118, 119–20
    Nietzsche's philosophy, 117
    psychic re-organization of the, 123
    solidaristic societies, 66
    Touraine on, 25–6
    see also identity
self-development, 8, 114, 120
self-regulation, 44, 45

Selznick, Philip, 91
semiotic displacement, 125, 127
Seneca, 148
Sennett, Richard, 6, 95
'sense of belonging', 20, 67
sequestration, 59–60, 61, 62
sexuality
  Christian Right, 63, 64
  commercialization of, 132
  Freudian theory, 118–19
  'Netsex', 130
  society as creation, 101
Silk, M. S., 115
Simmel, Georg, 1, 3, 22, 52, 101,
    104–7, 113, 153
simulacra, 5
slavery, 152
Small, Albion W., 2, 5
Smith, Adam, 31, 157
the social, 10, 31, 38, 155, 158
  challenged by neoliberal economic
    orthodoxy, 132
  conservatism, 40–1
  'death of', 6, 13, 15, 17, 103,
    131
  decentring of, 33
  Durkheim, 51
  new forms of, 14
  Nietzsche, 115
  pluralistic view of, 52
  Simmel, 104–5, 106
  society as structure, 45
social capital, 51, 84, 87
social change, 1–2, 13–14, 30
social cohesion, 17, 29, 69
social control, 16
social Darwinism, 152
social differences, 23
social elasticity, x, 102–3, 157–8, 169,
    171
social facts, 45
social games, 111, 112–13
social imaginary, 121, 122
social inclusion, 134

social interaction, 5
  Simmel, 105, 106, 113
  structuration theory, 109, 110
  virtual, 132
social justice, 65
social movements, 25, 28, 80, 83,
    85–6, 133, 135
social networking sites, 140–1,
    142
social order, ix, 29–30, 42, 165
social practices, ix
  cosmopolitanization, 144
  Nietzsche, 113
  solidarity, 22, 67
  structuration theory, 107
social relations, 10, 12
  conservatism, 41
  elasticity, x, 102, 103
  instrumental nature of, 65
  marketization of, 78
  'mobile connectivity', 140–1
  nostalgia, 47
  Simmel, 105
  society as creation, 19, 153
  society as solidarity, 22, 68, 97
  society as structure, 33, 34, 39
  stabilized, 44
  thin, 51
  Weber, 50
social system, ix, 8, 10, 107–8, 109
social welfare models, 65–6, 93
socialism, 22, 23, 30, 32, 135
sociality, x–xi, 14, 158
  destructive, 155–6
  globalization of communication,
    27–8
  'mediated socialities', 129–30,
    143
  postmodernist view of, 2
  Simmel, 105, 106
  society as creation, 101, 104
  society as solidarity, 18
  virtual, 137–8
sociation, 22, 27, 106

society
  catastrophic societies, 165–8
  changes in, 1–2
  communitarianism, 92
  as creation, viii, 15, 18–19, 20–2, 90,
    100–53, 159
  definitions of, viii–ix, 3–5, 9–10,
    12–13
  evolution of the concept of, viii–ix,
    168–9
  'feral societies', 159–63
  functionalist conception of, 22–3
  Giddens on, 107–8
  globalization, 23–4
  images of, 7–14
  instability of, 23
  radical transformation of, 171
  rejection of the concept of, 2, 5–7
  Simmel on, 104–6
  as solidarity, viii, 15, 16–18, 20–2,
    26–7, 65–99, 100, 143, 159
  as structure, viii, 15–16, 20–2, 26–7,
    29–64, 69, 100, 101, 143, 158–9
  'systemness', 19–20
  Touraine on, 25–6
  on verge of collapse, 155
sociology
  Bourdieu, 112
  challenges for, xi
  changes and transitions, 168
  classical, 10, 30–3, 41–2, 52, 69, 70–2
  companionship, 80
  concept of society, viii–ix, 8, 10, 22,
    23–4
  conservatism, 45–6
  cosmopolitanization, 145
  democratic participation, 25
  destructive socialities, 155–6
  foundational perspectives, 1
  German, 80
  globalization, 26–7
  individual/society relationship, 38
  Simmel, 104–5, 106
  solidarity, 69, 70–2, 83

structuration theory, 108
structure, 29, 30–3, 41–2, 52
solidarity, viii, 15, 16–18, 20–2, 26–7,
    65–99, 159
  Alexander's 'civil sphere', 82–90
  Bourdieu, 112–13
  Christian theology, 72–4
  communitarianism, 90–2
  contradictions of, 101
  Durkheim on, 12
  Habermas, 79–82
  lower-case and upper-case, 90, 98–9
  MacIntyre, 77–8
  'mediated socialities', 143
  Nietzsche, 74–7
  nostalgia, 100
  organic, 39, 41
  reassessment of, 92–7
  response to gang rape case, 156, 158
  social differences, 23
  sociation, 27
  Tönnies, 69, 70–2
  transnational, 97–9
  trust, 32
Somalia, 161
soul, 114, 116, 121
  'maladies of the', 123
sovereignty, 24, 31, 56, 145
Soviet Union, former, 13, 152
Spain, 94
spectatorship, 157
Spencer, Herbert, 31, 43, 170
Spinoza, Benedict de, 71
sport, 111, 112
St Augustine, 72, 73, 92
St Paul, 73, 74, 75, 76, 150
state, 13, 36–8
  civil society relationship, 79
  conservatism, 64
  Durkheim on the, 22, 32, 42–4
  rise of the, 53
states of emergency, 60–1
Stauth, Georg, 114
Stern, Joseph Peter, 115

'sticky societies', 66, 102, 158, 159
Stockhausen, Karlheinz, 124
Stoicism, 148–9
storage, 59, 60, 61, 62
the stranger, 61–2
structural-functionalism, 41
structuralism, 108
structuration theory, 101, 107–10
structure, viii, 15–16, 20–2, 26–7,
      29–64, 158–9
   abstract nature of, 100
   Bourdieu, 110–11, 112, 113
   Christian Right, 62–4
   classical sociology, 30–3, 52
   Durkheim, 39–45
   enclavement, 56–61
   globalization, 53–5
   Hegel, 36
   individualism, 69
   Marx, 36–8
   'mediated socialities', 143
   nostalgia, 46–51
   parallel communities, 61–2
   political deadlocks, 101
   response to gang rape case, 156, 158
   Rousseau, 35
   structuration theory, 107–10
the Subject, 25–6, 34–5
subjectivism, 110, 112, 114, 119
Sudan, 161
suffering, 157
Sweden, 96
symbolic identification, trauma of, 123
symbolic interactionism, 20
symbolic order, 125
'systemness', 8, 19–20, 108

taste, 111–12
Taubes, Jacob, 73, 74
taxation, 88, 93, 136
Taylor, Charles, 147, 150
Tea Party, 64
technology, digital, 128, 129–43
terrorism, 55, 62, 160–1, 169, 170

Thailand, 84–5
Thatcher, Margaret, 4, 6, 46, 66, 78,
      93, 164
'Third-Way' politics, 9, 93
Thompson, E. P., 65
time-space compression, 143
Tocqueville, Alexis de, 84
Tönnies, Ferdinand, 1, 29
   community, 11, 13, 17, 49, 80, 92,
      97, 98
   Durkheim's critique of, 12, 14
   friendship, 50
   globalization, 98
   influence on Habermas, 79
   solidarity, 65, 69, 70–2
Torpey, John, 56
Touraine, Alain, 23, 24, 25–6
trade unions, 94–6, 164
transnationalism, 146, 160
trust, 31–2, 50, 78, 80, 84, 134–5
Tunisia, 28, 133
Turkle, Sherry, 130
Turner, Bryan, 114
Twitter, 28, 142, 162

Ubermensch (overman), 76, 116
uncertainty, 23
the unconscious, 117–18, 119, 120,
      122–3, 127
United Kingdom
   Anti-Social Behaviour Act, 60
   de-unionization, 96
   Internet users, 139
   liberalism, 31
   London riots (2011), 161–3
   migration controls, 171
   privatization, 134
   public institutions, 87–8
   public utilities, 136
United States
   Alexander's 'civil sphere', 84
   Americanization, 127
   Californian gang rape case, 154–5,
      156, 158

United States (*cont.*)
    Christian fundamentalism, 62–4
    cities, 52
    critiques of multiculturalism, 86
    debt, 136
    de-unionization, 94–5
    financial crisis, 96
    incarceration, 57
    Internet users, 138, 139
    migration controls, 171
    military expenditure, 136
    Moral Majority, 18, 63
    racial inequality, 91
    religious conflict, 88–9
    scandals, 133
    security doctrine, 55, 56, 62
unity, 8, 9, 37
    community solidarity, 69
    Simmel, 106
    solidarity, 17, 97
universalism, 18, 23, 38, 104, 105,
    148
Urry, John, 26, 165–6
utilitarianism, 31, 41, 67

values
    Christian, 62–3, 74
    civil religion, 89
    class solidarity, 78
    common, 20
    communitarianism, 91, 92
    cosmopolitan, 80
    Nietzsche's call for 'revaluation of',
    76, 114
    psychological internalization of,
    42
    religious, 41
    solidarity, 97
Vergesellschaftung, 22, 50, 106–7
Vietnam, 138, 170
violence
    honour killings, 158
    London riots, 161–3
    Nietzsche on, 113

terrorism, 55, 62, 160–1, 169, 170
    see also war
virtual fluidity, 137–40
virtual wars, 141–2
von Gierke, Otto, 50, 71

war, 12, 55, 56, 62, 171
    virtual wars, 141–2
war on terror, 54, 55, 56, 58–9, 61, 62,
    147
water security, 168
Weber, Max, 1, 42
    asceticism, 77
    bureaucracy, 33
    capitalism, 41
    charisma, 76
    cities, 52
    community, 22
    dark vision of society, 31
    economic action, 32
    influence of Christianity on, 78
    love, 68
    Nietzsche compared to, 114
    rationalization, 59
    resentment, 17
    role of the state, 43
    the social, 104
    social order, 29
    social relations, 50
    society as an iron cage, 34, 47
Wellman, Barry, 140
WikiLeaks, 27, 138, 142
Wilde, Oscar, 3
Williams, Raymond, 3
Wittgenstein, Ludwig, 111
Wollheim, Richard, 120
women, 71, 85

xenophobia, 58–9, 62

YouTube, 155
Yugoslavia, former, 152

Zola, Émile, 124